Routledge Revivals

Jesus in the Tide of Time

First published in 1980, *Jesus in the Tide of Time* considers the historical Jesus and studies the ways in which he has subsequently been regarded by different people in different cultures.

The book examines the political, social, economic and religious background to Jesus' life. It also looks at what is known about Jesus as a historical personality, and considers the use of symbolic figures by the early Christians to represent him. It highlights the attitude towards the person of Jesus as an indicator of the culture of the particular period and place throughout history, and questions whether different cultures, periods and individuals manufacture Jesus in their own image.

Jesus in the Tide of Time will appeal to those with an interest in the history of Christianity, religious history, and social history.

Jesus in the Tide of Time

An Historical Study

By John Ferguson

First published in 1980
by Routledge & Kegan Paul

This edition first published in 2021 by Routledge
2 Park Square, Milton Park, Abingdon, Oxon, OX14 4RN
and by Routledge
605 Third Avenue, New York, NY 10017

Routledge is an imprint of the Taylor & Francis Group, an informa business

© 1980 John Ferguson

All rights reserved. No part of this book may be reprinted or reproduced or utilised in any form or by any electronic, mechanical, or other means, now known or hereafter invented, including photocopying and recording, or in any information storage or retrieval system, without permission in writing from the publishers.

Publisher's Note
The publisher has gone to great lengths to ensure the quality of this reprint but points out that some imperfections in the original copies may be apparent.

Disclaimer
The publisher has made every effort to trace copyright holders and welcomes correspondence from those they have been unable to contact.

A Library of Congress record exists under LCCN: 81150815

ISBN 13: 978-0-367-75074-9 (hbk)
ISBN 13: 978-1-003-16087-8 (ebk)
ISBN 13: 978-0-367-75072-5 (pbk)

Book DOI: 10.4324/9781003160878

Jesus in the Tide of Time:
An Historical Study

John Ferguson

President, Selly Oak Colleges, Birmingham
Formerly Dean and Director of Studies in Arts,
The Open University

Routledge & Kegan Paul
LONDON AND HENLEY

*First published 1980
by Routledge & Kegan Paul Ltd
39 Store Street,
London WC1E 7DD and
Broadway House,
Newtown Road,
Henley-on-Thames,
Oxon RG9 1EN
Set in 11/12 IBM Journal
and printed in Great Britain by
Lowe & Brydone Printers Ltd
Thetford, Norfolk
© John Ferguson 1980
No part of this book may be reproduced in
any form without permission from the
publisher, except for the quotation of brief
passages in criticism*

British Library Cataloguing in Publication Data

*Ferguson, John, b. 1921
Jesus in the tide of time.
1. Jesus Christ
I. Title
232   BT202*

ISBN 0 7100 0561 X

FOR LESLEY

Contents

Preface		page ix
Abbreviations		xi
1	Palestine in the First Century	1
2	Jesus	25
3	The Person of Christ	55
4	The Early Church: Types and Symbols	82
5	Christ and Culture	119
6	Son of God	145
7	Son of Man	168
8	Summing-Up	213
	Index of Biblical References	234
	General Index	237

Preface

Another book on Jesus? When John Hinnells asked me to write originally I had the same sensation. Yet when I came to brood on it, the chance to write about such a seminal and challenging person could not be resisted, and I could see the opportunity to do something which is, I think, new in asking questions about the way different ages and different cultures have reacted to him.

I am myself a Christian. But I did not want to write another account of the Christ for Christians. Nor did I want here to write evangelically. If confrontation with the historic Jesus leads people to commit themselves to him, that is his doing and theirs. I have tried to write as objectively as possible; no doubt my presuppositions affect my presentation, but I have tried to let them obtrude as little as possible. I hope therefore that the result will be of interest to many people as a study of historical and cultural values, no matter what their own beliefs.

Some parts of the book, notably the sixth and seventh chapters, are inevitably selective and impressionistic. It will be easy to point to omissions. What is here is an honest attempt to record significant emphases as they appear to me. One point I think I should make. In the last chapter I come to the conclusion that the Wesleyan and Evangelical movements of the late eighteenth century preserve a healthy balance between Jesus as Son of Man and as Son of God. This was not a predetermined view. It was not a conclusion I was expecting to draw. I am not a Methodist, and my theology is not that of the Evangelicals. The study was not designed to the conclusion; the conclusion came out of the study. And it is of course open to any reader to say that their views, though balanced, were wrong.

One or two debts of gratitude. First to John Hinnells, for his encouragement and helpfulness. Then to Lesley Roff who in the busy-ness of her work as short-courses officer at Cranfield found time, in friendship and interest, to type the manuscript. And to my wife for yet another of her remarkable indexes, and to Brenda Rea for typing this.

Abbreviations

Aug.: Augustine	*C. Faust.*	*Contra Faustum (Against Faustus)*
	De Trin.	*De Trinitate (On the Trinity)*
	Ep.	*Epistula (Letter)*
Calvin	*Inst.*	*Institutes of the Christian Religion*
Diod. Sic.: Diodorus Siculus		
Eus.: Eusebius	*Laud. Const.*	*Laudatio Constantini (Panegyric of Constantine)*
Hermas	*Sim.*	*Similitudines (Similitudes* or *Parables)*
Ign.: Ignatius	*Eph.*	*Epistula ad Ephesios (Letter to the Ephesians)*
Iren.: Irenaeus	*Haer.*	*Adversus Omnes Haereses (Against All Heresies)*
Jer.: Jerome	*Adv Lucif.*	*Adversus Luciferum (Against Lucifer)*
Jos.: Josephus	*Ant.*	*Antiquitates Judaicae (Antiquities of the Jews)*
	BJ	*Bellum Judaicum (The Jewish War)*
Nov.: Novatian	*Trin.*	*De Trinitate (On the Trinity)*
Phil.: Philo	*Flacc.*	*In Flaccum (Agaisnt Flaccus)*
	Leg.	*Legatio ad Gaium (The Embassy to Gaius)*
Theophil.: Theophilus		
	Ad Autol	*Ad Autolycum (To Autolycus)*

These are abbreviations of works cited in the text.

ET In the Bibliographies stands for English translation. The figures following titles of early works usually refer to book, chapter, section, subsection.

I
Palestine in the First Century

JUDAISM

Jesus of Nazareth grew up in a Jewish family in a Palestine which had been permeated by Greek influences for three centuries, and was now a part of the Roman Empire.

The folk-memory of the Jews went back to an early migration from Mesopotamia by their forefather Abraham, from 'Ur of the Chaldees'. Ur was in fact one of the cities of Sumer. There is no special reason to doubt such a tradition of emigration, and we can trace the main stages on the route, each of which has been claimed to have associations with Hebrew traditions: Mari with its colossal palace including an archive of 25,000 cuneiform tablets; Haran, a religious centre which the Biblical Abraham calls 'my country'; and then, as they turned southwards, Ebla, a rich and prosperous site in North Syria, where sensational finds were recorded in the 1960s and 1970s. We cannot of course be certain of such folk-memories; but the Jewish people later believed them to be true, and Abraham later became the type of faith in leaving his homeland and going out to an unknown future.

An even more emotive tradition was associated with a period in Egypt, due initially to shortages in Palestine. According to this tradition, the Israelites were in Egypt for twelve generations, beginning in prosperity, and ending in persecution and adversity. They were rescued by a national leader named Moses: it is a strange name, Egyptian in form, a suffix meaning 'son of'. He led the people to withdraw from Egypt, and at the Sea of Reeds a disaster overtook the pursuing Egyptian forces. There is no trace of this in Egyptian records, but that is not unexpected. Disasters are not always recorded in the archives of an autocracy, and, in any case, the episode, central to Jewish history, was peripheral to Egyptian.

Central to Jewish history it was. The first five books of the Bible enshrine the Jewish Torah, the basis of the religion of Judaism, and Exodus, the book of the deliverance, is the second of these. The deliverance was actual and historical, and it held the promise of future political deliverance in time of oppression and spiritual deliverance in time of trial. In one form or another this is one of the greatest of the titles of the God of the Israelites: 'I am the Lord your God who brought you out of the Land of Egypt, out of the house of bondage' (*Exod*. 20.2); 'It is the Lord our God who brought us and our fathers up from the land of Egypt, out of the house of bondage' (*Josh*. 24.12); 'Thus says the Lord, the God of Israel, "I brought up Israel out of Egypt, and I delivered you from the hand of the Egyptians and from the hand of all the kingdoms that were oppressing you" ' (1 *Sam*. 10.18); 'Thou didst bring a vine out of Egypt; thou didst drive out the nations and plant it' (*Ps*. 80.8); 'Therefore, behold, the days are coming, says the Lord, when it shall no longer be said, "As the Lord lives who brought up the people of Israel out of the land of Egypt" but "As the Lord lives who brought the people of Israel out of the north country and out of all the countries where he had driven them" ' (*Jer*. 16.14.5); 'He brought them out of darkness and gloom and broke their bonds asunder' (*Ps*. 107.14); 'O Lord, thou has brought up my soul from Sheol' (the land of death) (*Ps*. 30.3). The testimony is persistent and eloquent.

Who was this liberating God? Moses, exiled from Egypt for killing an Egyptian, took refuge among the Midianites, and married into them. While he was pasturing his father-in-law's flocks on the slopes of a mountain he had a mystical encounter with a God called by a holy name usually transliterated as Yahweh, and given the meaning 'I AM' or 'I AM WHO I AM'. This divine being announced himself the God who had guided the fortunes of Abraham and his successors without being known to them by name (*Exod*. 3.6; 6.2); he called Moses to be his instrument in the deliverance from Egypt, and promised his people 'a land flowing with milk and honey'. After the escape the refugees came to Mount Sinai, and there entered into a solemn covenant with Yahweh. This produced a unique religious relationship. Most tribal gods, Chemosh of Moab for instance, had their being totally intertwined with the life of their people. If Moab was annihilated, Chemosh ceased to exist. But Yahweh stood to his people in a free relationship; his being did not depend on theirs. This in turn offered the seeds of a later universalism; the God who is independent of his people may be seen as independent of all peoples; the God who unknown has guided his people may be seen as, unknown, guiding other peoples: 'Did I not bring up Israel from the land of Egypt, and the Philistines from Caphtor and the Syrians from Kir?' (*Amos* 9.7). Furthermore, associated with the story of the Covenant is the Decalogue or Ten Commandments, and it seems probable that we should say that some form of moral code dates from the original Covenant; Yahweh from the first made moral demands of his people.

The settlement of the Israelites in the land of Canaan was gradual and by no means a single operation. Archaeological evidence is conflicting. The evidence from Hazor shows destruction at about 1225 BC, which is compatible with the Bible story; the evidence from Ai shows that the city had by then been desolate for a thousand years; the evidence from Jericho is subject to conflicting interpretations. The land they were entering was a political, cultural and religious hotch-potch, though the evidence of archaeology is now enabling us to take a more positive attitude to the Canaanites than was previously possible. Such a positive attitude did not exist in Israelite tradition. The precarious unity of the Hebrew tribes depended upon them keeping their moral and religious identity. The nature and fertility gods and goddesses, Astarte and Baal especially, formed a dangerous temptation on both accounts.

Out of this slow period of wars, incursions and settlements emerged a united monarchy under a king named Saul, maintained, secured and extended by his successors David and Solomon. The prophet Samuel was reluctant to anoint a king: Yahweh alone was King. But he submitted to popular pressure, and the king became God's anointed representative, a concept seared deep into the memories of the people later. Three other things of vital importance happened during this period round about 1000 BC. First, David captured from the Jebusites their hilltop fortress named Zion, and established there his capital of Jerusalem. Second, David was by tradition a musician, and there is no reason to doubt that he began the collection of religious songs we call the Psalms, which grew across the centuries to become the hymn-book of the Jewish people, and so close to the mind of Jesus that, on the edge of death, he called out the opening words of the twenty-second Psalm. The early Christian writers have the Psalms at their fingers' ends, and are for ever quoting or referring to them. Third, Solomon built Yahweh a temple in Jerusalem, and this temple became the centre of his worship.

But Solomon's rule had become increasingly oppressive, and with his death the kingdom broke into two, the ten northern tribes forming the kingdom of Israel and the two southern ones the kingdom of Judah. It was a period of instability. To the south lay the imperial power of Egypt, slumbering in the decay of its glory. To the east, at the other end of the great loop of irrigated land known as the Fertile Crescent, was Mesopotamia. Here, first Assyria and then Babylon rose to military power. The Palestinian tribes formed a buffer, and their political leaders seesawed:

> Ephraim is like a dove,
>   silly and without sense,
>   calling to Egypt, going to Assyria.
>   (*Hos.* 7.11)

The black obeslisk of Shalmaneser III, now in the British Museum, shows Jehu, king of Israel, prostrating himself before the ruler of Assyria. It was a time also of religious apostasy. When there was a bad harvest or when there was political danger, there were plenty of people to trek off to the Baalim. But it was also this period which saw the emergence of the figure of the prophet or *nabi*. These men of God were not predicting the future but proclaiming a message from God, not foretelling but forthtelling. Their message was first of God. Isaiah, who stood alongside kings, has a mighty vision of Yahweh high upon a throne in a purity which makes the prophet's own presence shameful and painful. Amos, a shepherd from the hills, saw Yahweh as the God of all peoples. His prophecies denounce in Yahweh's name both the kingdoms for their lies and oppressions; they denounce the peoples round about for their attacks on his covenanted people; but they also denounce Moab for atrocities committed against Edom. Israel and Judah are not involved, but Yahweh still cares. But if their message starts from God it comes down to Man. Amos is the great preacher of social justice, inveighing against those who sell honest men into slavery because they cannot repay the price of a pair of shoes, or who tamper with the scales so as to cheat their customers. Hosea is the preacher of love, who denounces violence as he denounces apostasy, and yet sees Yahweh still loving his people as he himself continued to love his unfaithful wife. Of all the prophets Hosea seems to have been the one with whom Jesus was to find the closest affinity. Jesus stood, and was seen to stand, in the tradition of the prophets (*Mark* 8.28), and Islam places him firmly in that succession.

It was during this period that the Messianic hope began to be voiced among the Jewish people. The word Messiah simply means 'Anointed', as kings, priests and prophets were anointed and thereby endowed with higher power, as it was believed. 'The Messiah' is not spoken of in that phrase at this period. But we find emerging the hope of a new deliverance by Yahweh, and a restoration of the united kingdom under an idealized ruler in the line of descent from David who will be endowed by Yahweh with righteousness, wise counsel, sound judgment and peace.

One other important event was the religious reform carried out in Jerusalem in 621 BC by King Josiah. In the course of repairs to the Temple a book was found purporting to be Mosaic. As a result of this discovery the Temple itself was purified, and established as the only place where sacrifice might be offered. We may suspect that other sanctuaries were sometimes syncretistic with the fertility cults, and a single central shrine could be more easily controlled; at the same time it emphasized the monotheism which had emerged as the Jewish faith; and no doubt there were political implications in the strengthening of Jerusalem and establishing a strong point of national unity. It is probable that the fifth book of the Bible, *Deuteronomy*, reflects these reforms, whether or not it was the book so mysteriously discovered.

Politically, the reforms had little immediate chance. In 612 BC Nineveh fell to the rising power of Babylon. Fifteen years later Nebuchadrezzar of Babylon captured Jerusalem, and deported a number of leading citizens including the young king Jehoiachin; a poignant record of his exile was found on a clay tablet in Babylon recording the allocation of a quantity of high-quality sesame oil to Jehoiachin, king of the land of Judah. The puppet-king left behind played power-politics with Egypt. In 587 BC or 586 BC Nebuchadrezzar sacked Jerusalem and razed it, Temple and all, and deported the people to Babylon.

The Babylonian Exile lasted less than fifty years but again provided an immensely potent folk-memory. It was yet another experience of oppression and deliverance. Deliverance came in the end from Cyrus the Mede. The writing was on the wall for Babylon, and the tough, militaristic Zoroastrian Cyrus was implausibly hailed as Yahweh's anointed. But in the meantime four things had happened of profound significance. First, Jeremiah, one of the greater prophets, had proclaimed a new covenant between Yahweh and his people. 'This is the covenant which I will make with the house of Israel after those days, says the Lord; I will put my law within them, and I will write it upon their hearts; and I will be their God, and they shall be my people' (*Jer.* 31.33). These words were to be deeply entrenched in the mind of Jesus. Second, only a few years before, Jerusalem had been established as the one place for the full worship of Yahweh. So the exiles sang:

> By the rivers of Babylon we sat down and wept
>   when we remembered Zion.
> There on the willow-trees
>   we hung up our harps ...

> How could we sing the Lord's song
> in a foreign land?
> (*Ps.* 137. 1-2, 4)

Yet they found marvellously, miraculously, beyond expectation that they could sing the Lord's song in a foreign land. They yearned for Jerusalem, but they could still worship Yahweh. So the idea grew that Yahweh did not live in temples made by human hand, and did not depend on the sanctity of a single spot. After all, it was not in Jerusalem that they had first encountered him, and they could find him — or he could find them — in Babylon as he had found them in Egypt. So the universalism of Yahweh was strengthened. Third, at Babylon they saw the pomp and ceremony attending to the city-god Marduk, worship on a scale they had never dreamed of. Yet Marduk was (to them) non-existent, the false idol of a single city. How much greater then must be Yahweh, whose fiat ran among all peoples! So from the period of exile comes the exalted vision of one of the greatest of all religious geniuses, whose very name we do not know, but whose words were incorporated in *Isaiah* 40-59:

> Who has set limits to the spirit of the Lord? . . .
> Why, to him nations are but drops from a bucket,
>   no more than moisture on the scales;
>   coasts and islands weigh as light as specks of dust . . .
>   All nations dwindle to nothing before him,
>   he reckons them mere nothings, less than nought . . .
> Do you not know, have you not heard,
> were you not told long ago,
> have you not perceived ever since the world began,
> that God sits throned on the vaulted roof of earth,
>   whose inhabitants are like grasshoppers?
>   He stretches out the skies like a curtain,
>   he spreads them out as a tent to live in;
>   he reduces the great to nothing
>   and makes all earth's princes less than nothing . . .
> Do you not know, have you not heard?
> The Lord, the everlasting God, creator of the wide world,

grows neither weary nor faint;
no man can fathom his understanding.
(*Is.* 40. 13-28)

Fourth, that same prophet incorporated into his work a vision of the Servant of Yahweh. The language is mysterious and ambiguous. Sometimes the Servant seems to be a single individual, who actually died for his people. Sometimes he seems to symbolize the Israelites as a whole. But through the theme of the sacrificial obedience of one who is despised and rejected by man runs a hope of resurrection by the divine power of Yahweh.

The Persian victory made possible a return to the homeland. There are accounts of an immediate return in 538 BC, but our effective evidence dates from 520 BC. Some priority was given to rebuilding the Temple, which was completed and rededicated in 516 BC. But the centuries which followed were a period of poverty, hardship, dependence and obscurity. The curtain is lifted briefly during the time of Ezra and Nehemiah in the fifth century, and falls again.

One other thing needs to be said about this period. From the sixth century we can date the beginning of the Diaspora or Dispersion of the Jews. On one side they were swept willy-nilly to Babylon, and, while some returned, others remained. On the other, some went, presumably of their own volition, to Egypt, perhaps enlisting as soldiers. They settled at Elephantine, and were certainly there in 525 BC. They had an elaborate Temple in honour of 'Yahu', though the papyri suggest some compromise over strict monotheism or even monolatry. The Temple was destroyed in an uprising in 410 BC, and the Elephantine Jews consulted Jerusalem about the rebuilding.

THE GREEKS

In 338 BC Philip of Macedon annexed Greece. Two years later he was succeeded by Alexander, who crossed the Hellespont in 334 BC, annihilated the power of Persia in three years and annexed their former possessions. When he died in 323 BC he had led his armies halfway across Asia and deep into the Indian subcontinent. His empire split into warring kingdoms. Palestine was somewhere near the border between the domain of the Ptolemies in Alexandria, established as a Greek city in Egypt, and that of the Seleucids which eventually found a capital at Antioch-on-the-Orontes in Syria. Both kingdoms were Greek, as were Macedon and (later) Pergamum. Alexandria and Antioch were not merely political and economic rivals; they vied with one another in their passion for Hellenic culture.

The Hellenistic Age is sometimes seen as an age of decline. Certainly there is nothing in it quite like the cultural achievement of Athens during the 120 years from 470 BC to 350 BC — but that is without parallel in history. In the classical period the political and social structure of Greece had depended on the city-state, the *polis*, a limited area geographically (from less than 2 to 3,300 sq. miles) centring on a single township, with a total population of anything from a few thousand to a quarter of a million, proudly self-governing and independent. These remained in the Hellenistic and Roman periods and provided effective local government in significant independence of the distant monarchs to whom they were subject, and a focus for civic loyalty. People *belonged* to Cyrene or Tarsus or Gadara.

The *polis* remained, but it had to find its being within cosmopolis. The secret of the Hellenistic and Roman periods was to retain the values of the city-state within a large dominion, to blend centralization and decentralization, to combine the positive values of a large political unit with a strong sense of local responsibility. Travel became easier. Trade routes opened up to India, even to China, to Russia, even to the Baltic, to Africa even south of the Sahara, to Western Europe and the gates of the Atlantic. There was greater mobility. The poet Theocritus was born and bred in Sicily, moved to Cos, and from there to Alexandria: poems of his maturity seem associated with Sicily, Egypt, Cos, Rhodes, Miletus and perhaps Lesbos. Flavius Zeuxis, an ordinary worker from Hierapolis in Phrygia, during the Roman Imperial period, announced on his tombstone that on voyages to Italy he had passed Cape Matapan 72 times. Alexandria and, later, Rome became cities as we understand the word, with a large cosmopolitan population, and inner-city problems.

This new world involved a new outlook. In language the old dialects slipped away and were replaced by a standard or common (*koinē*) form of Greek (BBC Greek as it were), the language of the New Testament. The gods of the city-state, Athene of Athens, Hera of Argos, Artemis of Ephesus and the rest, were not enough, especially as the new overlords were inveterate builders of city-states which inevitably lacked tradition, and the names of Alexandria, Antioch, Seleuceia, Ptolemais, Berenice, Attaleia and the like began to bespatter the map. So ruler-worship came in as a unifying force for the new kingdoms, Sarapis was invented as a god for a far-flung empire, Isis, the divinity of the land of Egypt, made comprehensive and universal claims, Zeus was the centre of a new monotheism, the Sun, an obviously universal power, attained a new prominence. So too with the philosophers. Stoics and Epicureans alike announced that national divisions are unnatural and all mankind are one.

At the same time the individual felt himself in the grip of world-forces which he could not control. He turned in on himself. This has been called the age of 'the failure of nerve'. The artist or writer was no longer working within the framework of a single city-state. So there was a restless search for variety, for new themes in the homely or the exotic, for the miniature or the monumental, for the exploration of the inner personality. Such themes as a drunken old woman, a boy struggling to take a goose to market, or, in literature, a woman taking her son to the schoolmaster for a whacking, or Apollonius's picture of Medea as a young girl experiencing first love are typical of the period.

The philosophies of the period pursue *autarkeia*, self-sufficiency, 'non-attachment' as Aldous Huxley calls it. The two great philosophies of the age were Epicureanism and Stoicism. For Epicurus the object of life could only be pleasure. But Epicurus did not treat pleasure crudely. He saw, and said, that our impulse to pleasure starts from the body,

Palestine in the First Century 11

from food and sex, but does not finish there. He was a pessimist; he believed the most pleasurable action to be that which gives the smallest excess of pain over pleasure: his keyword is *ataraxia*, freedom from disturbance. Hence morality, asceticism, renunciation of political, military and economic ambition. Disturbance comes from desire and fear. Desire can be controlled by self-discipline, fear by a proper scientific and religious understanding.

> God is not an object of fear.
> Death is not an object of sensation.
> Good can be easily attained.
> That which we fear can be easily endured.

Science shows us that the world is composed of atoms and void; it enables us to understand fearful phenomena such as thunderstorms and earthquakes; it tells us that death is annihilation, the peaceful dissolution of the atoms of soul and body. The gods are blissful beings, not concerned with us, though effluxes emanating from them can help the man who is rightly attuned to receive them.

The Stoics were pantheists. All is God, and God is all: we may call him Zeus or Nature or Fate or Reason (*Logos*) or Universe (*Cosmos*) as we will. He is in each one of us; each of us has within us a Holy Spirit; each of us has a Ruling Principle which is a spark of the divine fire. It is in ethics, however, that Zeno, the founder of the Stoics, was most original. Virtue is absolute. Nothing is good but virtue and nothing bad but vice; all else is indifferent. Among things indifferent some, such as good health, will be preferred, but never at the expense of virtue. Virtue is one and indivisible; it is impossible to possess one virtue without possessing them all; he who offends in one point is guilty of the whole law; if you are not a saint, you are a sinner. Emotions – pleasure, grief, fear and desire – are corrupting, and to be controlled, or rather eliminated. All that stands in the path of self-sufficiency, even pity, is vicious. External events are determined, since all is God and God is all; he does not determine the response of our will. Follow Nature and all will be well.

Meantime the ordinary man turned Fortune into a goddess.

In the great cosmopolitan city of Alexandria the Jews settled in their thousands. They were found in all parts of the city, but had a quarter which was peculiarly their own. They seem to have formed a quasi-autonomous corporation within the city. Here they were exposed to the Greek language, which they adopted, dropping their own Aramaic. Here the so-called Septuagint, the Greek version of the Jewish scriptures, was produced. Here too they were exposed to, and absorbed something of Greek science and scholarship, culture and ways of thought. There was mutual respect and tolerance : it is told that Ptolemy III ceremoniously visited the Temple at Jerusalem and presented a thank-offering.

The Dispersion was not confined to Alexandria and Mesopotamia. Philo reckoned that there were a million Jews in Egypt by the first century AD (*Flacc.* 2.523) with communities stretching as far as the boundaries of Ethiopia (6.43). The Seleucid Antiochus transplanted 2,000 Jewish families, already in Mesopotamia, to Phrygia and Lydia (Jos. *Ant.* 12.3.4). Josephus says that in the war of AD 66-70, 18,000 Jews were killed in Damascus alone (*BJ* 7.8.7). Philo quotes a letter from Herod Agrippa to Caligula: 'Jerusalem is the capital city, not of a single country, but of most, because of its colonies in Egypt, Phoenicia, Syria, Coele-Syria, Pamphylia, Cilicia, most of Asia Minor as far as Bithynia and the distant parts of Pontus' (*Leg.* 2.587); he proceeds to list Greek cities and islands with substantial Jewish populations. *The Acts of the Apostles* gives evidence that at the festival of Pentecost after the death of Jesus there were gathered on pilgrimage to Jerusalem 'Parthians, Medes, Elamites; inhabitants of Mesopotamia, of Judaea and Cappadocia, of Pontus and Asia, of Phrygia and Pamphylia, of Egypt and the districts of Libya around Cyrene; visitors from Rome, both Jews and proselytes, Cretans and Arabs' (2.9-11). So Strabo says 'It is not easy to find any place in the habitable world that has not yet received this nation, and in which it has not made its power felt' (Jos. *Ant.* 14.7.2.115). No doubt, but the process was mutual, and Hellenistic culture rubbed off on these sophisticated Jews of the Dispersion.

The influence was not merely among the Dispersion. It penetrated Palestine. New cities were founded with Greek constitutions and Greek practices: old ones were adapted, Raphia, Gaza, Ascalon, Azotus, Ptolemais, the future Caesarea. The Decapolis, ten Greek cities first mentioned as a league in the New Testament, but older in individual origin, had a mixed Greek and Semitic population. The lists vary slightly. Scythopolis, west of Jordan, is said to have been the largest: the rest, if we accept a reasonable list, lie east of Jordan — Capitolias, Abila, Hippos, Gadara, Pella, Gerasa, Dion, Kenath and Raphon.

'In recent times', said Hecataeus of Abdera, writing in the first half of the third century BC, 'under the foreign rule of the Persians, and then of the Macedonians, by whom the Persian Empire was overthrown, intercourse with other races has led to many of the traditional Jewish ordinances losing their hold' (Diod. Sic. 40.3). This is the comment of a detached observer, and must carry weight.

The great symbol of Greek culture was the gymnasium: the very name implies naked exercise, not normally practised by the Jews. Bevan's description has justly remained celebrated:

The first great interest which filled and informed the life of a Greek as he grew to manhood centred in the gymnasium. The gymnasiums were as much of the essence of a Greek state as the political assemblies. They expressed fundamental tendencies of the Greek mind — its craving for harmonious beauty of form, its delight in the body, its unabashed frankness with regard to everything natural, we might say that unsuspiciousness concerning nature, which, if man is indeed a double being, spirit and flesh at war, hardly corresponds to the maturer view, but which still today marks the Hellenic strain in our civilisation. The gymnasiums also served other by-ends beside the one of bodily training; they were the social centres, in which the life of a Greek youth got those interests which go with companionship, the spur of common ambitions, and *esprit de corps*. From the days of Alexander and his successors we find as a regular institution in Greek cities guilds of young men called *epheboi*, attached to the gymnasiums and organised under state control. A young man might remain in the ranks of the *epheboi* for a year. He wore a distinctive uniform, some variety of that Greek country dress — the dress worn for hunting, riding, travelling — which consisted of a broad-brimmed hat, a *chlamys* brooched about the shoulders, and high-laced boots. But the wealth and pride of the city to which he belonged were told by the material of his garb, by its colour and embroidery. In state processions the body of *epheboi*, wearing sometimes even crowns of gold, formed a brilliant cluster in the spectacle.

The Jews participated. In Egypt they had long had the right to do so, and there is evidence that some did. At Iasus they certainly did. In Jerusalem itself Jason-Jeshua got permission in 175 BC to establish a gymnasium and a body of ephebes, and to enrol the men of Jerusalem as citizens of Antioch (1 *Macc*. 1.14-5; 2 *Macc*. 4.9-14; Jos. *Ant*. 12.251). There was, of course, already a gymnasium in Antioch. Herod built gymnasia in Damascus, Ptolemais (Acco) and Tripolis, perhaps developing older foundations. We know of gymnasia in Aradus, Philadelphia, Petra, and the Phoenicians at least were well-known in intercity contests. What was happening in Jerusalem was only an extension to the homeland of what was happening outside; indeed it was only a logical extension of a deeply permeating Hellenism, and we are told that it was welcomed by the upper classes in the capital.

The other symbols of Greek culture were the stadium, theatre and hippodrome. In Alexandria the Jews participated in athletic contests. Paul certainly knew all about them and used them in vivid metaphor of his own career. There were theatres at Gerasa — two of them — and Kenath and probably elsewhere, and there were certainly Jews who knew their Greek tragedy. One Ezekiel wrote a tragedy in Greek on the subject of Moses, complete with episodes, messenger's speech and choral interludes. More, as Horace Kallen amply demonstrated in a neglected book, the author of *The Book of Job* undoubtedly knew his Aeschylus and probably his Euripides; he structures his work as a tragedy, with prologue, lyric interludes, and epilogue. As to a hippodrome, Herod established one in Jerusalem itself.

The Greek language was already well established. In the

third century BC it was bilingual scholars from Jerusalem who went to Alexandria with the blessing of the high-priest Eleazar, on the invitation of Ptolemy Philadelphus to translate into Greek the Torah and the Prophets. The Jewish historian Eupolemus actually derived the name Jerusalem from Greek words. The inscription over the Court of the Gentiles, like the inscription over the cross of Christ, was in Greek and Latin. Only a Greek-speaking crowd could have misunderstood Jesus's words *'Eli Eli lama sabachthani'* as a cry to Elias. Paul addressed the Jerusalem mob in Aramaic to startle and pacify them, not because they could not understand Greek (*Acts* 21.40). Fragments of a Greek text of scripture have even been found in the Qumran caves. The Murabba'at finds, somewhat later but from a remote area, are also significant: they show that in that unsophisticated place in the second century AD marriage contracts and business contracts between Jews were written in Greek. The Galilee, the main area of Jesus's ministry, was a network of trade-routes and a conglomeration of peoples; it was called 'Galilee of the Gentiles'. Spoken Greek was a matter of ordinary commercial, political and social necessity. Outside the Galilee the reverse was true, at least of the upper classes. They would acquire a fluency in reading Greek, but it was regarded as disreputable to speak Greek fluently (Jos. *Ant.* 20.11.2). Greek names are common among Jews in the Hellenistic Age, Theodotus, Theophilus, Dositheos and Dorotheos, and double names like Apollonius-Jonathan (no inhibitions about an idolatrous Greek name any more than Christians had later over a name like Dionysius or Monnica) or Jason-Jeshua or Heras-Ezekiel.

Greek thought began to inform Jewish literature. We have noticed this in *Job*. *Ecclesiastes* is tinged with Epicureanism and shaped as a diatribe; the author was also familiar with Aristotle (2.3) and the Stoics (1.9-10, 17; 3.16-17; 9.11-12). *The Wisdom of Solomon* actually asserts that the Divine Wisdom teaches the four cardinal virtues of Plato (8.7) and expresses a Platonic hope of individual immortality (3.1-4). *The Song of Songs* is a typically Hellenistic love-idyll, a Jewish version of a Theocritan pastoral. 4 *Maccabees* is influenced by Stoic thought. Pythagorean thought reached through and affected Artapanus' *Life of Moses*, and even some of the stricter sects, Pharisees and Essenes: the evidence of Josephus on this point has been confirmed by the Qumran discoveries. There were others too, whose work has not survived, besides the dramatist Ezekiel — historians such as Demetrius, Eupolemos, Aristeas, Cleodemus, Jason of Cyrene; the philosopher Aristobulus who used the allegorical method to expound the Torah; poets such as Theodotus who wrote a Homeric poem *On Shechem* and Philo who composed an epic on the theme of Jerusalem with all the obscure learning of the age. When the other and better-known Philo set himself to his monumental synthesis of Greek and Hebrew thought, he was building on very strong foundations.

The second century BC saw a revolt against Greek domination, headed by the Maccabees. It is important to see that their rising was occasioned by the specific issue of idolatry, the profanation of the Temple of Yahweh by a statue of Zeus, not by general Hellenization. It no doubt checked the spread of Hellenization. It could not and did not undo the work of a century and a half. The Hasmonaean rulers who enjoyed a century of semi-independence after the uprising bore Greek names such as Alexander and Aristobulus. Their coins were inscribed in Greek as well as Aramaic. An alliance with Sparta, originally in 300 BC, was renewed in the second century. The letter from Jonathan in 1 *Maccabees* 12 actually calls the Spartans 'brothers'. It does not matter whether the letter is genuine; the important point is that it was accepted as genuine, and that belief in the kinship was long-lasting (2 *Macc.* 5.9; Jos. *BJ* 1.515; *Ant.* 12.255).

Even after the Romans had come the permeation by Greek culture continued. The last half of the first century BC saw the rule of Herod the Great. He was a usurper, and hated by the patriots. But he ruled for a long time, and his policies must have moulded the thought of people throughout the country. Josephus calls him 'more friendly to the Greeks than to the Jews' (*Ant.* 19.7.3). The great Temple he built for Yahweh was a Greek temple. The other public buildings of the period, including the hippodrome, were Greek. The coins now bore Greek inscriptions without the Aramaic. We may, if we like, discount the Greek thinkers and authors at Herod's court; we cannot discount the Greek loan-words in *The Mishna*, which are numerous, nor the fact that *The Mishna* permits a bill of divorce to be written in Greek (*Gittin* 9.8). More, the Scroll of the Torah might be written in Greek. The first teacher named in *The Mishna* bears the Greek name Antigonus. The Nash papyrus suggests that Hebrew was still in liturgical use in Egypt in the first century BC, but before long even the *Shema'* was authorized in Greek. The fact that a law was passed somewhat before AD 70 forbidding Rabbis to teach their sons Greek shows that up to that point they were doing so.

In general, then, the evidence is that by the time of Jesus Jewish culture was well mixed in with the prevailing Hellenistic culture. The Judaism to which he came was Hellenistic Judaism.

THE ROMANS

The Romans provided an additional complication. They had been fishing in eastern waters since the Hannibalic wars, but were reluctant to take over imperially: the narrowly based senatorial oligarchy were afraid that they would have to let others into a share of power if they extended their administrative commitments too widely. Eventually circumstances forced them, and in 146 BC they took over Greece, and in 133 BC inherited Pergamum. Judas Maccabaeus had perhaps negotiated with the Romans in 161 during their period of non-intervention. His brother Jonathan also had no success, but their brother Simon was recognized by the Romans. Rome, having moved into the east, was in fact steadily undermining the power of Syria, and it was this as much as anything which caused the Greek rulers of Syria to leave the later Hasmonaeans to their own devices.

It was a state of affairs which could not last. The first century BC saw a succession of military autocrats at Rome establish temporary periods of dominance through a devastating series of civil wars. By the 60s the leading soldier was Cn. Pompeius, Pompey the Great. His ambition was to settle the East and extend Roman power to the Euphrates. He established the Roman province of Syria. Judaea was at the time in a state of some turmoil. This did not suit Pompey's book. He marched on Jerusalem, was held up for three months before he could capture the mountain-citadel, and went into the inner shrine of the Temple and was amazed to find no image there. He limited the territory of Judaea and put in a puppet to rule at Jerusalem.

At Rome there was an uneasy coalition between Pompey, Crassus and Caesar. Crassus had military ambitions in the east. He plundered the Jerusalem Temple on his way to his doom and death. Caesar and Pompey, left without a buffer, clashed, and Caesar won. He was favourably disposed to the Jews, and when he was assassinated in 44 BC, the Jews were among his chief mourners. The liberators made for the east, and the Epicurean Cassius was proconsul of Syria. He died at Philippi; there was a new triumvirate of Caesar's heir Octavian (the future Augustus), Lepidus and Mark Antony. By 31 BC Octavian achieved sole power. Before that Herod had been set in power by Antony's legions, despite Cleopatra's hatred of him; after Antony's defeat he was quick to ingratiate himself with Octavian. Ruthless, suspicious and tyrannical, he none the less brought prosperity, and the country was more at peace than his own palace. But despite the splendour of the Temple he built, the religious Jews scorned and hated him. The Pharisee who wrote *The Assumption of Moses* draws an unforgettable picture:

> An insolent king shall succeed them, who will not be of the race of the priests, a man bold and shameless, and he shall judge them as they deserve. And he shall cut off their chief men with the sword, and shall destroy them in secret places, so that no one may know where their bodies are. He shall slay the old and the young, and he shall not spare. Then the fear of him shall be bitter in their land. And he shall execute judgments on them as the Egyptians executed upon them, over thirty-four years, and he shall punish them.

So the eye of faith saw the tyrant as the instrument of God.

Herod died. The Romans were content to have puppet-rulers rather than take over direct responsibility for a notoriously difficult land. Herod had four sons left alive. They appealed to Augustus to decide between them; the Jews sent an embassy asking for a Roman administrator rather than any of the Herods. Augustus divided the country between three of them, Antipas being tetrarch of the Galilee and Peraea, Philip tetrarch of the north-east, and Archelaus ethnarch of Judaea, Samaria and Idumaea. Archelaus was such an appalling ruler that he achieved the remarkable feat of uniting the Jews and Samaritans against him. He was banished in AD 6, and the emperor decided to administer this key-territory through a procurator drawn from the middle-class, inferior in rank to the senatorial governor of Syria but with general administrative independence, governing from Caesarea. It was this takeover which occasioned Quirinius' census, which was connected with taxation: he took the opportunity of having a proper census of the whole of the province of Syria. The census created unrest and Judas of Gamala and a Pharisee named Zadok organized an uprising, which was ruthlessly crushed.

The first procurator, Coponius, ruled for only three years; he was succeeded by M. Ambibulus, and he by Annius Rufus, each for a seemingly uneventful three years. After that longer periods became the norm. Valerius Gratus governed from AD 15 to 26; he appears to have had some control over the office of high-priest, and there were actually five during his governorship. He was succeeded by Pontius Pilate, whose name has recently been found in an inscription at Caesarea. He was there for ten years. The picture in the gospels has led unwary readers to think of him as a weak man. In fact he was a strong man, headstrong perhaps and lacking in tact, but undoubtedly decisive.

In the meantime the other two sons of Herod had held on to office for a long period. Philip ruled for thirty-seven years, and won the praise of Josephus for his mild and peaceable rule, his prompt and equitable justice, and the fact that he travelled freely within his territory and never went outside it, so that he was always available in time of need. Antipas followed his father's tradition as a great builder, establishing a new capital named Tiberias in honour of the emperor in the best region of the Galilee. He was evidently a shrewd ruler, and though his territories were potentially turbulent, we can be certain that there were no disturbances of any importance, or Josephus would have mentioned them, and indeed Antipas would not have found favour with the mordantly able Tiberius. Antipas is associated with the execution of the prophet John the Baptist; it is possible that he saw John's followers as a danger to the peace and thought it better to have him out of the way, but our records show him as reluctantly acceding to the execution in fulfilment of a rash promise. In fact the episode was indirectly concerned with a disturbance of another kind. Antipas' first wife was daughter of the Nabataean king Aretas. He threw her over for Herodias, and Aretas retaliated by military action. Tiberius was willing to give military support to a man he trusted, but died before action was taken, and his successor Gaius, nicknamed Caligula, doubted Antipas' loyalty and banished him, with Herodias, to Gaul.

It will be clear in this way that there was little or no cultural influence from Rome at the time of Jesus. Latin was, with Greek, the official language, and no doubt the procurator's headquarters in Caesarea saw life lived the Roman way, and the same will have been true on a smaller scale for the garrison in the Antonia tower in Jerusalem. But for the rest Jerusalem was largely untouched, and the Galilee totally so. The culture of the eastern part of the Roman Empire was Greek.

What there was in Judaea proper was the Roman military and imperial presence. Pilate was tactless in parading this; his soldiers carried idolatrous emblems (as the Jews thought) within Jerusalem. Taxation was another sore point, and another of Pilate's tactless acts was to impound for secular use in developing Jerusalem's water-supply money given to the Temple treasury for sacred purposes. But even if Pilate and his successors had been souls of tact, sooner or later, unless the Jews had taken the very different road of Jesus, there would have been violent uprisings, simply because of alien dominion.

JEWISH PARTIES

At this period there were four main parties among the Jews.

At the time of the Maccabees we find a group called the Chasidim, who were religiously purist and politically quietist. Their successors were known as Pharisees, or separated ones. Josephus dates their origin to the time of Jonathan, but we cannot really trace them back beyond the last quarter of the second century BC. They were austere in their religious observances, progressive and constructive in many of their social actions. They were responsible for development in synagogue worship and more widely in education. They had considerable popular influence, and often themselves came from the working class, herdsmen, smiths, wood-cutters, petty traders. They were not a large group and did not number more than 6,000. In our records of the life of Jesus they appear as opposed to him because of the freedom with which he treated religious observances, but in fact the representation is one-sided (though no doubt they did so oppose Jesus) and the result something of a caricature. Jesus was far closer to the Pharisees in outlook than either was to the Sadducees, and there is little or no indication of Pharisaic opposition to the followers of Jesus later.

The Sadducees originated at much the same time. The name is perhaps derived from Zadok, the great high priest of Jewish tradition. They were an aristocratic, politically powerful group, from whom the high priests and elders were largely drawn. The French would call them *bien pensants*. For political reasons they favoured association with the Graeco-Roman world; for the same reason they opposed religious narrowness. They therefore confined their religious observance to the Torah and did not accept the body of interpretative tradition which had grown up around it. For similar reasons they did not believe in an afterlife, or in intermediate spiritual beings such as angels. It was their political manoeuvring which led to the execution of Jesus: 'It is expedient that one man should die for the people, and that the whole nation should not perish' (*John* 11.50).

A third group, also formed about the same time, were the Essenes. They were closer to the Pharisees than to the Sadducees; indeed they might with more justification have been called the separated ones, since with them pietism and religious purism led to withdrawal into separated communities. Our knowledge of them for a long time was mainly from Josephus, but the discovery of the Qumran community by the Dead Sea has afforded us a closer knowledge of one such group and its life and beliefs. They were a community of the new covenant who had gone apart to practise devotion to the Torah, and to await the apocalyptic end when Yahweh would overthrow the powers of evil and inaugurate his Kingdom. It is striking that the theological writings of this purist group are shot through and through with Hellenistic modes of thought, especially with Stoic theology, determinism, astrology, and belief in spiritual beings.

The fourth group are usually called the Zealots. It has been argued that the name should strictly be confined to the group formed around John of Gischala in the AD 60s. However, Josephus explicitly traces the origin of the movement to the rising of Judas of Gamala in AD 6. The Zealots were intense in their religious dedication, like the Pharisees and Essenes, but, unlike these, did not follow a policy of political quietism or withdrawal, but of violent resistance to alien government, and especially from any Gentile act which offended religious susceptibilities. Whatever name we give to the movement, it existed from the moment of Roman rule, and continued throughout the period up to the fall of Jerusalem. We can trace its members under a variety of names. One is *sicarius* or dagger-man; another is Cananean; another is the Aramaic *barjona*; yet another is the term 'brigand' or 'robber'.

It will be noticed that the division between these four parties is partly religious: the Sadducees being less stringent in religious observance than the other three. It is partly in what one might call ecclesiastical polity, the Sadducees favouring a hierarchical structure, the Pharisees wanting a much broader base among the common people, the Essenes seeking the dedicated community. It is partly a matter of political action, the Sadducees favouring involvement even at the cost of compromise, the Pharisees quietism, the Essenes withdrawal, and the Zealots violent protest. It is essential to see that for the Jews religion, ecclesiastical government and politics were not three independent fields but aspects of one single theocratic outlook.

BIBLIOGRAPHY

It is inevitable that one is influenced by the books on which one was trained, and I have turned particularly to W. O. E. Oesterley and T. H. Robinson *A History of Israel* (London 1932), and to the excellent but slighter N. H. Baynes *Israel Amongst the Nations* (London 1928) and H. W. Robinson *The History of Israel* (London 1938). Also, more recently, B. W. Anderson *The Living World of the Old Testament* (London² 1967); J. Bright *A History of Israel* (Philadelphia 1959); M. Noth *The History of Israel* (ET London² 1960). For the ideas I have learned to swear by three books: H. W. Robinson *The Religious Ideas of the Old Testament* (London 1913); N. H. Snaith *The Distinctive Ideas of the Old Testament* (London 1947); W. A. L. Elmslie *How Came Our Faith* (Cambridge 1948). See also S. H. Baron *A Social and Religious History of the Jews* vol. 1 (New York 1952). It would be possible to compile an immense bibliography, but I do not believe that anyone will go far wrong with those guides.

For the Greek period we now have Martin Hengel's indispensable *Judaism and Hellenism* (ET Philadelphia 1974). Also useful are V. Tcherikovier *Hellenistic Civilization and the Jews* (Philadelphia and Jerusalem 1959), S. Lieberman *Greek in Jewish Palestine* (New York 1942), and *Hellenism in Jewish Palestine* (New York 1950), and the older N. Bentwich *Hellenism* (Philadelphia 1919). I was brought up on, and still find lucid and attractive, E. Bevan *Jerusalem Under the High-Priests* (London 1924). See further my own paper 'Athens and Jerusalem' in *Religious Studies* 8 (1972) 1-13, on which I have drawn extensively. Note also H. Kallen *The Book of Job as a Greek Tragedy* (New York 1918); I. Lévy *La Légende de Pythagore de Grèce en Palestine* (Paris 1927); E.R. Goodenough *Jewish Symbols in the Greco-Roman Period* 12 vols (New York 1953-65).

For the Hellenistic Age generally it is hard to better W. W. Tarn *Hellenistic Civilization* (London³ 1952). See also my own *The Heritage of Hellenism* (London 1973).

The best treatment of the Stoics is in German : M. Pohlenz *Die Stoa*, 2 vols (Göttingen 1948-9). See also the brief but palmary F.H. Sandbach *The Stoics* (London 1975). For a useful anthology M. Hadas (ed.) *Essential Works of Stoicism* (New York 1964) For Philo see H. A. Wolfson *Philo* 2 vols (Cambridge, Mass. 1947) For the Romans in Judaea E. M. Smallwood *The Jews under Roman Rule* (Leiden 1976).

For further background A. C. Bouquet *Everyday Life in New Testament* Times (New York 1954); H. Daniel-Rops *Daily Life in the Time of Jesus* (ET New York 1962).

2
Jesus

THE PROBLEM OF THE SOURCES: THE FOUR GOSPELS

It is notoriously difficult to reconstruct the life of Jesus. Günther Bornkamm says bluntly, 'No one is any longer in a position to write a life of Jesus', but that is overstated.

Our primary source comprises four 'gospels' or proclamations of good news. They were not originally so entitled. Their putative authors go by the names of Matthew, Mark, Luke and John, and their earliest titles are simply *According to Matthew* and the like. But the generic term 'gospel' is important as indicating that they are not and are not intended to be historical narratives or literary biographies. They are gospels, proclamations of good news, calls to faith, extended preachments. It has been often and rightly pointed out that the words spoken by the early Christian leader Peter at the festival of Pentecost form a synopsis of *According to Mark*:

> Men of Israel, listen to me: I speak of Jesus of Nazareth, a man singled out by God and made known to you through miracles, portents, and signs, which God worked among you through him, as you well know. When he had been given up to you, by the deliberate will and plan of God, you used heathen men to crucify and kill him. But God raised him to life again, setting him free from the pangs of death, because it could not be that death should keep him in its grip. (*Acts* 2.22-4 NEB)

Mark similarly is structured around, first, miracles, portents and signs, and then the account of Jesus' execution followed by the affirmation that he rose from the dead. It does not sound like a biography. But the fact that it is not biography or history does not mean that it has no connection with biography or history. Had there not been a historical Jesus, and had he not said and done some at least of the things attributed to him, there would have been no gospel to proclaim. In particular, one article in the later creed of the Christians, that Jesus 'suffered under Pontius Pilate', places his death in a firm historical context. Pontius Pilatus, as we have seen, was procurator of Judaea from AD 26 to 36.

We do not know the dates at which the four gospels were written, but most scholars would place them all in the second half of the first century AD: that is to say that they were all published within the lifetime of people who could recall the main events they describe. The first three, *Matthew*, *Mark* and *Luke*, are closely interrelated, and are called synoptic because they have a broadly unified standpoint. It is fairly clear that *Matthew* and *Luke* in their present form draw on *Mark*, though some scholars have argued for the primacy of *Matthew* in one form or another. *John* tells the same story, though his selection of incidents and some details of chronology are different; he records the same teaching, but in different language; he is more politically aware, and at the same time more spiritual and mystical. *John* is normally dated to about AD 95; a papyrus fragment of the work written in about AD 130 was found in Egypt, and refuted the claims of those who considered it to be a late second-century work. Some critics, maintaining its total independence from the other gospels, date it as early as AD 80. *Luke* is from the same pen as *Acts*, as the two introductions make clear. *Acts* leaves its central figure Paul in prison. It is on the whole unlikely that the book would finish like that if Paul were dead. He was executed in about AD 65. If the deduction is correct (and the only reasonable alternative would be that the author had planned, but failed to write, a third volume), then *Acts* must be dated to AD 62 or thereabouts, and *Luke*, the 'former treatise', perhaps to AD 60. This would put *Mark* back to the early 50s. *Matthew* in its present form may be almost any date from AD 65 to 80.

The gospel-writers had earlier traditions to draw on. A strong case can be made out for an earlier collection of Jesus's sayings, used by *Matthew* and *Luke*, originally compiled as a manual of moral instruction for converts; this is usually called Q, a symbol devised to contrast with P (traditions going back to Peter), and perpetuated as the initial letter of *Quelle* ('source'). *Matthew* and *Luke* each had its own special source, and some scholars have suggested that *Mark* represents the traditions of the church at Rome, Q those of Antioch, *Matthew's* special source that of Jerusalem, *Luke's* that of Caesarea. Many would add that *John* represents the special traditions of Ephesus.

All the gospels are built up of fragmentary passages loosely connected with one another. One of the scholarly movements in between the two world wars, called *Formgeschichte* or *Form-criticism*, tried to identify these snippets or *pericopai*, and to show why they were preserved within the church, by classifying them under different heads. There are *paradigms*, *apophthegms* or *pronouncement-stories* (as they are variously called), preaching material enshrining some saying, often in the vaguest of contexts. There are *tales*, *miracle stories*, *wonder stories* or *novellen*. Here the interest is generally not in words but in action. Here there is a much closer attention to detail; sometimes we might almost say that there was pleasure in the story for its own sake. The function of these is to act as signs of Jesus's power. There are *myths* and *legends*. Both words bear in popular usage the meaning of something unreal or untrue, but this is not their real meaning. A myth enshrines a religious message, a legend is something which ought to be read. Both may be fact or fiction. Interestingly only two of the shorter legends are really about Jesus, one telling how as a boy he stunned the men of learning by the acumen of his questions, one telling of his escape from a mob at Nazareth. But the narrative of his execution may be included here. There are *sayings*, which were preserved as part of the teaching about the Christian way of life. These may be subdivided into Wisdom sayings, Prophetic and Apocalyptic sayings, Laws and Community regulations, Sayings in the first person (though this overlaps the other divisions) and parables. There are *controversies* which were preserved to guide and strengthen the followers of Jesus in the controversies they in turn had to face. Radical criticism has suggested that much of this material was altered or even invented after the time of Jesus, that its origin rather than its preservation was due to the Church, or, at best, that we simply do not know and cannot get back behind the appearance of the *pericope* in the life of the Church. That however is overstated, and the value and truth of Form-criticism does not depend on such extreme assertions.

But although the gospels are built out of pre-existent material, each bears the stamp of an integrative hand and a distinctive personality. Two of them are attached to the name of close associates of Jesus. It is almost certain that Matthew the tax-collector cannot have written the gospel in its present form. Papias, a bishop from Asia Minor in the early second century, tells us that Matthew wrote *The Logia* (whatever they may be) in Hebrew. The author of the gospel quotes the Jewish scriptures in Greek. *The Logia* ('oracles' or something like it) has by some scholars been identified with Q, by others with a selection of relevant prophecies. But an attractive hypothesis identifies it with the systematic oral teaching given by Matthew, perhaps in Jerusalem, which underlies the gospel. At any rate it is reasonable to think that even if Matthew did not write the gospel which bears his name he was involved with the transmission of the material on which it distinctively draws. *John* claims to depend on an eye-witness, 'the disciple whom Jesus loved', and it shows a close knowledge of the geography of Palestine, and this eye-witness is usually identified with John, the Son of Zebedee. On the other hand there are some difficulties, particularly in the style of Jesus, to attributing the authorship to this John. Now three letters in the New Testament are attributed to John, and in two of them he calls himself 'the Elder'. This is not a title which an apostle would be likely to claim. Papias tells us of two Johns, one 'the Elder' whom he knows personally, and one, a direct disciple of Jesus, who had passed on. The most widely accepted account is that the gospel was written by John the Elder and incorporated the evidence of John 'the disciple whom Jesus loved'. But *Mark* also has a similar incorporation of firsthand evidence, if we can trust Papias, who calls Mark Peter's interpreter. Furthermore, Mark and Luke were well-known figures in the early Church. Mark is sensibly identified with John Mark, in whose mother's house the Christians in Jerusalem used to meet (*Acts* 12.12). Mark was a cousin to the great missionary Barnabas, and was in Rome with Paul and Peter. So he had access to a number of people who were close to Jesus, and, if we are right in thinking that he includes an otherwise pointless story about a young man wearing a linen cloth who narrowly escaped arrest with Jesus (*Mark* 14.51-2) as an account of something that happened to him, he was close to the events himself. Luke, a much-loved doctor, almost certainly did not know Jesus in the flesh, but he travelled widely with Paul, and visited Jerusalem and other Christian communities. He was probably himself an early member of the Christian community at Antioch. So although Jerome says of his two books, 'He wrote the gospel from hearsay but *Acts* as an eye-witness', the hearsay was not without authority. The four gospels form an impressive body of primary evidence.

Further, precisely because the four authors are selective, but differently selective, they complement one another. Not merely do they represent four different local church traditions, and the memories of three separate close associates of Jesus, but each of the writers has his distinctive interest. *Mark* is a book of fairly simple literary style, endowed with touches of realistic description, presenting a sophisticated theology. Mark was writing primarily to affirm that Jesus was the Messiah. This involved him in wrestling with two problems, one why Jesus was not more readily recognized as the Messiah and did not openly so proclaim himself, the other how the Messiah could die an inglorious death. So he shows Jesus's whole career as Messianic; he depicts Jesus as triumphant over the supernatural forces of evil; and (to encourage the Christians of his own day) he shows Jesus triumphant through suffering, and promising his followers similar sufferings through which they too would become triumphant. *Matthew* is the most comprehensive of the gospels, whether in terms of the life or teaching of Jesus. It is clearly written by a Jew for Jews. Matthew asserts that the New Covenant depends on the Old, but transcends it. His aim is to show that

Christianity is the true consummation of Judaism, and that Jesus is the true Messiah. He argues, sometimes straining his argument, that the fulfilment of the words of the prophets is to be seen in Jesus. He claims that Jesus fulfils and transforms the three most precious concepts of the Jews, the chosen people, the Temple and the Torah. By contrast Luke is a Greek writing for Greeks; the great Origen said that this gospel was composed for converts from the Gentiles, and Jerome commented on the elegance of the style, 'smacking of secular rhetoric'. The stories are beautifully told: even if the parable of the Good Samaritan is an authentic record of Jesus's narration, it is to Luke that we owe the account of the Walk to Emmaus. Luke's gospel is theological enough, but it reads less like a sermon, and perhaps owes something to lives of Epicurus, themselves written to exalt one who in his own way brought 'the prescription of salvation'. Luke, writing for Greeks, was concerned to assert that Jesus offered salvation to all: 'The Son of Man came to seek and to save the lost.' Matthew carries the family-tree of Jesus back to Abraham, the ancestor of the Jewish people, Luke carries it back to Adam, the ancestor of all mankind. So Luke too is concerned with the poor, with the place of women in society, with social justice. *John* has an air different from that of the other gospels, though the differences are less than might appear at first blush; the synoptic gospels are in measure Johannine, and the Johannine gospel synoptic. John's express purpose in writing is that his readers 'might believe that Jesus is the Christ, the Son of God, and believing, have life in his name' (20.11). John handles his theology in a more obviously interpretative manner, using typology and symbolism, and bringing together wide resources of contemporary thought to do so.

As we must ask whether individual *pericopai* have been invented or modified to suit the needs of the Church, so we are bound to wonder how far the individual gospel-writers have adapted their material to suit their particular purposes. Certainly some discrepancies seem explicable in these terms. But it remains true that there was pre-existing material for them to adapt, and that they were concerned with some kind

Jesus

of record of the meaning of actual events which took place in Palestine round about AD 30. The gospels, because they interpret, need interpreting. But they are rooted in history. There is a Jesus of history behind the Christian faith. As Prof Léon-Dufour has put it, 'The fact of Jesus is presented as a life.'

OTHER SOURCES

Other sources for the life of Jesus are for the most part slight.

Paul's letters are in general earlier than the gospels. Paul did not know Jesus during Jesus' natural life, but he had access to many people who had known him. He tells us very little about Jesus's life, except for the Last Supper with the disciples, and the Crucifixion and subsequent events. But his Christian ethical teaching, although he sometimes imposes his own interpretations, is in fact an earlier record of the ethic of Jesus than the gospels provide.

We shall not expect to find much about Jesus in contemporary pagan writers. One more execution in an outpost of empire was neither here nor there, and Anatole France's story of Pilate in old age being asked about Jesus and replying, 'Je ne m'en souviens pas' is *ben trovato*. Suetonius mentions riots in Rome in AD 49 'at the instigation of Chrestus'; this may be a garbled account of a conflict between Jews and Christians. Tacitus tells of the persecution of Christians by Nero, and knows that 'they got their name from "Christ", who was executed by sentence of the procurator Pontius Pilate in the reign of Tiberius.' Pliny encountered Christians in Bithynia in about 112, but though his account of the Christians is important he knew nothing about 'Christ' except that he was hymned as a god.

The Jewish historian Josephus, in the eighteenth book of *Jewish Antiquities*, has a reference to Jesus:

> Now there was about this time Jesus, a wise man, if it be lawful to call him a man, for he was a doer of wonderful works, a teacher of such men as receive the truth with pleasure. He drew over to

him both many of the Jews, and many of the Gentiles. He was the Christ. And when Pilate, at the suggestion of the principal men amongst us, had condemned him to the cross, those that loved him at the first did not forsake him; for he appeared to them alive again at the third day; as the divine prophets had foretold these and ten thousand other wonderful things concerning him. And the tribe of Christians, so named from him, are not extinct at this day. (18,63 tr. W. Whiston)

One thing, however, is certain: Josephus did not write those words. They are clearly a Christian affirmation, and Josephus was not a Christian. But Josephus was a historian of the Jews, and it is probable that his work included some less adulatory reference to Jesus. It is possible that this has disappeared entirely, and the new paragraph been substituted. It is more likely that the Christian interpolator modified what he found. If so, Josephus probably stressed two things about Jesus, his performance of seemingly miraculous acts, and his teaching. It is noteworthy that the passage mentions Jesus as a teacher of Gentiles as well as of Jews. The passage is further evidence, if needed, for crucifixion by Pilate.

It should also be mentioned that the Slavonic and Old Russian versions of Josephus have interpolations, on which Robert Eisler built a brilliant but insubstantial fantasy. This was unwise, but there are interesting details — that Jesus was greeted as a second Moses, that he broke the Torah and did not observe the sabbath, that his word had power, that he performed healing miracles, that many people thought he could rid them of the power of Rome and urged him to use the Mount of Olives as a base for an assault on the Roman garrison, that he refused, and (in the Old Russian) that there was an inscription in the Temple referring to 'Jesus, a king who did not reign'.

We are aware of, and in some cases have fragmentary remains of, a number of other gospels. For the most part these are worthless. One group comprises patently fictitious inventions to fill up the gaps in the canonical gospels, for example on the childhood of Jesus. Another group was written to support theological views which did not emerge till the second century. A few of the others, such as *The Gospel according to the Hebrews*, seem to preserve some independent traditions; but they do not substantially alter the account we are able to give of the life and teaching of Jesus.

Similarly, there are a number of sayings of Jesus preserved for us in various sources, but not appearing in the gospels. Some are quoted in other parts of the New Testament. Some are preserved on a papyrus found in Egypt: one of the most interesting of these runs: 'Wherever there are two, they are not without God's presence; and where there is one only, I say, I am with him. Raise up the stone, and there you shall find me; cleave the tree, and I am there.' Some are quoted by the Christian fathers. Some come down to us from Moslem sources. Occasionally what is transmitted is not a saying but an anecdote. Such sayings and anecdotes tend to accumulate around well-known people. Socrates is a good example, but one need only reflect on the stories about Sir Thomas Beecham or Fred Trueman to realize that they need treating with caution. The most likely to be authentic are those which there is no obvious reason for inventing. Stories and sayings which do not fit the stereotype merit careful scrutiny. But again, although there are a few stories and sayings of considerable interest, our account of Jesus would not be essentially different if these had not been preserved.

JESUS: BIRTH

We know little for certain about Jesus' birth. *Mark* has nothing to say about it. Nor has *John*, a fact of particular interest when we reflect that John and Mary, Jesus' mother, were closely associated with one another, and, according to a story which we need not doubt, came to Ephesus together.

In *Matthew* and *Luke* there are stories of the birth of Jesus which have given to the celebration of Christmas some of its best-loved images. According to these stories, Jesus' mother Mary, though engaged to be married to a certain Joseph, was a virgin at the time, and conceived him without sexual intercourse. The birth took place at Bethlehem; Luke associates it with a census carried out by the governor Quirinius. There was no accommodation available, and the baby was born in an outhouse or stable. Luke tells of angels appearing to shepherds to proclaim the birth of the Messiah. Matthew tells of the appearance of a wonderful star, and of three eastern astrologers following it to Bethlehem, and offering rich gifts, and of king Herod's fear of a rival king leading him to murder the children in Bethlehem, a massacre from which Jesus escaped because his parents, supernaturally warned, took refuge in Egypt.

What can we say about these stories?

First that the chronology is impossible. Herod died in 4 BC. P. Sulpicius Quirinius became proconsul of Syria in AD 6, when he carried out a notoriously unpopular census: in any case a Roman census was not possible in Herod's reign. Second, it is not likely that the Romans would have required people, especially women in an advanced stage of pregnancy, to go to the homes of their ancestors for the purposes of census. (We have an edict from Egypt by which people were required to return to their own homes for census purposes, but that is a different matter.) Third, that Paul, our earliest witness, knew nothing about a virgin-birth, but on the contrary stressed the fact that Jesus was born naturally, so, in Paul's theology, taking upon himself all the taint of inherited evil. Both Matthew and Luke give genealogies of Jesus (which contradict one another), tracing his parentage back through Joseph. We perhaps should not make too much of this since, by the institution of levirate marriage, legally descent was calculated through the mother's first husband rather than through the physical father. But we can be certain that the people looked on Jesus as Joseph's son (*Luke* 4.22), though we may note in passing an early sneer that he was illegitimate (*John* 8.41).

The association of Jesus' birth with the Roman census, the hated instrument of Roman oppression, was of high symbolical significance. Jesus, as we shall see, was identified with the Messiah, who was the awaited liberator from Rome. He was executed by the Romans. It was natural to set his whole life in the framework of Roman rule. Furthermore, by the time the gospels were written the Christians were fascinated by looking for passages in the Jewish scriptures which might be linked with Jesus. Thus, the Messiah had to be born in Bethlehem (*Mic.* 5.2). He would be born of a 'virgin' (*Isa.* 7.14); the original Hebrew meant no more than 'young woman' but it was misinterpreted. Offerings of gold, frankincense and myrrh were well-attested gifts for a king (*Ps.* 45.8; 72.15; *Is.* 60.6; *Song of Songs* 3.6). Jesus had to be called out of Egypt because of the saying, 'Out of Egypt have I called my son' (i.e. Israel: *Hos.* 11.1). We must then say that these stories do not seem to be part of the tradition derived from Peter or, more importantly, from Mary; they are packed with internal contradictions and improbabilities; and we see good reasons why they might emerge. It is best to be sceptical.

Curiously enough, one part of the narrative which may be historical is the brilliant star. Kepler long ago showed that in 7 BC there was a close conjunction of Jupiter and Saturn in the constellation Pisces, which would give the effect of a star of abnormal brightness; again in 3 – 2 BC there was a series of remarkable conjunctions. But this does not give us a precise date for Jesus' birth: it is more likely that it was later recalled that there was a bright star 'at about the time he must have been born'.

CHILDHOOD AND YOUTH

Apart from the fantasies of the Infancy Gospels (there is a charming story of Jesus making birds out of mud: he then speaks to them, and they fly away), we have little record of Jesus' younger days. One story told how when Jesus was 12 his parents took him up to Jerusalem for the Passover, and how he gave them the slip when they were returning, so that they had to go back for him, finding him listening to and questioning the experts in the Temple.

At that point Joseph was still alive. By the time Jesus was 30 Joseph was clearly dead: he has no part in the later story. He may not have lived long. He was a carpenter. Every Jewish father brought his son up to a trade, and it is a near-certainty that Jesus was trained as a carpenter. Mark calls him just that (6.3): so in the second century does the pagan Celsus. Later stories tell of him helping his father at work. Another says that when he set up in business himself a notice over his door ran 'His yokes fit easily, and the burdens on them ride lightly.' This may be merely an adaptation of words spoken by Jesus in another context (*Matt.* 11.30). On the other hand, Jesus may well himself have adapted to his teaching words he had used literally elsewhere. Certainly metaphors and similes from carpentry came readily to him: he told for example of a man trying to get a speck of sawdust out of his mate's eye, while all the time there was a plank in his own (*Matt.* 7.3-5).

Jesus was the eldest son. Mark tells us of four younger brothers (James, Joses, Judas, Simon) and some sisters – how many we do not know (6.3 cf. 3.30). James, 'the Lord's brother' was later a prominent member of the Jerusalem church, presiding over it, a man of exemplary holiness and a martyr. Some interpreters, anxious to preserve the perpetual virginity of Mary, have argued either (following Epiphanius) that these were half-brothers and half-sisters, children of Joseph in a supposed early marriage, or (following Jerome) that they were cousins. Neither is the natural interpretation of the words. If Jesus had at least six younger siblings, and Joseph died while he was still a teenager, or not long after, then the secret of the hidden years is not difficult to discern. Jesus became the family breadwinner, and it was only when his brothers and sisters were old enough to fend for themselves that he felt the call to a different life.

One other episode from his youth must be mentioned. Judas of Gamala, who according to Josephus founded a 'fourth philosophy' among the Jews (that of those later called Zealots) raised an armed insurrection, and captured Sepphoris, a few miles north of Nazareth. It did not last. The Roman general Varus suppressed it ruthlessly, razed Sepphoris, and crucified the insurgents along the roadside. The boy must have seen the smoke and the corpses.

Meantime his character had been forming, strong and devout.

JOHN THE BAPTIST

Jesus was about thirty when the transformation took place. Luke dates it to the fifteenth year of Tiberius' reign, that is somewhere about AD 29; this is likely to be approximately right. The change is associated with the dramatic appearance of Jesus's cousin John, an ascetic who lived simply in the wilds with coarse home-made clothing and food he gathered for himself. John recalled the image of the prophets of old. Like them he warned of the imminent judgment of God. 'The one who is to come' would soon reveal himself; he was already among them (*John* 1.26). He would winnow the people, garner the good grain and reject the chaff. The axe might fall at any moment. So John called the people to honesty, generosity, integrity. Josephus called him 'a good man who encouraged the Jews to practise virtue and to behave properly to one another and to be devout towards God', but that is a colourless picture of his dynamic and terrible denunciations. He called the people to repent, that is, to change their outlook and purposes, and used a rite of baptism by immersion in the river Jordan. Converts to Judaism were expected in this manner to wash away their pagan past; but that the 'children of Abraham' should also be expected to do so was something new. Even so, this was only a preparation for a more cataclysmic baptism 'in the Holy Spirit and fire' on the part of 'the one who should come'.

The crowds flocked to receive baptism, Jesus among them. Jerome quotes a fascinating passage from *The Gospel according to the Hebrews*. Jesus' mother and brothers go to be baptized and ask him to come along. Jesus' answer is 'Why, what sin have I committed that I should go and be baptized by him? – unless perhaps these very words are a sin of ignorance.' At any rate Jesus went, putting himself alongside the serving soldiers, collaborators, figures from the religious establishment, and those whom the latter would despise. All our records concur in affirming that Jesus in his baptism had a profound spiritual experience. From this moment is to be dated his consciousness of his vocation.

THE WILDERNESS

His immediate response was withdrawal for six weeks into the wilds from which John had emerged. Here Jesus wrestled with the nature of his mission. The record, which must go back to Jesus himself, vividly and picturesquely told, recounts three temptations. They were not temptations to do anything cheap or mean, his character was already too steadfast for that to afflict him. They were subtler temptations, to pursue good ends by wrong means, means that were not God's. One was to use paranormal powers to secure food, for he was hungry out in the wilds. Some interpreters have treated this as a simple temptation to selfish action. But his answer 'Man shall not live by bread alone' has a wider application than to his own immediate hunger; in answering the temptation by an appeal to the Torah (*Deut.* 8.3) he is placing even the meeting of material needs under the authority of God. This came out later in his teaching: 'Set your mind on God's kingdom and his justice before everything else, and all the rest will come to you as well' (*Matt.* 6.33).

The second temptation was to secure political power on the devil's terms. The Messiah was expected to be the leader of a violent liberation movement. The most obvious means, to worldly wisdom, of securing political power, was to raise an army, and there were plenty of Jews ready to volunteer for such a campaign. The Zealots, or their immediate predecessors, fostered such a policy. But Jesus had a different vision of God and his ways, and he consistently refused to use violence to achieve his ends. He taught that the Son of Man, the new man, the true man, must suffer, and when one of his followers, who had shortly before identified him as the Messiah, protested, Jesus cut him short, calling him the Tempter; it is precisely this temptation that Peter was renewing.

The third temptation was to use paranormal abilities to compel men's assent by a spectacular miracle. Jesus must have been already conscious of abnormal gifts; he used them to help others; but he knew that such a knock-me-down demonstration of power could not — almost by definition could not — evoke the faith and trust and love which he saw as the basis of true living. God is not to be put to the test like that.

George Caird, in his commentary on this passage, writes well: 'Luke tells us that the devil departed from Jesus for the time being. Jesus had won an initial victory, but these same temptations were to recur throughout his ministry. The insistent demands upon his compassion, the enthusiasm that would make him a national hero, the suspicion that required a sign from heaven — all this was to end only with the mocking cry, "If you are the King of the Jews, save yourself!" '

JESUS IN THE GALILEE

From his period of withdrawal Jesus for a period seems to have followed John as a baptizer, but, on John's arrest for criticizing the local ruler, moved into the Galilee, whose inhabitants called it proudly '*the* Region'. It is a well-marked area, some fifty miles by thirty in extent, well-watered by streams from the hills, and exuberantly fertile. 'The soil', writes Josephus, 'is rich and fertile everywhere, covered with plantations of trees of all kinds. Its fruitfulness encourages even the laziest to take the trouble to cultivate it' (*BJ* 3,3,2). It was thickly populated, even if Josephus' figure of 3 million is overstated; there were villages and small towns dotted about everywhere. The population was very mixed; it was popularly known as 'Galilee of the Gentiles', and everyone was expected to be able to speak Greek. It was a network of roads, some of them important trade-routes. The Greek cities of the Decapolis were hard by.

Jesus' period in the Galilee was marked by four features.

First, he was a preacher and a teacher. He was addressed as 'Rabbi' not just by his own devoted followers, but by strangers as well. His basic message is concisely expressed by Mark (1.15): 'The time has come; the Kingdom of God has drawn near. Repent and believe the good news.' He preached in the open air; he spoke in synagogues. He proclaimed his message publicly; he discussed it privately with any who wished to come to him. His aim was to encourage his hearers to an awareness of the immediate presence of God and to induce from them the response of changed lives, and a new spirit of service in a new community. His teaching was vivid and brilliantly brought home by illustrations from everyday life and short stories and parables.

Second, he was active in healing. It is clear that he had unusual gifts. Sometimes these were gifts of discernment; he was quick to get at the roots of illnesses which we would call psychosomatic. A good example is the account of the paralytic whose friends lowered him in a stretcher from a roof-top to bring him to Jesus. Jesus knew that his immobility arose from his sense of guilt, and declared the forgiveness of his sins; from this he was able to walk away, carrying his stretcher. But sometimes the healing seems to have been physical; it flowed through Jesus' fingers as the power of God at work in his world. Jesus, undemonstrative as he was about his healing work, saw his power in throwing down the demons of disease as evidence of God's present rule.

Third, his work led him into controversy. The Sabbath, itself an admirable institution, a day of rest not merely for those in authority but for those whom they might otherwise exploit, and a day of worship and a reminder that all creation was God's, had become hedged round with formalistic interpretations and legalistic restrictions: for example it was regarded as legitimate to travel twelve miles but not more, to write one letter but not two, to untie a knot with one hand but not with two, to fasten a pail to a well with a band but not with a rope, to tie the ends of a broken lute-string but not to replace it, to eat food but not prepare it, and so to take vinegar to relieve toothache and swallow it (food) but not to spit it out (medicine). Jesus challenged these restrictions. He not merely healed on the Sabbath, maintaining that it must be right to do good on any day; he even justified his disciples for plucking ears of wheat and rubbing them in their hands (technically reaping and threshing), so casting scorn on petty interpretations. 'The Sabbath is made for man, not man for the Sabbath.' But Jesus seemed to be undermining the Torah, though he insisted that he was in fact fulfilling it. So with his moral teaching. He deepened the commandments of the Torah, by saying for example that it is not enough to refrain from the act of adultery but that the desire to commit adultery is itself condemnable; he extended them, as by calling for the love enjoined towards the neighbour to be extended to the enemy; and at times he contradicted them flagrantly, as when he said that people must be prepared to disown their parents for his and the gospel's sake. The religious establishment, always suspicious of popular preachers, found such unorthodoxy deeply disturbing, and we have records of a number of clashes.

Fourth, he attracted a large and varied following. He singled out twelve from among these as his close confidants. Several of them were fishermen from the Lake of Galilee. One was a tax-collector, that is a collaborator or Quisling who was working with the Roman occupying power. Some seem to have been seeking a military answer to Roman oppression. Simon the Zealot was almost certainly one (though it has been argued that a 'Zealot' in the time of Jesus, though not when the gospels were written, simply meant a religious enthusiast). Judas Iscariot may have been another; one explanation of his sobriquet is that it represents the Latin *sicarius* or dagger-man. Simon Barjona, leader of the Twelve, may have been a third, since *Barjona*, which may mean 'son of John', was another nickname of the guerrillas, and it was Simon who had and used a sword at the time of Jesus's arrest. The Twelve were all Jewish by religion but not by race or nationality, and one of them, Philip, had a Greek name. They were representative of a wider entourage which included a number of women. It was not socially possible for these to travel out on the preaching mission, but in every other way they seem to have been full and important members of the community growing around Jesus, and some of them were among his closer friends. Jesus in fact treated women with a respect and seriousness rare in his age. Even Rudolf Bultmann allowed this as something we could authentically say about the historical Jesus. He spoke freely with them in public. He stood firmly against the sort of dual morality by which a man sows his wild oats while a woman becomes culpably damaged goods. He was not ashamed to be seen with such women, and drew more than one to change her life. Respectable people looked askance at some of the company he kept; as he ironically remarked, 'The fit and well don't need the doctor' (*Mark* 2.17).

THE TEACHING

Jesus' teaching starts from God. His proclamation was of good news about God. His characteristic word for God is 'Father'. The idea of God as Father was commonplace enough, but Jesus gave it a new dimension by restoring its intimacy. His own prayers, and the prayer he commended to his followers began 'Abba', a word so intimate that it is almost to be translated 'Daddy'. The illustrations he uses are not from idealized and inevitably aloof human fathers but from ordinary family relations. He tells of a son who goes away and wastes his patrimony, but is still welcomed by his father on his return. That father is not abnormally saintly but normally human. God is close, and Jesus calls others to the attitude of simple trustfulness he had himself. He had come to a consciousness of himself as 'Son of God'; he gave to others the possibility of becoming children of God. Of course the language is anthropomorphic; it is anthropomorphic because it is personal.

Jesus spoke continually of the kingdom, rule or reigning of God, declaring that it was already upon his hearers. This meant that God was confronting them now, where they were. Jesus pointed to his own work: 'If by the finger of God I drive out the devils, then be sure the kingdom of God has come upon you.' In Jesus' presence, says C. H. Dodd, 'the dark forces within, which ravage the souls and bodies of men, were overcome and their victims made new', and this was a sign of God's present sovereignty. The old was being swept away; there was a new beginning, and it was focused on Jesus himself. John, the gospel-writer, saw it as a coming of light into the world; the darkness might reject it, but could not quench it. But to reject the light was itself a form of judgment; it meant living in darkness. In a mysterious saying Jesus declared that the kingdom of God was 'within' or 'among' his hearers. The meaning is uncertain. The sovereignty of God is within for it exists wherever men and women accept God as sovereign. It is in the midst, because Jesus himself, fully accepting and expressing the sovereignty of God, is in their midst, and because it is found in a visible community. Towards that community Jesus was working. He spoke a good deal of the Son of Man. Most people think that he was speaking of himself. But it was normal in Jewish teaching to personify a nation or group by a single individual figure, and it is possible that 'Son of Man' refers to the new humanity, the new people of God's kingdom. The Kingdom, in Jesus' vision, is growing unseen but triumphantly, like a tiny seed burgeoning into a great bush.

The kingdom transforms normally accepted values.

> Happy are you poor;
>   the kingdom of God is yours!
> Happy are you who are hungry now;
>   you will be filled.
> Happy are you who weep now;
>   you will laugh!
> (*Luke* 6.20-1)

In *Matthew* the catalogue is extended, ending

> Happy are the pure in heart;
>   they will see God!
> Happy are those who work for peace;
>   God will call them his children!
> Happy are those who are persecuted because
>   they do what God requires;
>   the kingdom of heaven belongs to them.
> (*Matt.* 5.7-10)

In Matthew's account Jesus gives to his disciples a new way of life. The single word which sums this up is 'love', and in a public encounter with a lawyer Jesus summed up the whole duty of man as love towards God and towards the neighbour. The story of the good Samaritan who helped the victim of highway robbery, and the injunction to show practical goodwill towards a Roman soldier impressing a Jew to carry his pack are clear indications that for Jesus neighbourliness knows no bounds, and love is action not attitude (*Luke* 10.25-37; *Matt.* 5.41). The word for 'love' in our Greek text is not *eros*, possessive, acquisitive love including sexual passion, capable of being sublimated into higher aspirations, nor *philia*, natural or reciprocated love, but *agape*, which means the patient, tolerant, persistent seeking of the wellbeing of another, regardless of any merit in them or response from them. 'How often am I to go on forgiving my brother if he goes on wronging me?', Peter asked Jesus. 'Is seven times enough?' 'Seven times?', replied Jesus. 'No! Seventy times seven' — that is indefinitely.

All this, even with Jesus' illustrations, does not form an ethical code. It does form an ethical commitment, a direction. Jesus was deeply concerned about behaviour. Men are known by their fruits. It is no good saying, 'Lord! Lord!' without living rightly. The nations will be judged not by whether they have acknowledged God but whether they have fed the hungry. But Jesus had no time for demonstrative do-gooding, or cold and proud uprightness and uptightness; he preferred to see warmth pouring out from a person even if their lives had been astray.

THE MESSIANIC BANQUET

One episode, which appears in all four gospels, is often called 'The Feeding of the Five Thousand'; Matthew and Mark indeed tell the story twice in versions with little significant difference. The episode was the culmination to the Galilean ministry. The disciples had returned from a preaching mission with a story of success. Jesus wanted to get away from the crowds with them for a quiet retreat. They took a boat across the lake; the crowds flocked round the shore. Jesus saw them 'as sheep without a shepherd' (a phrase with some roots in the Messianic traditions), and his heart went out to them, and he spent the day teaching them. When it was getting late, the disciples wanted to send the crowd away, but Jesus divided them into groups of 150 and sat them down. As Hugh Montefiore has said, it looks like a military operation, the organization of an army, but it did not lead to a military action. Then, according to the story, Jesus took a few loaves of bread and small fish, prayed over them, and they proved enough to satisfy the crowd. It is a curious story. It is not easy to accept a simple miracle, and the rationalizing explanations (as that everyone had brought a picnic but was hiding it, and Jesus's example of sharing led them to share) are not wholly convincing. But something happened, and Dodd is right to concentrate attention on its significance. John calls it a sign. Acted parables, symbolical actions reinforcing teaching, were a regular practice of the prophets; there is a good example in *Acts* 21.10 when Agabus takes Paul's girdle and uses it to tie his own hands and feet to symbolize Paul's future imprisonment. To break bread together then is a symbol of community. But Jesus also used the idea of a feast to signify the blessing of God's kingdom, to be revealed in the future but available now. And at the feast Jesus is the host. This is a Messianic banquet. In John's narrative, at the end the people want to make Jesus king, that is to challenge the power of Rome; they identify him with 'the one who is to come'. But Jesus will not allow this, and slips away. What seemed like a military operation has taken on a different meaning – the establishment of a sharing community.

THE MESSIAH

We have seen something of the expectation of the Messiah as a liberation leader, and of the hope that Jesus might turn out to be that Messiah. 'We hoped that he would be the one who was going to set Israel free', said one of his followers after his death (*Luke* 24.21). This last dramatic episode represented a turning-point. We can see in it Jesus's acceptance of the rôle of Messiah and his unexpected interpretation of that rôle. This meant that he was politically endangered, but that he also lost popular support. He left the Galilee. He did not turn away from the Jews, but he seems at one point at least to have deliberately passed through Gentile territory when another route would have been more direct (*Mark* 7.31), and we have a number of records of encounters with Gentiles; we have noticed that Josephus thought of him as a teacher of Gentiles as well as of Jews. The kingdom he proclaimed within a Jewish context was a universal kingdom.

Two episodes of some importance now took place. At or near Caesarea Philippi Jesus had a conversation with his followers. He asked them what people were saying about him. Various answers were given, that he was John the Baptist (now executed) reincarnated, or Elijah or one of the prophets. 'What about you?' he asked 'Who do you say that I am?' 'The Messiah', said Peter. Jesus praised him for his insight, and told them not to make it public. He then went on to tell them that the Son of Man must suffer. Jesus thus brought together, so far as we can see for the first time, the Messianic expectation and the vision of the Suffering Servant held by the great prophet of the Exile and contained in *Isaiah*. It was at this point that Peter, who had just before expressed the colossal hopeful insight, renewed the temptation Jesus had faced and rejected, and received Jesus' rebuke, a rebuke as forceful as the earlier commendation. But Jesus now went on to a new thought. Those who would come with him must shoulder the cross. Jesus, who had repudiated the way of violence, still expected to be executed as a revolutionary; for crucifixion was a Roman punishment for rebellion, not a Jewish punishment for blasphemy.

A few days later Jesus went up into the hills with three of his closest associates, and there went through a profound mystical experience in which they shared. A sensation of brilliant light is spoken of by many mystics in their moments of spiritual illumination, and there are well attested examples of the same sensation being shared by onlookers at the moment of the mystics' ecstasy. On the hilltop they saw Jesus transfigured, and two visionary figures with him, and said that they heard a voice, 'This is my dear son; listen to him.'

Jesus now made his way towards Jerusalem, knowing that

he was putting his head into a noose. It was the time of the Passover, and the city was crowded with pilgrims. He rode in on a donkey, and as he rode the crowds scattered palm-branches on the way and greeted him as the Messiah. Many of them must have been thinking on the vision of a Messiah who would ride in on a white horse to raise the liberation army.

> Look, Lord; raise up the son of David as their king
>   at the appointed time, God
>   to rule over your servant Israel.
> Arm him with might to break the tyrants.
>   Cleanse Jerusalem from the destructive oppression
>   of the Gentiles.
> In wisdom and justice let him drive out the sinners
>   from God's inheritance,
> crush the sinner's arrogance like an earthenware pot,
> crush his whole being with a mace of iron,
> blot out with a word the lawless Gentiles,
> put the Gentiles to flight with his mere threats.
>   (*Psalms of Solomon* 17.23-7)

But Jesus quite deliberately aligned himself with another prophetic passage from *Zechariah* (9.9-10). The king who comes humbly on a donkey comes to put an end to war and armaments and to speak peace to the Gentiles. As Jesus came within sight of the city he shed a tear. There were two ways before Jerusalem, the way of peace which would lead to salvation, and the way of war which would lead to destruction. He offered his people the first; but he knew that they were set on the second. Thirty odd years later it happened, and Jerusalem was sacked; we can still see the soldiers carrying off the *menorah* or seven-branched candlestick on the Arch of Titus in Rome.

JERUSALEM AND DEATH

On entering the city he made his way to the Temple, then retired to the nearby village of Bethany for the night. Next day he returned and flung down a challenge to the religious establishment. During the festival the outer court of the Temple was a market for money-changing and the purchase of sacrificial animals. Jesus entered the court in flaming anger, ordered the traders out, threw down the money-changers' tables, and shepherded the animals away, shouting, 'It is written "My Temple shall be called a house of prayer for all the nations", but you have made it a robbers' den.' The stress on 'all the nations' is noteworthy. It should be said that the popular picture of Jesus flailing a great whip at the traders has no authority in our records. There cannot have been a riot, or the Roman garrison on guard overlooking the Temple would have intervened. It was a remarkable display of personal authority. It was not a *coup d'état*; there was no attempt at a take-over. It was a challenge to the administration of religion by those in power. 'You cannot serve God and Money', he said on another occasion. But there was a positive message as well. In the vision of Zechariah, which Jesus was following, the day is looked for when men of all nations will go to Jerusalem to worship, and then there will be no trader in the Temple (14.21). The Zealots wanted Jerusalem cleansed from the Gentiles; Jesus wanted Jerusalem cleansed for the Gentiles.

Our records now tell of increasing confrontation between Jesus and the Jewish authorities. They laid verbal traps for him, but he was too skilful to fall into them. At the same time he told denunciatory parables which they knew were directed against them and their hostile rejection of the prophetic vision in favour of worldly security. John tells of a meeting of the Council in which the high priest Caiaphas summed up the issue by saying, 'It is more to your interest that one man should die for the people than that the whole nation should be destroyed' (*John* 11.47-53).

As the crisis drew near Jesus spoke to his disciples in mysterious apocalyptic language of the approaching new age. There would be a period of disaster, war, false Messiahs, persecution of his followers, natural cataclysms. Those who held out to the end would be saved; they would see the Son of Man coming in the clouds with great power and glory; the present generation will live to see it all. But no one knew the exact moment of revelation; they must therefore be constantly on the watch.

In the latter part of the nineteenth century liberal Christianity tended to ignore or play down this apocalyptic element in Jesus' teaching. In 1901 Albert Schweitzer, musician, musicologist, theologian and, later, missionary doctor produced an interpretation of Jesus centred solely on his eschatology. Neither does justice to the wholeness of Jesus' thought. To ignore the eschatology is to distort the evidence. Moreover there has been a change, at least of emphasis, from the bright vision of the natural growth of the kingdom which Jesus gave earlier to the dark prophecy of its unexpected bursting on to a period of terror. But the ethical teaching which Jesus gave to his disciples is not based (as a 'temporary ethic') on the imminent expectation of the end of the world but rooted in the very nature of God.

What then are we to say about this picturesque discourse?

Broadly speaking, there are three possible views.

The first is simply that Jesus was mistaken. This is the natural explanation. Christians have tended to reject it for dogmatic reasons. But Jesus in his full humanity was a child of his time, with all the ignorances and limitations of first-century human kings. He himself admitted that he did not know the precise details of what would happen (*Mark* 13.32). To accept this kind of fallibility in him is in no sense to denigrate what he was.

The second is that he was speaking about two things which have become blurred in our record. He was giving a sensitive insight into the near future, the persecution of his followers and the catastrophe hanging over Jerusalem as soon as the Jews turned to violence; he was also speaking of an ultimate destiny at some point in the indefinite future. Luke in particular is careful to make the distinction clear.

The third is that he was using imaginative language to describe what was actually happening. C. H. Dodd has taught us to think of 'realized eschatology', that is the present reality of the ultimate. Jesus had proclaimed that in his power over the forces of darkness the kingdom of God was already present among his hearers. Similarly John in his gospel (it is not quite clear whether he is attributing the words to Jesus or whether they are an editorial comment) sees present, not future, judgment in the rejection of the light. According to this view Jesus' apocalyptic is a drawing of the curtain from the real meaning of events, and his prophecy is a declaration of timeless truth rather than of future happenings.

The Jewish authorities now got hold of one of Jesus' intimate followers. The name of Judas has become a byword for treachery. But Judas' motives are obscure. Mark and Luke simply say that he went to the priests with information, for which they subsequently paid him. Matthew has an elaborately worked up story about a financial bargain, and subsequent repentance. John gives no details at all. It is unlikely that Judas was motivated by greed; Jesus did not pick that sort of person, and anyway the sum was nugatory. It is more likely that he was governed by misguided idealism; if he did belong to the Zealot wing he will have been puzzled and angry at Jesus' failure to capitalize on his triumphant entry or his successful cleaning-up of the Temple, and may well have thought to force Jesus' hand by threatening his arrest. But we do not know. For the priests time was urgent; they must get rid of Jesus before the Passover. But they could not risk riots if they arrested him in daylight, and Jesus took care to avoid the city after dark. They had to have inside knowledge of his whereabouts. Judas gave them that.

Meantime Jesus and his disciples met for supper in a private house. Whether or not it was the official date for the Passover meal, it was their Passover. It was a solemn occasion. Jesus gave a demonstration of service by washing his friends' feet. At supper he took bread, spoke words of blessing, broke it, and shared it with the others saying, 'Take this; this is my body.' Exactly what he meant by the words is controversial. What is not controversial is that he spoke them, and that his followers continued to share bread, actually and symbolically, in memory of that last meal. He also passed round a common cup, and after they had drunk said, 'This is my blood of the covenant, shed for many.' We can see something of his meaning here. The old covenant had taken place at Sinai between Yahweh and his people. This was the new covenant, of which

Jeremiah had spoken, the covenant associated not with Law but with Love, the covenant of God with his new people, the new community, the new Israel. By tradition such agreements were ratified by the sacrifice of an animal. Jesus was offering himself as the self-sacrifice to ratify the covenant of active, caring, sharing, nonviolent love.

John tells us that some of Jesus' most profound utterances were spoken on this occasion. They are impossible to summarize adequately. Briefly, he spoke of himself, seeing this as his moment of glorification; he was going to his Father, in obedience to and love of his Father; he would seem to be beaten by worldly powers, but that was not really so. He would leave them and return to them. He was so close to the Father, that the Father was at work in him, and anyone who wanted to know what the Father was like had only to look at him. He spoke of the disciples. They must have faith, and set their anxieties at rest. They must have love, the same quality of love for one another that he had shown them. For their lives depended on him; they were branches of the vine. So they would have peace, not peace as the world understood it, freedom from strife, but freedom in despite of strife; this was his gift to them. He spoke of the future. He promised them persecution, he also promised them a supporter in all their dangers, whom he called the Spirit of Truth or the Holy Spirit.

Now the end was near. They went out to a familiar rendezvous on the lower slopes of the Mount of Olives outside the walls, a garden called Gethsemane. Then Jesus went on one side to prepare for his ordeal. When he returned he was filled with calm determination. An armed guard, directed by Judas, appeared through the trees. Peter began the violent resistance for which Judas may have hoped, but Jesus put a stop to that firmly. The disciples scattered and Jesus was left under arrest.

At this period local courts did not have, under Rome, legal powers of life and death. They sometimes took them illegally, but this was not an occasion for such action. Jesus was brought before the Sanhedrin and condemned for blasphemy. They confronted him with his Messianic claims; our records of his answer vary, but he did not deny them. These however were not regarded as blasphemous. What was blasphemous was his claim to forgive sins, his arrogation to himself of a special relationship with the Father-God, and his apparent identification of himself with 'one like a son of man' seated at God's right hand and invested in prophecy with world-rule.

The high priests now had to make a capital charge stick with Rome. The Messianic claims offered just that. The Messiah was king of the Jews, a challenge to the Emperor's authority. Supporting charges were popular agitation and encouragement of refusal to pay taxes. The charges were purely political. Pontius Pilate, the governor, was not an unjust man. He would like to have ruled the business out of court. But he was an appointee of Sejanus, the recently discredited chief minister at Rome, and there was a witch-hunt on against Sejanus's supporters. The Jews threatened an adverse report to the Emperor. It would have been enough to break Pilate. He gave way. He asked Jesus, 'Are you the king of the Jews?' 'So you say', said Jesus, neither admitting nor denying; John adds, however, that he drew attention to the absence of armed forces. Pilate made a last attempt to save Jesus; he accepted the conviction but offered to discharge the prisoner. Three freedom-fighters were under arrest; the priests quickly worked up their supporters to shout for the release of one of these instead. Jesus and the other two were led away to death by crucifixion. Jewish custom demanded that as it was the Sabbath next day, the bodies should be taken down before sunset. That afternoon the other two were finished off. Jesus was found to be dead already, and was given hasty but decent burial through the good offices of a friend in high places.

AFTERMATH

The story of Jesus in our records does not finish there. It goes on to the conviction that Jesus rose from the dead, and we cannot ignore that conviction. It was based on two sorts of evidence. One was the fact that the tomb was found to be empty two days after the execution. The other was a number of people who claimed to have met Jesus during the days that followed.

Broadly, six explanations of this have been offered by different critics. The first is fraud on the part of the disciples. The second is self-delusion. The third is that Jesus was not actually dead when taken down from the cross but in a trance from which he later recovered. The fourth is that the reported events of physical survival are a mythical expression of spiritual survival. The fifth is that the disciples in some sense experienced the continuing presence of Jesus though not with the physical body he experienced before his death (in one of the stories he appears in a locked room). The sixth is that there was an actual physical and material resurrection of the dead body.

Four things seem certain. First, some tremendous experience hit Jesus' followers. They had abandoned him at his arrest; within a few weeks they were courting arrest themselves to tell others about him. Second, they declared unequivocally that this was Jesus' rising from the dead (whatever, exactly, that might mean), and it was on this firm conviction that the Christian Church was founded. Third, that some of the records are not compatible with the normal physical behaviour of a normal physical body. Fourth, that appearance of this kind lasted for a few weeks only and then came to a stop. It is probably best therefore to accept that the disciples had a series of profound mystical experiences in which they were aware of the continuing presence of Jesus, but not to press explanations further.

After the last of these appearances there followed ten days of waiting, and then came a fresh, and different, series of mystical experiences, sometimes of ecstatic inspiration, sometimes of quiet guidance. There was no vision of Jesus here, but they associated the experiences with the promise he made at the Last Supper, and spoke of the Holy Spirit, the Spirit of God or the Spirit of the Messiah (Christ).

BIBLIOGRAPHY

The gospels: A convenient conspectus of modern scholarship will be found in W. Barclay *The First Three Gospels* (London 1966) or in A. M. Hunter *Introducing the New Testament* (London^2 1957); Barclay has a good bibliography. Also the useful but miscellaneous and uneven collection of papers H. K. McArthur (ed.) *In Search of the Historical Jesus* (London 1970). The Pelican New Testament Commentaries are also generally excellent.

Other sources: A convenient, indeed for the most part a brilliant summary will be found in F. F. Bruce *Jesus and Christian Origins Outside The New Testament* (London 1974). Texts in M. R. James *The Apocryphal New Testament* (Oxford 1924).

Life: I owe much to two marvellous studies both of which carry immense learning lightly: C. H. Dodd *The Founder of Christianity* (London 1971); L. Grollenberg *Jesus* (1974 ET London 1978). I must confess to evading difficult details of chronology; they do not affect the general picture. Vincent Taylor *The Life and Ministry of Jesus* (London 1954) deals with these in a sensible, sensitive and scholarly way.

It is perhaps worth saying that one of the contributors to J. Hick (ed.) *The Myth of God Incarnate* (London 1977) lays down six criteria by which New Testament evidence may be accepted: (a) coherence; (b) incidental information; (c) material embarrassing to the later Church; (d) material Paul says was handed on to him; (e) material incorporating Aramaic and Hebrew words; (f) widespread tradition. On this basis he accepts twelve points about Jesus as relatively clear: (i) his public preachment of the reign of God; (ii) his link with the Baptist; (iii) his healings; (iv) the fact that he saw himself as the one in whom the Reign was being manifested; (v) as the Messiah; (vi) as the Son of Man; (vii) his interpretation of the Messiah in terms of a unique relation to God; (viii) emphasis on love as an interpretation of the kingdom; (ix) on love in life; (x) on love in the new community; (xi) his interpretation of his coming death as the means to a new relationship; (xii) his death on the cross followed by a later conviction that he was alive.

3
The Person of Christ

SON OF MAN

The early Christians were persuaded of the full humanity of Jesus. Whatever view might be taken of his conception, no one doubted that he came to life through the normal processes of human birth. The Word became flesh (*John* 1.14). Jesus grew up to be a normal human being. He was hungry (*Mark* 11.12) and thirsty (*John* 4.7; 19.28). He was moved by emotions of pity (*Mark* 1.41) and anger (*Mark* 3.5). He was subject to weariness (*Mark* 4.38; *John* 4.6). He wept at the death of Lazarus (*John* 11.35) and at the prospective fate of Jerusalem (*Luke* 19.41). As he prepared for his betrayal and death he was in agony so that his sweat became like great drops of blood falling down upon the ground (*Luke* 22.44). The author of *Hebrews* affirms that Jesus faced every temptation which other humans face (4.15). At the last he underwent a humiliating death (*Phil.* 2.8).

The title 'Son of Man' is ambiguous. There is no doubt at all that it goes back to Jesus himself. Except once, in the recorded words of the first martyr Stephen at the moment of his final vision and death, it appears only in the gospels and always from Jesus' lips.

Its primary meaning is one who is fully human.

> God is not a mortal that he should lie
> not a son of man that he should change his mind.
> (*Num.* 23.19)

> What is man that you think of him,
> the son of man that you care for him?
> (*Ps.* 8.4)

So the prophet Ezekiel hears a divine voice addressing him as 'Son of man', or, as we would say, simply 'Man!' The fact that Jesus chose to use this phrase should warn us against interpreting his message with too much of an otherworldly slant; a son of man works in this world. Even with this simple explanation we are left with an ambiguity between the meaning 'a man' (normally human) and '*the* man' (exemplarily human).

But 'Son of Man' had also acquired Messianic associations. The primary source for these was the apocalyptic vision in the seventh chapter of *Daniel*, where the prophet saw 'what looked like a human being' ('one like a son of man'), surrounded by clouds, and given authority, honour and royal power. This human figure seems to have symbolized the new Israel. This figure blurred and fused with a mythical figure widely found in the Near East, Primal Man (*archanthropos*) or Great Man or Perfect Man or Heavenly Man (*Urmensch*). Hippolytus, bishop of Rome in the early third century, has a long discourse on the theme in the fifth book of *The Refutation of All Heresies*, citing primal figures from Greece, Assyria, Phrygia, Egypt, Chaldaea, Samothrace, Thrace and elsewhere.

We can see the new concept in a Jewish apocalyptic work of the first century BC, *The Similitudes of Enoch*, which survives only in Ethiopic, linked with visionary passages from slightly different periods. Here the Son of Man is a supernatural figure, pre-existing from the beginning of the world (48.2), and endowed with sovereignty and judgment over all (62.6; 69.27).

> And there I saw one who had a head of days,
> And his head was white like wool,
> And with him was another being whose countenance
>   had the appearance of a man,
> And his face was full of graciousness like one of the
>   holy angels . . .
> 'This is the Son of Man who has righteousness . . . .'
>   (46.1-3)

The Person of Christ   57

> And he sat on the throne of his glory,
> And the sum of judgement was given to the Son of Man.
> (69.27)

This supernatural sovereign and judge is also called 'the Righteous One' (38.2 cf. *Acts* 3.14 of Jesus), 'the Elect One' (40.5 cf. *Luke* 9.55) and the Messiah (48.10). There is not much doubt that *Enoch* has influenced the New Testament writers, especially when we read of the Son of Man:

> He shall be a staff to the righteous whereon to stay themselves,
> And he shall be the light of the Gentiles,
> And the hope of those that are troubled at heart.
> (48.4)

But was Jesus himself thinking of this Messianic ruler from *Enoch* when he used the phrase 'Son of Man'? T. W. Manson argued that Jesus' use was based solely on *Daniel* and that he was not referring to himself in isolation but to the whole Messianic community. Manson examined carefully all the passages in which the phrase appears, and came to a conclusion which usefully links this corporate view with the application of the term to Jesus:

> It will be convenient to state at once the theory which will be maintained in the following pages. It is that 'Son of Man' in the Gospels is the final term in a series of conceptions, all of which are found in the Old Testament. These are: the Remnant (Isaiah), the Servant of Jehovah (II Isaiah), the 'I' of the Psalms, and the Son of Man (Daniel). It has been argued above that it is the idea of the Remnant which is the essential feature about each of these: and it is now suggested that Son of Man in the Gospels is another embodiment of the Remnant idea. In other words, the Son of Man is, like the Servant of Jehovah, an ideal figure and stands for the manifestation of the Kingdom of God on earth in a people wholly devoted to their heavenly King. How, then, does it come about that in the Gospels the term 'Son of Man' is so often and so obviously a designation of Jesus himself? The answer to this question is that the restriction of the denotation of the term is the outcome of the prophetic ministry of Jesus. His mission is to create the Son of Man, the Kingdom of the saints of

the Most High, to realise in Israel the ideal contained in the term. This task is attempted in two ways: first by public appeal to the people through the medium of parable and sermon and by the mission of the disciples: then, when this appeal produced no adequate response, by the consolidation of his own band of followers. Finally, when it becomes apparent that not even the disciples are ready to rise to the demands of the ideal, he stands alone, embodying in his own person the perfect human response to the regal claims of God.

(The Teaching of Jesus 1963 edn. p. 227-8)

I should myself be inclined to see the term as more fluid from the first, as ambiguous between the new community and Jesus' own vocation. Something similar can be seen in the Suffering Servant, who seems to be at one moment a definite individual (perhaps the exiled king Jehoiachin, imprisoned and finally executed) and at another the commonalty of Israel. If Jesus was applying the term to himself, despite the superhuman aura attaching to it in *Enoch* it is likely that he chose it for its human connotations. We can see on the one hand that 'Son of Man' allowed a universalist meaning, whereas the common Jewish Messianic title 'Son of David' (which Jesus seems to have repudiated: *Mark* 12.35-6) would have had a nationalist slant. On the other hand we can see that 'Son of Man' with its explicit emphasis on humanity made easier Jesus' equation of the Messiah or the Messianic community with the Suffering Servant, and the majority of the occasions when Jesus uses the term come after Peter's acknowledgment of him as the Messiah and begin from his own teaching that the Son of Man must suffer.

'Son of Man' then, though it has other overtones, is a phrase which does full justice to Jesus' humanity.

SON OF GOD

In general the gospels show Jesus as a human being endowed with exceptional powers, and with a special relationship with God and a peculiar vocation. But there are some passages which suggest that not merely did the Church, reflecting after the event, see Jesus as a divine being, but that during his lifetime his contemporaries already were puzzled and mystified. There was a note of authority attached to his teaching (*Mark* 1.22) — not merely to his teaching but to his actions (*Mark* 1.27). A Roman centurion recognized this note of authority and found it familiar. 'I am a man set in authority' (this probably underlies the 'under authority' of our text). 'I say to one man "Go" and he goes, and to another "Come" and he comes, and to my slave "Do this", and he does it.' So, without understanding, he knew that Jesus would not have to go in person to heal his batman (*Matt*. 9.5-13).

The sort of questions which arose in the minds of his contemporaries were eloquently formulated by R. W. Dale in his sermon on the Trinity:

> Who is this that places persecution for his sake side by side with persecution for righteousness' sake, and declares that whether men suffer for loyalty to him or for loyalty to righteousness they are to receive their reward in the divine Kingdom? Who is it that in that sermon places his own authority side by side with the authority of God, and gives to the Jewish people and to all mankind new laws which require a deeper and more inward righteousness than was required by the Ten Commandments? Who is it that in that sermon assumes the awful authority of pronouncing final judgment on men (Matt. vii, 21-23)?.... These are not words that we ever heard before, or have ever heard since, from teacher or prophet. Who is he? That question cannot be silenced when words like these have been spoken.

Dale could have extended his list of questions. Who is this that declares that whoever has seen him has seen the Father? Who is this that asserts his authority over the traditional institutions of his people? Who is this that prophesies that heaven and earth will pass away but his words will not pass away? Who is this that declares that all authority whether in heaven or on earth is given him? Who is this that dares to call the failure to believe in him sin? Who is he?

The answer they came up with was that he was what he was because of his relation to God. They saw this as the secret of his authority: 'If I by the finger of God cast out demons, then has the kingdom of God come upon you' (*Luke* 11.20). So when after a bad night's fishing, Peter on Jesus' advice cast his nets in a different place and netted a huge haul, he went down on his knees and said, 'Go away from me, sir! I am a sinful man!' (*Luke* 5.8). There was something numinous, awesome, holy about Jesus. (The word there rendered 'sir' can bear a more exalted significance, both temporally and spiritually: 'my lord'.) The transfiguration led Peter to suggest (not knowing what to say) making three booths or tabernacles, one for Jesus and one for each of the other mystic figures who appeared alongside him. Even at the moment of Jesus' death something about him wrung from the centurion on duty, 'This man was undoubtedly a son of God.' (*Mark* 15.39)

From the centurion that did not mean any claim to uniqueness. There were plenty of sons of the gods in Greek and Roman myth, and some like Asclepius-Aesculapius or Heracles-Hercules were themselves deified. But in a Jewish context such a phrase was different, and it is clear that the suggestion that Jesus was *the* Son of God was the principal reason for his condemnation by the Sanhedrin (*Luke* 22.70-1).

The idea underlying the phrase 'Son of God' is a complex one. We should note first, as with 'Son of Man', the use of 'son of' to express close identification with the word following. Thus 'son of lies' means an inveterate or, as we might say, congenital liar. 'Son of God' thus would mean one wholly at one with God. But there are wider associations. First there is the sonship of Israel. 'Thus says the Lord, Israel is my firstborn son' (*Exod.* 4.22). 'When Israel was a child, I loved him, and out of Egypt I called my son' (*Hos.* 11.1). Second, there is the idea that an individual by special grace is adopted as son. So through Nathan Yahweh says of Solomon 'I will be his father and he shall be my son' (2 *Sam.* 7.14). There is no question here of identification, since Yahweh goes on to say that he will chastise Solomon when the king goes astray, but he will not abandon him. Third, these two strands come together in the second Psalm, where the Messiah is spoken of as son in a passage much canvassed and applied to Jesus by early Christian writers (2.7: *Acts* 13:13; *Heb.* 1.5; 5.5 cf. *Matt.* 3.17). There is however no clear evidence outside the New Testament that 'Son of God' was a current Messianic title, though some New Testament passages suggest it (*Mark* 3.11; 5.7; *Luke* 4.41; *John* 1.49; 11.27 'You are the Messiah, the Son of God, the one who comes into the world'; *Matt.* 14.33; 16.16 'You are the Messiah, the Son of the living God'; 26.63 'I adjure you by the living God, tell us if you are the Messiah, the Son of God'; 27.40).

Correlative to this is the idea of the fatherhood of God. In *Deuteronomy* God's behaviour to Israel is compared with that of a father (1.31; 8.5 cf. *Ps.* 103.13). Hosea has the unforgettable image of the father-God teaching Ephraim to walk (11.3). Through Jeremiah Yahweh calls himself a father to Israel (31.9) and Israel prays to him as such (3.4). 'You are our Father' is a repeated prayer in *Isaiah* (63.16; 64.8). Prayers of this kind are familiar in Judaism. 'Our father in heaven' is a frequent invocation in Jewish prayer. The Midrashim, post-Christian in their collection, but pre-Christian in much of their material, make much of the idea of God as Father. More, there is a special sense in which the just man may see God as his Father, and this comes out strongly in the Hellenistic period. In the second chapter of *The Wisdom of Solomon* 'they', the earthly rulers (but with something of Edward Lear's 'They' about them), scorn the poor and honest man, who claims to be the servant of Yahweh and asserts that God is his Father (2.16). It is this that undergirds the prayers to God as Father in the Wisdom literature (14.3; *Eccles.* 23.1; *Tobit* 13.4). It is not too much to say that the Fatherhood of God is a characteristically Jewish concept.

Yet Jesus' use of it was offensive to Jewish religious susceptibilities. Jesus uses the word 'Father' of God with three different connotations. In the widest God is the Father of all mankind; so the Father makes his sun to rise and sends his rain for all men, Jews and Gentiles, saints and sinners. This might be offensive to the national exclusiveness and self-righteousness of some of the respectable Jewish leaders, but it was hardly blasphemous. In the second usage he is speaking of the relation of God to the community of believers, the new Israel. This is his normal use; he frequently speaks to his hearers (it matters little whether they are committed disciples or those he is hoping to draw into a new commitment) of 'your Father' (e.g. *Mark* 11.25-6; *Luke* 6.36; 12.30-2). This is especially prominent in *Matthew*, and it is an extension of the Old Testament usage. Again this might become offensive when Jesus said unequivocally that the Jews of his day did not follow God as their father (*John* 8.42), but it was not abnormal or blasphemous.

But Jesus also claimed that God was his Father in a special and unique sense. This was associated with two mystical experiences; the records say that at his baptism and at the transfiguration there was a voice declaring him Son of God. This then becomes not a question of 'our Father' or 'your Father' but of 'my Father' (e.g. *Luke* 2.49 Jesus as a boy in the Temple, even before the mystical experiences; 22,28; *Matt.* 7.21; 10.32-3 and often; *John* 5.17 and very often, especially in the controversies with the Jews and the last discourse to the disciples). The key-passages are those in which Jesus claims a unique relationship to God. 'All things have been delivered to me by my Father, and no one knows the Son except the Father, and no one knows the Father except the Son and any one to whom the Son chooses to reveal him' (*Matt.* 11.27); 'I and the Father are one' (*John* 10.30); 'He who has seen me has seen the Father' (*John* 14.9). The more extreme form-critics attribute all these passages to the early Church, and do not accept them as genuine sayings of Jesus. But Jesus did offend the Jewish authorities enough for them to feel that his blasphemy was worthy of the death-penalty, and there is no reason to doubt the core of the record.

John also used a term from Greek philosophy in his exploration of the being of Jesus. This was Logos, the 'Word' of the Authorized Version. We shall be looking at this more closely in the next chapter; for the moment we may note that it brought together the power of Yahweh in the Jewish story of Creation, with a Stoic word for God, based on the idea of order, balance and reason behind the universe. It makes Jesus pre-existent, more than man, but (though Stoic

The Person of Christ

usage would support the meaning) not necessarily God.

Certainly as the Christians came to reflect on their experience of Jesus, they came to regard him as more than an ordinary man. The climax of this in the gospels comes in one of the stories of Jesus appearing to the disciples after his death. Thomas, who had not been present at an earlier manifestation, was openly sceptical. Jesus suddenly appeared among them, and invited Thomas to examine his wounds. Thomas said, 'My Lord and my God' (*John* 20.28). We may have some scepticism about the historicity of the episode, if only because the phrase 'My Lord and my God' sounds like a counterblast to the emperor Domitian's claim to be just that — *dominus et deus* — but it shows what was happening in the Church. The younger Pliny, governing Bithynia in AD 112, investigated the Christians, and found that they met before dawn on a fixed day and sang an antiphonal hymn to Christ as a god. This will have been the sort of hymn, perhaps the very hymn, which almost two generations before was being sung, probably in Ephesus:

> And so in honour of the name of Jesus
>> all beings in heaven, on earth and in the world below
>> will fall on their knees,
> and all will openly proclaim that Jesus Christ is Lord,
>> to the glory of God the Father.
>>> (*Phil.* 2.10-11)

So too in the last book of the Bible, perhaps written at much the same time as *John*, the seer had a vision of the Lamb (symbolizing Jesus) and the songs sung to him:

> The Lamb who was killed is worthy
>> to receive power, wealth, wisdom and strength,
>> honour, glory and praise!
>
> To him who sits on the throne and to the Lamb
>> be praise and honour, glory and might
>> for ever and ever!
>>> (*Rev.* 5.11-12)

THE TWO NATURES

So the Christians saw these titles, 'Son of Man' and 'Son of God', as expressing the humanity and divinity of Jesus. Paul wrote to the church at Colossae: 'The full content of divine nature lives in Christ, in his humanity' (*Col.* 2.9). As the direct experience of Jesus ebbed, doctrine about him became more important. Across the centuries the central core of Christians became clear that no formulation was acceptable which did not affirm Jesus as both man and God. To some extent the twofold nature came to be expressed in the double name by which he was called, Jesus Christ, especially as Christianity came to spread outside circles where the original title 'Messiah' was meaningful. Theologians today are known to contrast the Jesus of History and the Christ of Faith. The large majority of doctrinal controversies in the first few centuries of Christianity had to do with the Person of Christ. There was in fact a double problem. One was how to do justice to an experience of Jesus which regarded him as fully human and fully divine. Alongside this, once some formula had been agreed, was the reconciliation of the monotheism which had long been rigid among the Jews, and was in fact characteristic of much of the most enlightened thought of the Roman Empire, with belief in the divinity of Jesus. The apologist Aristides insisted that Christianity was more monotheistic than Judaism (14-15), but it was no light matter to maintain this in detail.

THE EBIONITES

The Ebionites were a sect of Jewish Christians going back to the early days of Christianity. They seem to have flourished particularly on the east bank of the Jordan. It is difficult to discern a clear picture through our scanty, scattered and hostile information, but it seems that they effectively remained a sect within Judaism, continuing to stress the essentiality of the Torah, and holding that Jesus was a kind of Moses reborn, the human son of Joseph and Mary, who was inspired by the Holy Spirit at the moment of his baptism. Up to that point he was outstanding for virtue, Son of God only in an ethical sense in which any man might become a Son of God. But as a result of his exceptional justice, prudence and wisdom he became worthy to be the Messiah, and at his baptism received a new power, the power of the Messiah. This gave him a prophetic ministry and the capacity to perform miracles. The power of the Messiah left Jesus before his death; it was the human Jesus who suffered and died. The Ebionites were notable for their ascetic lives; in general it seems true to say that they believed in Jesus's humanity but not in his divinity.

DOCETISM

One of the first views which the main body of Christians repudiated was Docetism, the doctrine that Jesus was not really human but only seemed (*docein*) so to be. Such ideas were beginning to circulate in the first century. 'The blood of Christ was still fresh in Judaea', said Jerome characteristically, 'when his body was being called a phantasm' (*Adv. Lucif.* 23). In the Johannine letters we read: 'Many false prophets have gone out everywhere. This is how you will be able to know whether it is God's Spirit: anyone who acknowledges that Jesus Christ came as a human being has the Spirit who comes from God. But anyone who denies this about Jesus does not have the Spirit from God' (1 *John* 4.1-3). And again: 'Many deceivers have gone out all over the world, people who do not acknowledge that Jesus Christ came as a human being' (2 *John* 7). Such views arose principally from the notion that a suffering God was a contradiction in terms. But allied with this was a rejection of matter, a view associated with Platonism which held to the unreality of the material world, but not exclusive to it. Found alongside it also was the belief in revealed spiritual knowledge or *gnosis*. Gnosticism can be traced as a mood in the first century, before it became incorporated in systematic exposition in the second.

Saturnilus or Saturninus was a Syrian from Antioch, one of the earliest of the Gnostic system-makers. According to him, behind the world is a hidden, withdrawn God. From this being came an emanation in the form of a man. The seven creator-angels had a vision of this being, and created man who lay dark and helpless, unable to stir. The power above gave man the spark of life, and later sent the Saviour to rescue those who retained the divine spark. But matter was evil; marriage and flesh-eating works of the devil; and the Saviour was therefore pure spirit. Saturnilus himself seems to have been a moralist and ascetic of the highest character.

Another, better-known, representative of Docetist thought was Marcion of Sinope, notoriously anti-Judaic, thus treating the Creator as depicted in the Old Testament as a kind of anti-God. Marcion exalted the God of Jesus as the God of Love not of Law, and was deeply committed to the person of Jesus as Saviour. But the Jesus whom Marcion extolled was no human being but an angelic spirit descending from heaven to combat with the god of this world and to liberate the souls of the righteous from the dominion of death. Marcion was not at all interested in the historical events of Jesus's life, with one exception, only in the mythical message. The exception is, paradoxically, the crucifixion. Marcion, somehow, had room in his theology for a suffering, dying Saviour; how he reconciled this with his immaterialism we do not know.

As a third group we may note the Docetae themselves. In fact we know of two bodies so named, one in Alexandria, where the leader was Julius Cassianus, and one at or near Antioch, and perhaps influenced by Saturnilus and his predecessor Menander. We know little enough about these groups, but they had their own gospel-writings. *The Gospel of Peter* was accounted Docetist by bishop Serapion. It said of Christ on the cross, 'But he remained dumb, as one who feels no pain.' Julius Cassianus quotes from *The Gospel of the Egyptians*. We know little enough about it but can assume that it too was a Docetist composition. In general much of the apocryphal New Testament belongs to this school, with or without a strong Gnostic element. Thus in *The Acts of John* John at the Last Supper leans his head

The Person of Christ

against Jesus' breast only to find it gives him no support; the body of Jesus after death seemed solid at one moment, but at the next was 'immaterial and incorporeal and, as it were, nothing'. In *The Acts of Peter* and elsewhere God sends his Son '*through* the Virgin Mary', and the suffering on the Cross is similarly unreal.

Among the Gnostics of Alexandria the facts of Jesus' life tend to be buried in vast Blakean philosophical systems. The Gnostics tend to be alienated from the material world, and their salvationist schemes are forms of liberation of the soul from its physical prison. This naturally led to Docetist tendencies. The two leading Gnostics of the second century, Basilides and Valentinus, took different views. Basilides, a highly original genius, who seems to have been influenced by Indian thought, distinguished the human Jesus from the divine Spirit who entered into him at his baptism: the Jesus of history and the Christ of faith are thus originally separate but come together. We have a curious account of Basilides' view of the crucifixion, according to which Simon of Cyrene was crucified, and Jesus himself (the Christ-Spirit presumably) took the form of Simon and stood by and laughed at them (Irenaeus *Haer*. 1.24.4). It is surely garbled, but it may reflect Docetist views. Valentinus on the other hand took the view that Jesus had a body, but it was a spiritual body, not subject to normal physical laws. As in *The Acts of Peter* he passed through his mother, as water through a pipe. One follower of Valentinus named Mark combined the two views, and postulated a double baptism of Jesus, one a *psychic* baptism of the physical phenomenon, for the forgiveness of sins, and one a *pneumatic* baptism in which he received the Christ-Spirit for his. (Roughly, *psyche* refers to the human soul, *pneuma* to the divine Spirit.)

Docetism continued among the followers of Mani (third century), inevitably because of their dualism of matter and spirit. Mani himself seems to have held a view close to that of Basilides, distinguishing between Jesus *impatibilis* (not subject to suffering), living Spirit, and Jesus *patibilis* (subject to suffering), the soul of the material universe. But his follower Faustus (fourth century) denied the physical birth of Jesus, held that his body was immaterial, and denied the reality of his suffering and death (Augustine *C. Faust.* 2.1; 5.1; 11.1; 14.2).

One of the clearest opponents of any form of Docetism was Ignatius, bishop of Antioch, writing right at the beginning of the second century. Two passages are particularly forceful. To the Trallians he writes:

> So shut your ears if anyone ever talks to you with no mention of Jesus Christ, of the family of David, and of Mary, who was genuinely born, ate and drank, was genuinely a victim in the time of Pontius Pilate, genuinely was crucified and died, before the eyes of those in heaven, on earth and under the earth, who was equally genuinely raised from the dead, by his Father's hand, that same Father who shall similarly raise up in Christ Jesus us who believe in him, without whom we have no true life. If as some godless people — unbelievers, that is — say, his suffering was only a semblance (whereas it is their existence which is the semblance), why am I in prison, and why do I actually long to be exposed to wild beasts? In that case my death is gratuitous; in that case I am telling lies about the Lord. (9-10)

Similarly to Smyrna at greater length:

> I glorify Jesus Christ, the God who has given you wisdom in this way. I have noticed that you are established in an unshakable faith, as if nailed to our Lord Jesus Christ's cross in body and spirit and strengthened in love in Christ's blood, being fully persuaded in relation to our Lord that he was genuinely of the house of David in physical terms, and God's Son in relation to God's will and power, genuinely born of a virgin, and baptized by John so that 'all righteousness might be fulfilled by him', genuinely nailed up — physically — for us in the time of Pontius Pilate and the tetrarch Herod (and we as a result of his blessed suffering belong to the fruit of that tree), so as to raise high a banner, for all time through his resurrection for his saints and those who have faith in him, whether among Jews or Gentiles, within the single body of his Church. He suffered all this on our behalf for us to gain salvation; he genuinely raised himself; his suffering was no mere semblance as some unbelievers say — it is

their existence which is the semblance, and their future will match their philosophy: they will be incorporeal and immaterial. Personally I know, I have faith, that he was in the flesh after his resurrection. When he appeared to Peter and those round him he said to them: 'Take hold of me, touch me, look and see that I am not a disembodied spirit!' There and then they touched him and had faith, being one with him physically and spiritually. This was why they even scorned death and were proved superior to death. After his resurrection he ate and drank with them as a physical body, even though spiritually one with his Father. Dear people, I am warning you of this, knowing that you hold the same views as I do. I am protecting you in advance against beasts in human shape. You must not welcome them; if you can help it you must not even meet them; just pray for their repentance. It won't be easy, but Jesus Christ, our true life, has power for this. If these actions of our Lord were mere semblances, then so is my imprisonment a semblance. Why have I given myself up to death, to fire, to the sword, to wild beasts? Because to be near the sword is to be near God, to be in the presence of the wild beasts is to be in the presence of God. It is simply in the name of Jesus Christ that I endure everything so as to suffer with him, and it is he, the perfect human, who gives me power to do so. (1-4)

Ignatius is very impressive in the way he holds together the spiritual and the physical, and roots his faith firmly in historical events.

EMANATION

The Christians who won the day within the Church and were later regarded as orthodox found that the Gnostics did not do justice either to the human or to the divine aspect of Jesus. We have seen the tendency to Docetism. We can illustrate the other aspect by a brief and over-simplified summary of Valentinus' system.

The Pleroma, or fullness of the godhead, consists of thirty Aeons or spiritual beings, arranged in pairs or syzygies. First came four pairs, Abyss and Silence, Mind and Truth, Word

(*Logos*) and Life, Man and Church. From Word and Life came five more pairs, and from Man and Church six more pairs, completing the Pleroma. The thirtieth and weakest Aeon is called Achamoth, Sophia or Wisdom. She has an incestuous desire to know the Father of all; in her passion she produces formless Matter. Now Abyss and Mind produce the first Redeemer, Horus (the name of the reborn Osiris in Egyptian religion, and a Greek word meaning 'limit'), who fences off Wisdom from heaven, though she does not lose her heavenly origin. She now produces Iadabaoth, Child of Chaos, the creator-god of the Old Testament or Yahweh, Plato's divine craftsman. He tries to imitate the perfection of the Pleroma in the realm of matter and the eternity of the Pleroma in the world of time. The world and the living things in it are thus ultimately of heavenly derivation, but in need of redemption. Mind counters by bringing out two more Aeons, the perfect offspring of the Pleroma, Christ and the Holy Spirit, and yet another Aeon, Jesus, is formed from the unity of all the others. The divine Saviour comes down to redeem and wed Wisdom and bring her back to the Pleroma, and to redeem the souls of the Gnostics, who are the true children of their mother, from the realm of matter. Mankind is divided into three groups – the *carnal*, who are beyond redemption; the *psychic*, who live by faith and good works but not by light and knowledge, and who are redeemed from this world without attaining the Pleroma; and the *pneumatic*, the illuminated, the true Gnostics, who have perfect knowledge and a brighter destiny, and whose feminine souls will be united in the Pleroma with male angels.

Not merely did Jesus not take on a human body in a real way. However exalted, he appears as one of a number of spiritual beings, appearing at quite a late stage of cosmic history, and at two removes from the Ultimate (since he is the product of Mind). Jesus appears as a Mediator, neither fully God nor fully Man. We must remember that there was no dogmatic orthodoxy at the period. Valentinus was not departing from orthodoxy, for there was none to depart from. But the effect of any interpretation of the meaning of Christ's work was to induce others to ask what they really

The Person of Christ

did believe, and so to build up a consensus of orthodoxy.

The immense complexity of Valentinus' system does not seem to have, and has not, much to do with the historical Jesus of Nazareth. Yet we should not underestimate the impact of Jesus on Valentinus. The astonishing thing is that this highly original speculative philosopher from the cosmopolitan city of Alexandria should take as his Saviour-figure a Jewish carpenter arraigned for blasphemy and executed for revolutionary activities in an obscure corner of the Roman Empire a century before.

ADOPTIONISM

The second century saw the emergence within Christianity of a group who felt passionately the need to safeguard monotheism, which the belief in the divinity of Jesus seemed to challenge. Ignatius was writing such words as 'Our God, Jesus the Messiah, was conceived in Mary's womb' (*Eph.* 18). Again, at the beginning of 2 *Clement* we read, 'Brothers, we ought to think of Jesus Christ as of God, as of the Judge of the living and the dead.' There had to be a counter to the scornful, 'Then you believe in *two* gods' (Novatian *Trin.* 11-8; 27). There were two different approaches to this. The first is known as Dynamic Monarchianism or Adoptionism; the word 'dynamic' does not mean 'active' so much as indicating a potential which God brought to fruition. The Adoptionists stressed the real and full humanity of Jesus.

In the anonymous *Letter to the Hebrews* the writer begins from the eternal divinity of the Son. But running through the letter are traces of a view of a different kind. 'Because he was humble and devoted, God heard him' (*Heb.* 5.7). 'He learned obedience through suffering and so was made perfect, and it was as a result of this that he became Saviour and high priest. So Jesus endured the cross for the sake of the joy which was set before him' (*Heb.* 12.2). In these passages Jesus appears not as the pre-existent Son of God, but as the Man who (we might almost say) achieves Godhood by obedience. Something similar underlies the early hymn quoted by Paul in *Philippians*:

> He was humble and walked the path of obedience all the way
> to death —
> his death on the cross.
> *For this reason* God raised him to the highest place above
> and gave him the name that is greater than any other name.
> (*Phil.* 2.8-9)

In Hermas' *The Shepherd* the Holy Spirit is the pre-existent creative power, and God chooses a righteous man in whom the Spirit will act. He worked unceasingly with the Spirit, and did nothing to stain the Spirit with impurity, and so God adopted him to be the Spirit's companion (*Sim.* 5.6).

Ideas of this kind are found towards the end of the second century in Theodotus, a leather-worker who came to Rome from Byzantium and taught that Jesus was an ordinary human being who became Christ when the Holy Spirit came upon him at his Baptism. Theodotus appealed both to the New Testament record of Jesus' humanity, and to prophetic passages from the Old Testament, as when Moses tells the Israelites that God will send them 'a prophet like me', and therefore human (*Deut.* 18.15). Theodotus was excommunicated by Victor, bishop of Rome; doctrinal orthodoxy was by now an issue. But his school of thought continued into the following century when his views were carried on by another Theodotus, a banker by profession, who won the condemnation of Victor's successor Zephyrinus, and a little later by Artemon or Artemas, who exalted Jesus above the prophets but denied his full divinity, and was also excommunicated. The views of the school were assailed in a lost treatise *The Little Labyrinth*.

In the second half of the third century these views were renewed in a more original and carefully worked out form by Paul of Samosata, bishop of Antioch. Paul insisted on a monotheistic view of God in a single substantial being or *hypostasis*. Logos, The Word, and Sophia, Wisdom are aspects of this one God. This makes a real incarnation of the Logos impossible. The Word inhered in Jesus not as part of his essential being, but as a kind of superimposed quality. Jesus was not essentially different from the prophets (who also received

The Person of Christ 73

the Word of God). Bethune-Baker put the matter well in his *History of Christian Doctrine*: 'it was not that the Son of God came down from heaven, but that the Son of man ascended up on high.' Our records do not make clear at what point Paul thought the change took place, whether at baptism or after the resurrection, but Paul's views can be taken as an outstanding expression of Adoptionism. They were condemned more than once by synods, and in 268 he was deposed from his bishopric.

MODALISM

The other way of safeguarding monotheism lay at the opposite extreme. This was the view that there is no distinction within the being of God between Father, Son and Spirit, but that these are different masks or *personae* through which we experience the one God, or different modes of his operation. The propounding of these views is atrributed to a shadowy figure named Sabellius, and they are often called Sabellian. If so, we must date him to the early third century, contrary to some evidence which would place him later. There is no special reason to doubt the tradition that he came from Africa, but he may have moved to Rome at a fairly early date. We know of the views of the school chiefly through the criticisms of Noetus of Smyrna by Hippolytus and of Praxeas by Tertullian. Praxeas too came from Asia, and some scholars have thought the name a pseudonym ('Busybody') given to Noetus by Tertullian, but there is no real evidence of this, though their views seem to have been broadly similar. We know also of a missionary follower of theirs named Epigonus. The stress on the unity of the Godhead led the Sabellians to say that it was the Father who was born, suffered and died in Jesus. They were thus called 'Patripassians', because of their belief that the Father suffered. Tertullian charged Praxeas with crucifying the Father. Noetus gave an allegorical interpretation to the opening of *John*, and accused his opponents of believing in two gods. It is important to observe that the Church's rejection of Patripassianism was not on the grounds of the impassibility of God — if the Christians were going to come to terms with a belief that Jesus and the Father were one, they had to accept that in some sense God suffers — but on the grounds of 'confusing the Persons' and blurring the distinction between Son and Father.

THE ARIAN CONTROVERSY

We come now to the greatest of all the controversies about the Person of Jesus. Somewhere about AD 318 or 319 Alexander, bishop of Alexandria, had a confrontation with a presbyter named Arius. Alexander maintained that God was a Trinity (Father, Son, Spirit) in unity; Arius called him a Sabellian. Arius offered a counter-doctrine, which may (following Adolf Harnack) be summarized under eight heads: (a) There is One God, solitary, eternal. He was not always Father; that came with the creation of the Son. (b) The Word (Logos) and Wisdom (Sophia) are within this God, but as powers not as persons. (c) To create the universe, God brought into being an independent entity or substance called variously the Word, Wisdom, the Son. (d) The Son is separate in substance from the Father, and, like all created things, subject to change. (e) The Son is not truly and fully God and has a relative not absolute knowledge of the Father. (f) The Son however is above all creatures, himself the perfect creature, and we may call him God, 'the only-begotten God'. (g) Christ took a genuine body, but in him the Word took the place of the human *psyche* (soul). (h) The Holy Spirit was a creation of the Son, and stands alongside the Son as an independent substance but ultimately derivative.

Arius, a skilful publicist, formed a party and aroused debate. Alexander did not act precipitately, but in AD 321 held a Council at Alexandria, excommunicating Arius. Within the next years Constantine, who was already involved in a somewhat syncretistic way with the Christians, secured sole sovereignty of the Roman world, and tried to secure some rapport between Alexander and Arius. The outcome was an Ecumenical Council at Nicaea in AD 325. The Council at an

The Person of Christ

early stage anathematized the teachings of Arius; they would not accept that the Son was a created being, that he was of a different essence from the Father, or that the Father was ever devoid of the Logos. It was not so easy to achieve an agreed positive formulation. Eventually they uneasily agreed on the word *homoousios*, 'of the same substance', by contrast with the (later) Arian term *homoiousios*, 'of similar substance'. So the Church split over a single letter but a wealth of meaning. There were objections to *homoousios*; one was that it was not scriptural, another that it was dangerously Sabellian and had actually been condemned in the proceedings against Paul of Samosata. But it held the day.

It is not necessary to go into the details of the subsequent controversies, or the career of Athanasius, the ablest theologian of the day, bishop of Alexandria from AD 328, and an eloquent and learned defender of the conciliar position. Controversy remained through most of the century. Which party was dominant depended as much on imperial favour as on any other factor. On the whole through the first part of the fourth century the West stood by the formulation of Nicaea, but the East was by no means as clear. In AD 357 an Arian creed was promulgated at Sirmium ('the blasphemy of Sirmium' said Hilary of Poitiers, not mincing words), and two years later, with imperial support, Arian formulations were carried in the East at Seleuceia and in the West at Ariminum. It was of this year that Jerome said 'The whole world groaned and marvelled to find itself Arian.' After this however the strength of the Arian movement in the East decayed. A small but important Council at Alexandria made a distinction, not up to that point observed, between essence (*ousia*) and substance (*hypostasis*). Gradually the formula began to emerge that God was one in essence but threefold in substance. At Constantinople in AD 381 a Second Ecumenical Council reaffirmed the position reached at Nicaea; two years later the Arians were legally proscribed.

The Arians in fact were not wholly of one mind. There were those who favoured the term *homoiousios*, 'of like substance', to express the relation of Son to Father; others who preferred the noncommittal *homoios*, 'like'; and a third group who held to a more extreme position with the term *anomoios*, 'unlike'. The supporters of Athanasius, who had originally been far more divided than the Arians, gradually became on this issue far more united.

This was not the whole story. Arius, a man of passionate faith, was a zealous missionary. During a period of exile in Illyricum he seems to have fostered Christian missionary work among the Goths, and through them among the Burgundians, Lombards and Vandals. As the frontiers of the Western Empire began to crack these groups began to seep through, down France through Spain to Africa, and even to Rome itself. One of the great Gothic Arian Christians of the late fourth century we know, Ulfilas, who among other things gave to his people the scriptures in Gothic; both Auxentius and Philostorgius compare him to Moses. In this way Arianism remained prominent in much of the West, the Catholic Franks being the major exception, and Africa until the end of the sixth century.

This controversy had little to do with the humanity of Jesus. This issue was about his divinity; was he absolutely divine or only relatively so? Athanasius thought that Arius' formula, though Arius could defend it by scriptural quotation, did not do justice to the idea of Jesus as Son of God. In the end his view triumphed, but not without pain and schism.

THE PENDULUM SWINGS

Apollinaris or Apollinarius (*c*. AD 310-90) was a friend of Athanasius and a vigorous opponent of the Arians. He was concerned to assert that in Christ Godhead and manhood were part of a single nature ('a person, being one, cannot be twofold'), that Christ was fully God, and that there was no element of sinfulness or moral progress in the human life of Christ as in ordinary, natural human beings. Man, he said, consists of body, soul and spirit, the body and soul forming the natural, physical environment for the spirit. In Christ the body and soul were normal, but the human spirit was replaced by the divine Logos. The guiding principle in man is subject

The Person of Christ

to error; in Christ this cannot be so. So the Incarnation was the assumption by the Logos of a physical body not of a whole man; the Word was made flesh not man (*John* 1.14); he became like man and appeared in human likeness (*Phil.* 2.7); this is the mystery which appeared in the flesh (1 *Tim.* 3.16). So Jesus and the Logos are one person; divinity and humanity are inseparably joined in him; he is open to our adoration, because in him even his human nature is actuated and made divine by the divine Logos. Apollinaris adapted an illustration from Origen. If we think of the human soul of Jesus as a lump of iron and his godhead as fire, we can see that the fire penetrates the iron so that it acts like fire, and yet the iron retains its own character. So the body of Jesus had miraculous power for those who touched it, yet remained a human body. The Christians who rejected Apollinaris and his views were concerned about two issues. First they were concerned because Apollinaris said that Christ lacked an element of full human nature, and quote against him such passages as that which asserts that in every way, apart from sin, he was just as we are (*Heb.* 4.15). Alongside this they maintained that if the Logos had taken the place of one of the normal elements of human nature, then the Logos must have become subject to suffering and death, and this was a conclusion which they could not stomach.

Nestorius (*c*. AD 385-450) went to the opposite extreme. He was born in Syria, entered a monastery at Antioch, and was probably taught by Theodore of Mopsuestia. He was a great preacher and a zealous champion of orthodoxy, and when the bishopric of Constantinople fell vacant in 428 he was given precedence over the local candidates. He was especially fervent in his attacks on Apollinarianism. It happened that a theological controversy arose about the propriety of applying the term Theotokos ('Mother of God') to Mary. This was a favourite word of popular devotion. Nestorius however felt that it savoured of Apollinarianism, and did not do justice to the two natures within Christ; he proposed instead Christotokos ('Mother of Christ'). How could you, he asked, in an unfortunate witticism, say that God was three months old? It is difficult to reconstruct exactly what he thought, since he also stressed the unity of Christ, though it was a unity of conjunction rather than organic union. The unity, he claimed, was one of will, intent and purpose. This savoured of Adoptionism and was rejected. Nestorius was concerned to do full justice to Jesus as Son of God and as Son of Man, to his divinity and to his humanity, and held that each of these natures was self-subsistent, and that they were therefore incapable of merging. Unfortunately he fell foul of the most formidable ecclesiastical politician of the day, Cyril of Alexandria, perhaps the most unpleasant man ever to have been canonized. At the Council of Ephesus in AD 431, Nestorius' views were anathematized and he himself deposed. He retired to the monastery at Antioch, and was subsequently banished to Upper Egypt. But the movement he started had its own impetus and he lived to feel that he had been partly vindicated and truth was triumphing. His movement continued to flourish in Edessa and Persia. It survived under the tolerant rule of Islam, and survives today in the small group of the so-called Assyrian Christians.

So the pendulum swung again, and the views of Apollinaris were reopened by Eutyches (*c*. AD 378-454), a leading monk from Constantinople; he claimed to be reaffirming the teaching of Cyril as he combated Nestorianism. He was charged with confounding the two natures in Christ. He could not accept that Christ's bodily form was of the same substance (*homoousios*!) as ours. The result was inevitably a form of Docetism. He also held that there were two natures before their union in the Incarnate Word, but only one after it, thus becoming effectively the founder of Monophysitism (the doctrine of a single nature). Eutyches perhaps had not thought out his position very clearly; he wriggled under cross-examination. He was deposed, appealed to Rome, was retried and acquitted. But meantime Leo repudiated his doctrine, a change of emperor lost him imperial favour, and at Chalcedon in AD 451 he was finally deposed and exiled. At Chalcedon, the Fifth Ecumenical Council affirmed what became the orthodox faith: that Jesus Christ is perfect God and perfect man, consubstantial with the Father in respect of his deity, consubstantial with men in respect of his humanity, in two natures, without confusion or change, division or separation, the difference between the natures being removed by their union, or rather the individuality of each being preserved as they come together in a single person and a single substance. It was a subtle formula. But Gibbon was not wrong when he wrote of this episode: 'An invisible line was drawn between the heresy of Apollinaris and the faith of St Cyril; and the road to paradise, a bridge as sharp as a razor, was suspended over the abyss by the masterhand of the theological artist.'

As a postcript it is interesting to note the views of Leontius of Byzantium, who held that Christ is united with the Father in the essence of divinity, and with us in the essence of humanity, and thus forms an independent essence, a third thing, in which the word and flesh are united. This was unacceptable to the majority, but it was certainly a serious attempt to do justice to the dual nature of Christ.

MONOTHELITISM

One final controversy should be mentioned. The seeming irrevocability of the Chalcedonian definition was by no means the end of Monophysite Christianity. An important episode was the attempt of the Emperor Zeno, through Acacius of Constantinople and Peter Mongo of Alexandria, to reunite the factions by a new statement called the *henoticon* or assertion of unity. This condemned Nestorius and Eutyches, and reasserted the faith expressed at Nicaea and later by Cyril, but by careful omissions would have allowed Monophysites back into the Church. It was never accepted by Rome, and led to a temporary schism between East and West; the extreme Monophysites also rejected it. Similarly in the sixth century Justinian made energetic but unsuccessful efforts at reconciliation. By the end of the sixth century Monophysitism was firmly established as the faith of the Coptic and Abyssinian Churches, the Syrian Jacobites, and the Armenians.

In the seventh century however the political and military danger first from Persia and then from Islam led to an even more energetic effort at reunion. This was originally fostered by the emperor Heraclius in association with Sergius, the Patriarch of Constantinople, and consisted in the assertion of two natures in Christ but a single mode of activity (*energeia*). A similar idea was found in Cyril and declared theologically acceptable (though not by Sophronius, the future bishop of Jerusalem), and it led to a major movement of reunion in Alexandria. Unfortunately, the bishop of Rome, Honorius, in approving these developments replaced 'mode of activity' by 'will', and it was this which appeared in the *Exposition* or *Ecthesis* published by Heraclius in AD 638. This was approved in the East at Constantinople in Councils held in AD 638 and 639, but it was unanimously rejected by Honorius' successors, and withdrawn ten years later. No other compromise proved acceptable, and the doctrine of the single will went out from orthodox Christianity after the doctrine of the single nature.

THE PERSON OF CHRIST

These controversies reflect a very different world from the world of the New Testament, though we should not underestimate the controversies there or idealize the early Christians. They led to bitter antagonisms, political manoeuvrings, sometimes to factional violence. But it is just to observe that they arose from an intense devotion to the person of Jesus Christ. Within this devotion there were three strands. One was that any view of Jesus must be based on the scriptural record. Some, like Marcion, might reject the Jewish scriptures of the Old Testament, and concentrate on the New, but all are concerned with scriptural authenticity. The second was to do full justice to Jesus' physical, historical humanity. The third was to do full justice to the view which had emerged in the Church of Jesus' divinity. Most of the controversies were due to the sense that one or other of these was being denigrated.

BIBLIOGRAPHY

Adolph Harnack *History of Dogma* 7 vols (ET 1894-9) is still invaluable. G. L. Prestige's Bampton Lectures *Fathers and Heretics* (1940) is a useful selective survey, full of original observations. S. Cave *The Doctrine of the Person of Christ* (London 1925) is an excellent survey. For a modern treatment of the issues. D. M. Baillie *God was in Christ* (London 1948). For Gnosticism see H. Jonas *The Gnostic Religion* (ET Boston ^{2}1963). An up-to-date study of Monarchianism is much needed; so, even more oddly, is one of the Arians, though this inevitably finds a niche in the church histories of Duchesne, Lietzmann and others. For Apollinaris see C.E. Raven *Apollinarianism* (1923). For Nestorius see F. Loofs *Nestorius and his Place in the History of Christian Doctrine* (1914).

My account of Valentinus is drawn from my *Illustrated Encyclopaedia of Mysticism and the Mystery-Religions* (1976). For the figure of Primal Man see R. Reitzenstein *Poimandres* (Leipzig 1904). For Leontius see Patrick Gray *The Defense of Chalcedon in the West* (1979).

For the original term 'Son of Man' see C. H. Kraeling *Anthropos and Son of Man* (1927); W. Manson *Jesus the Messiah* (1943); J. X. Campbell in *Journal for Theological Studies* 48 (1947) 145-55. For 'Son of God' see the brilliantly compact M. Hengel *The Son of God* (ET London 1976).

4
The Early Church: Types and Symbols

THE SPREAD OF CHRISTIANITY

Jesus was a Jew, and never disowned his faith. His immediate followers were all of the Jewish religion. Christianity emerged as a sect within Judaism. But it was not long before it began to spread more widely, not merely among God-fearers, that is Gentile converts to Judaism, but also among those who had had no association with the Jewish faith. Something of this story is told in *The Acts of the Apostles* and reflected in the letters of one of its leading exponents, Paul of Tarsus. Jerusalem was a natural centre at first, but there seems to have been a group in the Galilee, which may be a survival from Jesus' own ministry (1 *Cor.* 15.6; *Acts* 9.31), and it was quite likely from here that the group in Damascus was formed (*Acts* 9.1-19). The fact that we have unusually full records of Paul should not lead us to disparage the work of other missionaries, Apollos for example and that elusive couple Priscilla and Aquila, Philip, and Barnabas who broke away from Paul and worked independently of him. Paul himself speaks of his refusal to preach where others had already pioneered the missionary work (*Rom.* 15.19-20); this suggests that others were at work in areas which he avoided — Palestine, tracts of southern and western Asia Minor, Bithynia, Mysia, and the south Balkans. We know of Christians in Bithynia, Pontus, Cappadocia, Tyre and Sidon, Puteoli and Rome. There must have been a lot of effective Christian preachers. Some may have got beyond the boundaries of the Roman Empire. The tradition linking Thomas with the foundation of the Church in India is not an impossible one. By about 200 Tertullian can make a rhetorical claim about the other end of the known world: parts of Britain, inaccessible to the Romans, have accepted the sovereignty of Christ.

There was a long and sometimes bitter wrestling before it was determined that those who turned to Jesus did not have to come via the Torah; in this struggle Paul, the former Pharisee, played an essential part. The Jewish world was permeated with Hellenistic culture, as we have seen. But the Graeco-Roman world was not permeated with Jewish culture. So, as Jesus was presented to Greeks and Romans new modes of presentation had to be worked out. It is most surprising that the title Christ was so easily absorbed. In the non-Jewish world it was applied to objects rather than to people, and the anointing of a person was a normal act of cleanliness, applied also to dead bodies. There is evidence that it was treated as a proper name, and assimilated to Chrestos, 'good', a more familiar name. But when thinkers turned to write about Jesus, they naturally used the categories of Greek philosophy (there was effectively no Roman philosophy other than that derived from the Greeks), and when artists turned to convey something of the Christian message, they naturally used the techniques which they had already mastered in painting or mosaic and sculpture, and reworked some of the familiar designs in the service of the new faith.

The Jewish background was not lost. It was in any case an integral part of the thinking of Jesus, so that his teaching is literally incomprehensible without it. Furthermore all the first-generation documents which were collected and treasured in the New Testament were written from within the presuppositions of the Jewish faith, even when the authors, like Paul, burst those bounds. So that sometimes we see a double approach, by which Old Testament symbols are applied to Jesus, and pagan symbols are applied to the Old Testament figures themselves.

THE APPEARANCE OF JESUS

One of the central commandments of Judaism, traditionally going back to the original covenant with Yahweh, was, 'Do not make for yourselves images of anything in heaven or on earth or in the water under the earth' (*Exod*. 20.4). For this reason, if for no other, we have no contemporary portrait of Jesus. We have no description of him from the gospel-writers. They were not interested in his physical appearance, but it is surprising that nothing has slipped in even incidentally, as it has, say, with Zacchaeus or, later, with Paul and Barnabas. It is a reasonable deduction that he was not abnormally tall or short (though some have erroneously read into the story of Zacchaeus, who had to climb a tree to see Jesus, that Jesus rather than Zacchaeus was short). It is likely that he will have had unadorned shoulder-length hair and a full beard, as this was the style of the young Jewish male, as we know from representations of prisoners-of-war.

There are a number of legends which purport to give some account of Jesus' appearance. One story tells how the apostles asked Luke, who in some traditions was a painter, to produce a likeness of Jesus. The painter prayed and fasted, sat down before his panel — and the likeness appeared miraculously. In another Abgar, king of Edessa, invited Jesus to his court, and asked the court painter to paint him. The artist was unable to do so, but Jesus leant his face against the artist's block and the likeness appeared. Another legend told how the woman who was cured of a haemorrhage tried to draw her healer. Jesus came to her house, wiped away her unsuccessful attempts with a cloth — and the true likeness was imprinted on the cloth. A more familiar story tells how Veronica wiped his face in pity on the last journey to Calvary, and found his features imprinted on the kerchief. All these are legends. They tell us that the likeness of Jesus was not preserved; they tell us also that there came a time when worshippers wished that it had been preserved. The latest episode in this saga is the Turin shroud. This is a strange story. It certainly seems, after the most careful scientific investigation, that this is a linen cloth dating from somewhere about the time of Jesus, which was used to wrap the body of someone who had been scourged and crucified, and which carries an imprint of the body in its fabric. Even if it were the shroud which wrapped Jesus, it would not tell us much about him. The man's height cannot be estimated; it was between 5 ft 4 ins and 6 ft 2 ins. He had a beard, and shoulder-length hair, with a face long rather than round. But that is all.

There are also some late literary references. Antoninus of Placentia made a pilgrimage to Jerusalem in the mid-sixth century and there saw a footprint of Jesus, 'small, delicate and well-proportioned', and a portrait showing a man of average height, handsome with curly hair, fine hands and long fingers (like a Van Dyck portrait). Andrew of Crete saw another painting, attributed to Luke, where the face was long, the eyebrows joined, the head inclined forward, the figure well-proportioned. Epiphanius is more precise still. Jesus was 6 ft tall with a long nose, a complexion the colour of ripe corn, black eyebrows, red hair, and looked just like his mother. In the fourteenth century there was a popular book called *The Letter of Lentulus*, purporting to be written by P. Lentulus, governor of Jerusalem. It is not known earlier and has no historical basis. It contains a full account of Jesus' looks: 'He had a face which demanded respect, so that those who looked at it experienced a combination of awe and love. His hair was nut-brown in colour, and fell straight almost to the ears, and then in waves to the shoulders, with touches of blue where the light fell. His complexion was ruddy; his nose and mouth were perfectly shaped. His beard was full without being particularly long, forked at the chin and of the same colour as his hair. He was slim with graceful arms and hands, and carried himself well.'

These are entertaining, but we can place no credence in them. We do better to trust Irenaeus in the second century, who knew Polycarp, and so had access to very early traditions, and who said, 'We are wholly ignorant as to what he looked like'; 'the physical features of Jesus are unknown to us.'

In fact we can trace two views, and they are both theological and neither has any historical basis. One takes off from *Psalm* 45.2, 'You surpass all mankind in beauty.' This was applied to Jesus — it is quoted in *The Letter of Lentulus* — and led, for example, Gregory of Nyssa, John Chrysostom,

Ambrose and Jerome, to describe Jesus as handsome. The other view has its origin in the Suffering Servant in *Isaiah*:

> He grew up before the Lord like a young plant
>   whose roots are in parched ground;
> he had no beauty, no majesty to draw our eyes,
>   no grace to make us delight in him.
> his form, disfigured, lost all the likeness of a man,
>   his beauty changed beyond human semblance.
> He was despised, he shrank from the sight of men,
>   tormented and humbled by suffering;
> we despised him, we held him of no account,
>   a thing from which men turn away their eyes.
>   (*Isa.* 53.2-3)

On this basis Justin said that he had no presence, no good looks, a rather despicable appearance, and Origen that he was poor and mean of stature. Some accepted both traditions; both belonged to scriptural prophecy and both must be true. So the apocryphal *Acts of Peter* declares, 'He was at one and the same time ugly and beautiful.' Clement of Alexandria, that humane and commonsensical man, was perhaps wiser to say 'For those who seek real beauty, only our Saviour is beautiful.'

It is worth remarking that the bearded Christ who is most familiar in Western art emerges as an art-type only in the fourth century. Up to that point he has been portrayed as beardless. This was mainly affected by certain pagan types, Apollo or Orpheus or (as the Good Shepherd) Hermes with a ram on his shoulders, and also some of the divinized humans such as Alexander the Great or Hadrian's favourite Antinous. Such beardless representations can be seen from a fairly early date in the catacombs, on fourth-century sarcophagi, on a fourth-century glass vessel in the British Museum, in the fifth-century mausoleum of Galla Placidia in Ravenna. When the bearded image began to appear, it also was influenced by a pagan type, the philosopher, and particularly Epicurus. Epicureans were not irreligious, but they were opposed to many of the accepted religious practices which they regarded as superstitious. In this they sometimes found themselves in alliance with the Christians. When in the second century the fraudulent Alexander of Abonuteichos set to work on his gullible victims he began by a litany against atheists, Christians and Epicureans. The fourth century saw numerous Epicureans swinging over to join the Christian church. It was natural then to portray Jesus in a way which would appeal to them. For a long time these two types, the divine youth and the bearded man of wisdom, remained side by side in the churches. They are only types, but that tells us something of how Jesus was regarded.

Augustine says that even in his day there were in circulation innumerable portraits of Jesus, all different, and that it was not possible for more than one of them to be accurate. He goes on that it does not matter how people imagine his mortal appearance, provided that they believe in the miracle of the Incarnation (*De Trin.* 8.4).

NEW TESTAMENT TITLES

We must return to the New Testament, and look at some of the titles and images under which the first Christians regarded Jesus, and which naturally passed into the imagination of their successors, for whom the New Testament record was their only access to Jesus apart from their own devotional life.

(a) Rabbi or Teacher. 'Rabbi', 'my Master' was a title of respect accorded to honoured teachers by their followers. Jesus was regarded as a teacher and an outstanding one (*Mark* 1.21-8); his authority over the spirits of disease was looked on as an extension of his authority as a teacher. The title 'Master' or 'Teacher' is frequently applied to him in the first three gospels; John prefers to keep the Hebrew word, and from its use by Mary in the story of her post-resurrection encounter with him in the garden (20.16) we can see it as the familiar form of address. According to Matthew Jesus rebuked the men of learning for their demonstrative aloofness, and their divisive use of the title, and said to his followers, 'You must not be called "Rabbi", for you have one Rabbi, and you are all brothers . . . nor must you be called

"Teacher", for you have one teacher, the Messiah' (23.8-10). Whether or not Jesus said the words — they seem out of character — they certainly represent the faith of the early Church. Jesus as Teacher is one of the favourite representations on the great sarcophagi of the fourth century; sometimes he is symbolized in the figure of the true philosopher. Even earlier, Clement of Alexandria had planned a trilogy in which he showed the Logos first as an exhorter, then as a moral tutor, and finally as a teacher, though he never in fact completed the work and left the final section unwritten.

(b) *Kyrios* or Lord. *Kyrios* does not necessarily imply divinity. It is the ordinary Greek word for an owner or boss, and is a form of respectful address to a social superior. When someone uses it to address Jesus, it need mean no more than a respectful 'Sir'; it might be used in speaking or writing to an official or a parent, for example. But there is also a religious usage by which it might be applied to a god such as Sarapis, or the Ptolemies as divine rulers of Egypt, and, in the East, of the Roman emperors; in the Septuagint it is used for Yahweh. Probably we do right to see some kind of progression in its usage. When Jesus at an early point in his ministry says 'The Son of Man is lord of the Sabbath' (*Mark* 2.28) we should spell 'lord' without a capital. But when in *John* Jesus at his Last Supper with the disciples says, 'You call me "Teacher" and "Lord" and rightly, for that is what I am' (13.13), we see 'Lord' as a title of special respect for Jesus, complementary to 'Teacher'. Even here we are not necessarily beyond normal human respect. But when Peter at Pentecost says, 'God has made this Jesus, whom you crucified, both Lord and Messiah' (*Acts* 2.36) he is going some way beyond that, and Paul gives it a still more exalted meaning — 'one Lord, one faith, one baptism' (*Eph.* 4.5) 'crucified the Lord of glory' (1 *Cor.* 2.8) — and oscillates freely between using the word as a title of God and as a title of Jesus.

(c) Saviour. 'Saviour' as a title of Jesus does not often appear in the gospels, though it is a title of God (*Luke* 1.47). Matthew associates the name Jesus ('Yahweh saves') with his destiny to save his people from their sins (1.21), and Luke has the angels telling the shepherds of the birth of a Saviour or

Liberator (2.11). John goes further and tells that the Samaritans recognized Jesus as Saviour of the world (4.42); again, we can acknowledge at least that such a concept was in being by the time the gospel was written. There is however plenty of evidence in the gospels that Jesus regarded his work as saving people. The saying 'The Son of Man has come to seek and save what is lost' has an authentic ring (*Luke* 19.10); perhaps still more the sarcastic words of the bystanders at the crucifixion, 'He saved others but he cannot save himself' (*Mark* 15.31).

But what does Saviour mean? It means a deliverer from evils of all kinds. But we can properly single out three predominant usages. It means a political liberator; the great Old Testament act of deliverance was the salvation from the power of Egypt. It means a healer or rescuer in the most practical materialistic sense; the cognate verb is used in respect of Jesus' acts of healing (*Matt.* 9.21; *Luke* 8.36) or his deliverance of the disciples from danger (*Matt.* 8.25; 14.30). It means one who gives spiritual deliverance, such as Jesus proclaimed to a woman of immoral life who showed a loving spirit in anointing his feet with myrrh (*Luke* 7.50). We must not lose any of these meanings. They are all authentically there in Jesus' own lifetime. But it is the third which later came to predominate. Jesus' claim to forgive sins was central to the Jewish leaders' claim that he was a blasphemer; it was central also to the positive claims of his followers about him. ' "Repent," said Peter, "repent and be baptized, every one of you, in the name of Jesus the Messiah for the forgiveness of your sins." ' (*Acts* 2.38). There emerged with this a theology, or, perhaps it would be truer to say, a succession of theologies, linking the salvific work of Christ in this third sense with his crucifixion and resurrection; the theologies extend from Paul to the twentieth century.

It should be added that this, like *Kyrios*, was a title applied to Hellenistic rulers. Adolf Deissmann in his great *Light from the Ancient East* showed how the titles of Jesus may often be paralleled in Hellenistic ruler-cult.

(d) Messiah. We have seen already the expectation of the

90 *The Early Church: Types and Symbols*

Messiah or Christ, God's anointed vice-gerent, and the hope that Jesus was this Messiah. The hoped-for Messiah was a political liberation-leader. He was also a spiritual deliverer, for ancient thought was not individualistic, and the establishment of a community of peace and righteousness was a spiritual deliverance. The concept of the Messiah further had both an immediate and an eschatological aspect. The very title 'Christian', first given to the followers of Jesus in Antioch, seemingly a variant on 'Chrestoi' ('Goody-goodies') shows that the title remained of cardinal importance.

(e) (f) Son of Man and Son of God. We have examined these titles in the previous chapter.

(g) Logos or Word. This is a concept unique to the prologue of *John*. In *Genesis* God speaks and it is done. The Greek critic who wrote *On the Sublime* regarded the verse 'God said, "Let there be light", and there was light' as one of the great moments of sublimity in literature. So the *memra*, the Word of God, was held to be with power, and it was this Word which came to the prophets. In the Greek world Heraclitus of Ephesus held that the material world was in a state of flux, but that behind was a principle of balance and rationality which he called Logos, a Greek term meaning something spoken, thought or calculated or the process of speaking, thinking or calculation, so that the translation 'word' only reflects one aspect of its significance. This was taken over by the Stoics in the Hellenistic Age, and brought together with the Platonic idea of a Mind behind the universe, and used as a term for God. It seems likely that it was in Alexandria that these two ideas came together; we see them in the Hellenizing Jew Philo; and it is possible that it was the Jewish Christian Apollos who brought them to Ephesus and led John to use this as a title and interpretation of Jesus and his work. It is interesting to reflect that in traditional Chinese thought there is a similar underlying principle, the Tao or Way, the Way the universe works, and that when the Chinese came to translate *John* they used Tao to render Logos.

(h) Judge. In general, both in the Old and the New Testament God is judge. But the Messiah was invested with the role of judge (e.g. *Isa*. 11.3), and although in his lifetime Jesus refused

The Early Church: Types and Symbols

to act as judge (*Luke* 12.14; *John* 8.15; 12.47), John saw his very presence as an act of judgment (3.19), and in the New Testament Jesus is explicitly called the judge of the living and the dead (2 *Tim.* 4.1 cf. 1 *Pet.* 4.5). This gives rise to many later pictorial representations of Christ in judgment. One of the earliest to survive is from S. Apollinare Nuovo in Ravenna. Jesus, gentle but impassive, sits enthroned with an angel on either side; on his right are the sheep, to whom he gestures, on his left the goats. We may perhaps single out two others, to both of which we shall be recurring. One is in the dome of the monastery church of Daphni outside Athens. Here by tradition is set the image of Christ Pantocrator, the All-Ruler. The pose, frontal and holding a book in his left hand, is standardized. The interpretation is not, and the artist at Daphni has portrayed Christ as judge, his eyes fierce and terrifying, his ascetic features set, his brow frowning. In total contrast is Michelangelo's image in the Sistine. His Christ is young, heroic and athletic, but the head is turned aside and the eyes implacably averted; he is impassive, imposing. The great mediaeval song of Thomas of Celano expresses some of the thought which informed the figure of Christ as judge:

> Day of wrath and doom impending,
> David's word with Sibyl's blending!
> Heaven and earth in ashes ending!
>
> O what fear man's bosom rendeth,
> When from heaven the Judge descendeth,
> On whose sentence all dependeth!
>
> Wondrous sound the trumpet flingeth,
> Through earth's sepulchres it ringeth,
> All before the throne it bringeth.
>
> Death is struck, and nature quaking,
> All creation is awaking,
> To its Judge an answer making.
>
> Lo! the book exactly worded,
> Wherein all hath been recorded;
> Thence shall judgement be awarded.

It is a curious development of a single image of a man who is recorded as saying 'I have not come to judge the world but to save the world.'

(i) Wisdom plays a vital part in the post-exilic period of Jewish history. Wisdom is first a gift of Yahweh (*Prov.* 3.13-20) and it is from the awe of Yahweh that it begins (9.10; 15.33; *Job* 28.28; *Ps.* 111.10). But as the thinkers saw Wisdom not as human insight but as the divine purpose in creation, Wisdom was personified with a cosmic status as an intermediary between Yahweh and his creation. In the hymn to Wisdom in the eighth and ninth chapters of *Proverbs*, Wisdom was Yahweh's first creation, and, according to the most widely accepted translation, was beside him like a master-craftsman in the rest of the work of creation. In *Ecclesiasticus* Wisdom is an emanation from God.

> I came out from the mouth of the Most High;
> I covered the earth like a mist.
> My home was in high heaven,
> my throne on a pillar of cloud.
> (24.3-4)

The same thought is elaborated in the first-century *Wisdom of Solomon*:

> In Wisdom there is a spirit intelligent and holy, unique in its kind, yet made up of many parts, subtle, free-moving, lucid, spotless, clear, invulnerable, loving what is good, eager, unhindered, beneficent, kindly towards men, steadfast, unerring, untouched by care, all-powerful, all-surveying, and permeating all intelligent, pure and delicate spirits. For Wisdom moves more easily than motion itself, she pervades and permeates all things because she is so pure. Like a fine mist she rises from the power of God, a pure effluence from the glory of the Almighty; so nothing defiled can enter into her by stealth. She is the brightness that streams from everlasting light, the flawless mirror of the active power of God and the image of his goodness. She is but one, yet can do everything; herself unchanging, she makes all things new; age after age she enters into holy souls, and makes them God's friends and prophets, for nothing is acceptable to God but the

man who makes his home with Wisdom. She is more radiant than the sun, and surpasses every constellation; compared with the light of day, she is found to excel; for day gives place to night, but against Wisdom no evil can prevail. She spans the world in power from end to end, and orders all things benignly.

(7.22-8.1)

Paul identified Wisdom with Christ (1 *Cor.* 1.24, 30), just as in *Revelation* it is Christ on the throne who makes all things new (21.5). The concept of the Logos, which also came out from the mouth of the Most High, is here linked. One of the most famous of all places of worship, Justinian's great church in Constantinople, was dedicated to Holy Wisdom, Santa Sophia, conceived as the Person of Christ.

(j) Paul calls Jesus, as well as the Wisdom of God, the Power of God (1 *Cor.* 1.24). The word (*dynamis*) is a particularly interesting one. It has a wide range of meanings in ordinary life and ordinary conversation, much as our own English word. We may particularly note its use for the external manifestation of inherent authority. Philosophically (Aristotle's rather special use is not in question here) it can be applied to a basic elemental force, such as heat; more generally in philosophy it means the property, quality, productive power, function, meaning or value of a person or thing. It has a specific use in ancient religious writing for a manifestation of the divine. So in an inscription from Lydia in honour of a god called Men we read 'There is one god in the heavens, great Men the heavenly, the great Power of the immortal god', a phrase which closely parallels Paul's.

NEW TESTAMENT TYPES AND IMAGES

John in particular is replete with sayings of Jesus beginning 'I am', and we will start from the images in that gospel.

(a) The bread of life (6.35, 41, 48, 51): meaning the bread that is life as well as the bread that gives life. Bread is the basic food, and in the celebration which reenacted the Last

Supper, the Christians believed that in taking the bread they were taking the life which was in Jesus, and Jesus himself into their very beings. What is more, bread comes into being through the 'death' of the grain, its burial in the ground, and its subsequent fructification (*John* 12.24). Loaves are found in early Christian painting and sculpture.

(b) The light of the world (8.12 cf. 1.4-5). Another basic image. It was particularly associated with the glory of God (e.g. *Ps.* 27.1). It appears in the recently discovered mosaic under St Peter's in Rome where Jesus is portrayed as Helios, the sun-god, driving his chariot across the sky. The idea then emerges of Jesus as the sun of righteousness.

(c) The door of the sheep (10.7, 9). This has less impact than most of the other images, though in funerary symbolism it merges with the old image of the door of death. It is beautifully used in a thirteenth-century mosaic in the dome of Florence Cathedral, where Hermes Psychopompus is replaced by a saint or angel.

(d) The good shepherd (10.11, 14). One of the most basic images. In *Luke* Jesus tells the parable of the lost sheep; the shepherd takes immense trouble to go and find it and bring it home on his shoulders. There was already an art-type of the Greek god Hermes doing just that, and another of Apollo, and this provided an image of Jesus found in painting, graffito, mosaic, relief sculpture. Other mosaics show Jesus as the shepherd with the sheep around him. Sometimes the shepherd stands between a sheep and a goat; there is in this a warning of judgment. Sometimes he sits and enchants the flock with music like Orpheus. It was a literary image too. Hermas' *The Shepherd* was one of the favourite books of the early Christians. Clement of Alexandria calls Christ the shepherd of the king's sheep, of the Word's sheep. Abercius put on his tombstone:

> I, Abercius, am a disciple of the Pure Shepherd,
> Who feeds his flocks and sheep on mountains and plains,
> Who has great eyes which look on all sides.

(This last is a blending with another pagan image, the many-eyed herdsman Argus.) In *The Martyrdom of Perpetua and*

Felicitas there is a vision of the divine shepherd milking the sheep; this too is delightfully portrayed on a fragment from a sarcophagus in the National Museum in Rome. One splendid fresco from the tomb of an unorthodox family of the third century, the Aurchi, blends the figures of shepherd and teacher; the shepherd is reading to his flock from a scroll.

(e) The resurrection and the life (11.25 cf. 1.4; 6.35; 14.6). Another basic image.

(f) The way, the truth and the life (14.6). Three images. The way is a rich symbol. The Pythagorean philosophers had seen the importance of choice in life and used the letter Y to symbolize this. It represents a road and the parting of the ways. They constructed two columns of opposites, lists of things good and evil, which lie along the two ways. Jesus used a closely similar analogy, of the narrow road leading to heaven and the broad highway leading to destruction. He now says that he is that narrow road. The earliest name for the Church and its faith was the Way. The triple image comes together by reference to two passages in the *Psalms*: 'Teach me your way; I will walk in your truth' (86.11) and 'You will show me the path of life' (16.11).

(g) The vine (15.1, 5). Another very rich image. It already existed as a symbol of Israel (*Isa.* 5.1-7; *Jer.* 2.21; *Ezek.* 19.10; *Hos.* 10.1; *Ps.* 80.8). The true vine then stands for the true Israel. Jesus himself is identified with the true Israel, the faithful Remnant. There is a parallel with the saying, 'I am the bread of life', since wine stood to thirst as bread to hunger, and equally had its part in the Eucharist. The image by which Jesus sees his followers as incorporated in him, and drawing their life from his as branches from the main vine, is vivid and picturesque. Furthermore, the vine already existed in Greek religious art as a symbol of Dionysus, so that the Christians were able to re-use a marvellous Dionysiac mosaic in the mausoleum of Constantia (S. Costanza) outside the walls of Rome. Similarly a sarcophagus in the Lateran Museum, from about 300, shows three surely Christian shepherd-figures towering above a sprawling vine, Cupids, and Psyche and Eros. The vine appears in the background of the Constantinian mosaic of Christ as the Sun-god, found under St Peter's.

(h) The Lamb of God (1.29). This is not used by Jesus of himself, but by John the Baptist of him. The idea is certainly sacrificial, but it is interesting that the particular Greek word is not used in the Septuagint of the Passover lamb, but is applied to the Suffering Servant (*Isa.* 53.7). This again became a potent image, as we see in *Revelation*, where it recurs, and sometimes in the mosaics and elsewhere. In the catacomb of Domitilla there is a prancing lamb with crook and milk pail; some interpreters take this to be the worshipper, but it is in isolation more likely to symbolize Jesus. Paulinus of Nola, who decorated the cloister of his church with Old Testament scenes, would not depict Jesus except as 'a snow-white lamb under a blood-stained cross'. The symbol of the lamb became immensely popular in art, often in the apses of churches, so much so that the Quinisext Council in Constantinople in 691 decreed in its 82nd canon that 'henceforth Christ was to be publicly exhibited in the form of a man not of a lamb'; the Council felt that the symbol had taken over from the reality.

OLD TESTAMENT TYPOLOGY

Already in the New Testament we see the early Christians thinking of Jesus not just in terms of Old Testament prophecy but in terms of a typology by which an Old Testament figure might represent some aspect of Jesus and his work. This was carried to a high art by the Christian Platonists of Alexandria, who specialized in allegorical interpretation, and it played some part in forming the system of artistic allusion to Jesus.
(a) Adam. Jesus appears as the Second Adam in the New Testament (*Rom.* 5.14; 1 *Cor.* 15.45), restoring the paradisal bliss lost in the original fall. Scenes showing the first man thus are taken as reminders of the renewal of humanity in Jesus. Adam and Eve appear, for example, above the font at Dura-Europos, on a third-century painted ceiling in Naples or, with other scenes of deliverance, on a sarcophagus from Velletri. A marvellous ivory diptych in Florence shows Adam in a state of innocence among the animals; we are meant to think of the new Adam and the restoration of man. This dates

The Early Church: Types and Symbols

from the late fourth century. But of course there is a wry irony in the parallel between Adam and Jesus. Leonhard Goppelt reminds us that Christ is also the antitype of Adam, or Adam of Christ: 'as in Adam all died, so in Christ shall all be made alive' (1 *Cor.* 15.22). But the concept of Jesus as the second Adam remains through Christian history, as in Newman's familiar hymn:

> A second Adam to the fight,
> And to the rescue came.

(b) Abel was regarded as prefiguring Christ in three ways, first, because he was an innocent shepherd, second because he offered a sacrifice which was acceptable to Yahweh, and third because he himself became a victim. Jesus had himself put Abel at the head of the list of prophets who were killed (*Matt.* 23.35) and Melito says that Jesus was 'in Abel murdered', but the author of *Hebrews* contrasted his death with that of Jesus 'whose sprinkled blood has better things to tell than the blood of Abel' (12.24). Abel also became a prefiguration of the source of encouragement to the early martyrs.

(c) Enoch is a mysterious figure appearing in the early pages of *Genesis* (5.18-24). Apart from his place in the succession we are told simply that he walked with God, and escaped death by being taken away or 'translated'. On both grounds he appears as a prefiguration of Jesus.

(d) Noah becomes a type of Jesus in that he rescues those with him from the power of death. He stands also for the end and the beginning, the end of one world and the beginning of a new one, the end of one life and the beginning of a new one, the omega and the alpha. The story of the flood is naturally used as an image of baptism, but the salvation from cataclysmic destruction has also for the early Christians an association with eschatology and the final judgment. Noah appears delightfully on a sarcophagus from Velletri, dating from the late third century. He is bobbing up triumphantly from a chest, which could hardly hold him let alone any other creatures, with the dove and the olive branch.

(e) The Abraham story offers a number of parallels appropriate to the Christian understanding of Jesus. The author of

Hebrews has a fine series of vignettes of faith in which Abraham is prominent. They form a kind of lesson in faith, an environment of faith for the Jewish Christian. The climax is in Jesus on whom faith depends from start to finish; there is a close parallel between Abraham leaving home without knowing where he was going because he was looking forward to a city with firm foundations and Jesus enduring the cross for the sake of the joy which lay ahead of him (11.8-10; 12.2). A specific example of faith is found in Abraham's willingness to sacrifice Isaac (11.17-9); 'Abraham', says Hebert, 'apparently throwing away the whole of the promised future by the sacrifice of his son, was a type of our Lord going to His death with His lifework apparently incomplete, and its objects quite unattained; yet putting His hands between God's hands and going forward.' But in this episode, which is illustrated for example in the catacomb of Marcellinus, the symbolism is complex. The figure of Abraham may call Jesus to mind because he symbolizes faith and perfect obedience. The figure of Isaac may represent Jesus because he, so to speak, dies and rises again. Melito calls Jesus 'in Isaac bound'. Centuries later, Louisa Twining in her *Types and Figures of the Bible, Illustrated by the Art of the Early and Middle Ages* (London 1855) set side by side Jesus on the way to Calvary and Isaac bearing a cross. The figure of the ram caught in the thicket may stand for Jesus, as the substitutionary sacrifice, especially as in this particular painting it is not a ram caught in a thicket but a lamb coming freely to the sacrifice.

(d) Melchizedek appears in *Genesis* 14.18 as 'King of Salem' and 'Priest of God Most High'; he offered Abraham food and drink when the latter returned from his campaign against the four kings. In *Psalm* 100.4 the Messiah is called 'a priest for ever after the order of Melchizedek'. The author of *Hebrews* took up both these passages, seeing Melchizedek as a prefiguring of Jesus, and using them to prove the superiority of Christ's priesthood over that of Aaron and the Levites. Thereafter the link with Melchizedek is firmly fixed in the Christian tradition, and Clement of Alexandria takes his offering of bread and wine to Abraham as a prefiguring type of the Last Supper and the subsequent celebration of the Eucharist;

Cyprian even uses this passage as an argument for the propriety of using wine rather than water in the liturgy. Abraham and Melchizedek are magnificently portrayed in the mosaic in S. Maria Maggiore in Rome.

(g) Jacob appears in Stephen's résumé of Jewish history. He was the original Israel, as Jesus brought into being the new Israel. He wrestled with God and demanded to know his name. Jacob's dream of a ladder linking heaven to earth and earth to heaven is taken as a type of the Incarnation. Melito says that Jesus was 'in Jacob exiled'. This refers primarily to the sojourn with Laban as a type of Christ's sojourn in Egypt.

(h) Joseph's chequered career offered typological parallels in plenty. He was sunk in a pit and pulled out again; he was sold; he languished in prison, and was released and exalted; so far as his father was concerned he was dead and came to life again; in all these ways he prefigured the resurrection. Austin Farrer in his well-known *A Study in St. Mark* makes a lot of the parallels with Joseph, even to the use of the word 'confounded' of his hearers (*Gen.* 45.3: *Mark* 6.50).

(i) Moses is a type of Christ in more ways than one. First, because he was the instrument of the first great act of liberation; the Messiah would re-enact the act of liberation. Second, because he was associated with the Old Covenant, as Jesus with the New, in which Law found its fulfilment in love. Third because Moses striking the rock so that water gushed out formed a fitting emblem of Jesus giving the Living Water (*John* 4.7-13). So we see this scene in the catacombs of Marcellinus and Calixtus, among others. Sometimes this symbolism is further extended. In some of the catacomb sketches, Jesus raising Lazarus is in fact Moses striking the rock, and so bringing new life, and if it were not for the swathed tiny figure of Lazarus we might so interpret it. Moses striking the rock appears on a fourth-century glass in the Ashmolean Museum, Oxford. The deliverance from Egypt has one of its earliest portrayals in the great mosaic cycle in S. Maria Maggiore, Rome.

(j) Joshua was an obvious and natural prefiguration of Jesus; he bore the same name, and it was he who led the Israelites into the promised land. Joshua appears as a prefiguration of

Christ in one of the fragments of Melito newly disinterred from a Georgian homiliary. Joshua is an important figure in the first surviving mosaic cycle of Old Testament pictures in a Christian context, that in S. Maria Maggiore, Rome, already mentioned.

(k) Samson was an Israelite folk-hero, a man of colossal strength and legendary feats, who fought against the Philistines, but was betrayed by his weakness for women. One of the famous episodes in his career was when he encountered a young lion and tore it limb from limb with his bare hands. Samson's fight with the lion was taken as a type of Christ's conquest of evil. Later he found that some bees had settled in the carcase. Augustine in one of his sermons (364.4) uses the image, and Isidore seems to give the figure a wider reference when he writes 'Samson represents the death and victory of our Saviour, perhaps because he snatched the peoples out of the devil's jaws, as Samson took the honeycomb from the mouth of a lion he found.' At Anzy-le-Duc in the twelfth century one of the carvers sculpted Samson killing the lion on to one of the capitals in the nave. Another story of Samson told how he marched away with the gates of Gaza on his back; this was taken as a type of Jesus bursting the gates of death.

(l) David has his place in the Messianic genealogies, and 'son of David' was one of the Messianic titles. David naturally and easily became the type of Christ. Paul preaching in Pisidia takes off from David as the one who will perfectly do God's will to 'his descendant Jesus' (*Acts* 13.22-3). Some of the parallels are directed to his encounter with the giant Philistine Goliath. Augustine sees this as foreshadowing Jesus' victory over Satan, and Cyril of Alexandria says that his sling prefigures the Cross. David's encounter with the lion, like Samson's, bears a similar meaning. David was a shepherd, which provides a link with Jesus' own imagery. He was also a musician, and the image of Jesus as the ideal musician entrancing his hearers is one used by the early Fathers. More curiously Augustine also takes the story of David and Bathsheba typologically, David representing Jesus, Bathsheba the church, and Uriah the Hittite (Bathsheba's lawful husband, to

The Early Church: Types and Symbols   101

all intents and purposes murdered by David) Satan.

(m) Jeremiah was living in the late seventh and early sixth century. He watched from a distance the Deuteronomic reforms of king Josiah, and saw the people slip back again into idolatry. He denounced this and saw his prophecies torn up. He opposed the policy of alliance with Egypt and military resistance to Babylon, and was imprisoned in abominable conditions. Yet he was closely aware of a personal call from a personal God, and spoke of a new covenant written on men's hearts. With his rejection, his personal suffering, and his lamentation over the doom of Jerusalem, he formed an obvious type of Christ.

(n) Jonah, swallowed by the sea-monster and regurgitated, became a type of Jesus risen from the tomb. Jesus had spoken about the sign of Jonah, but it does not appear that this is what he intended (*Matt.* 16.41; *Luke* 11.29-32), though in another passage Matthew places this interpretation on the words, and puts it into Jesus' mouth (11.39-42). Augustine spells out the analogy more fully: 'Christ passed from the wood of the cross, as Jonah from the ship to the sea-monster (or the power of death); the endangered crew are the human race, battered by the storms of the world; and as Jonah preached to Nineveh after his return to life, so the Gentile Church heard the Lord's word only after the Resurrection.' (*Ep. ad Deo-gratias*)

There are two third-century statuettes in the Cleveland Museum of Art showing, in a splendidly spirited rendering, Jonah being swallowed and regurgitated: the very type of resurrection. On the sarcophagi Jonah is the type both of Jesus' resurrection and of the hoped-for resurrection of the dead. It is interesting too that the figure of Jonah is sometimes reminiscent of Ariadne or Endymion on sarcophagi, where there is equally hope of life beyond the grave, awakened by the divine kiss. Augustine tells us further that these representations of Jonah, which sometimes, as in the Catacomb of St Lucina or on a fourth-century gem, brought together different aspects of the story in a single composition, were a common topic for pagan derision.

(o) Daniel in the lion's den frequently stands for the resurrection of Jesus and, on sarcophagi, the deliverance of the Christian from the power of death. Lions' heads represent the devouring menace of death on pagan sarcophagi. On a magnificent Christian sarcophagus at Tipasa we have the two lions' heads, and, in between, the good shepherd, offering a kind of dual symbolism. The superimposition of the figures of Daniel and Jesus must have been deeply meaningful to those who suffered martyrdom by being thrown to the lions.

(p) Similarly Shadrach, Meshach and Abednego being delivered from the fiery furnace form a type of Jesus's victory over death, and are to be seen linked together in a delightful representation in the catacomb of Domitilla. Just as Daniel will have had a special meaning for martyrs in the arena, so this story must have had a special meaning for those who in Nero's reign were covered with pitch and used as living torches. There is a further point which must remain speculative. In fully fledged Christian theology God is a Trinity in Unity, Father, Son, Spirit, three Persons and one God. The theology was worked out across the centuries, but it is implicit in the prayer with which *Matthew* ends (28.19). Was there any thought in the Christians who looked on the image of the Three Holy Children (as they are sometimes called) that God, Father, Son and Spirit, passed triumphantly through the baptism of fire represented by the cross?

(q) One of the incidental types of Christ comes from the Daniel apocrypha and the story of Susanna. This is worked into an elaborate allegory by Hippolytus. Babylon is the world; the Garden represents the calling of the saints. Susanna is the church; the two elders represent the persecutors, Jewish and Pagan. Christ thus becomes the rather colourless figure of the wealthy Joachim, Susanna's husband. But in the catacomb of Priscilla the figure of Susanna dominates both the elders on one side, and Daniel on the other. She stands in prayer, and her trial may be seen as a type of death and deliverance.

MATERIAL TYPES OF CHRIST FROM THE OLD TESTAMENT

The early Christians regarded Jesus as prefigured not merely by individual persons but also by some impersonal objects in the Old Testament.

First among these is the Ark: Origen makes this explicit. It was, after all, the Ark rather than Noah which preserved the Remnant from the Flood; indeed Noah was one of these so preserved.

A second image is that of the Good Land, the Promised Land, the Land flowing with milk and honey (*Exod*. 33.1-3). Here is *The Letter of Barnabas*, written at the end of the first or beginning of the second century:

> What does the other prophet, Moses, say to them? 'Look. These are the words of the Lord your God: "Enter the Good Land which the Lord promised to Abraham, Isaac and Jacob, a Land flowing with milk and honey."' What has knowledge to say? Listen. She says, Hope in that Jesus who is going to appear to you in the flesh. (6.8-9)

There is a contrast with the other Jesus — Joshua.

> Man is earth suffering, for Adam was formed from the surface of the earth. What then is the meaning of 'the Good Land, a Land flowing with milk and honey'? Blessed be our Lord, brothers, who has placed within us wisdom and understanding of his secrets! The prophet is speaking a parable of our Lord. 'Who shall understand, unless he is wise and knowledgeable and loves his Lord?' So since by remitting our sins he has made us new, he made a fresh type of us, as though he were creating us anew with the souls of children. We are the real subject of the scripture where he says to the Son: 'Let us make man after our own image and likeness, and let them rule the wild animals of the earth, and the birds of the sky and the fishes of the sea.' Seeing the beauty of our creation the Lord said 'Increase and multiply and fill the earth.' He was addressing the Son. I'll show you again how he addresses us. He made a new creation in these last days; the Lord says 'Look: I make the last things as the first.' So the prophet

referred to this in his pronouncement. 'Enter into a Land flowing with milk and honey, and have authority in it.'   (6.9-13)

The analogy is not quite consistent, but the general purport is that Jesus is the Good Land, and in him his people found fulfilment.

A third image, of a similar kind, is Jerusalem. Jerusalem is the city of God in which his people find their home, and the analogy is strictly similar.

The fourth great image of this kind is the Temple. Here the comparison goes right back to the New Testament.

> The Jews challenged Jesus' 'What sign', they asked, 'can you show as authority for your action?' 'Destroy this temple,' Jesus replied, 'and in three days I will raise it again.' They said, 'It has taken forty-six years to build this temple. Are you going to raise it again in three days?' But the temple he was speaking of was his body.
> (*John* 2.18-20 cf. *Mark* 14.58; *Matt.* 26.6)

For the Christians, whether Jewish or Gentile, the destruction of the Temple was evidence that God does not live in houses made by men's hands (*Acts* 7.48 directed to Jews; 17.24 to Greeks). They saw Jesus as the one in whom God lived uniquely. The equation had been made explicit by the visionary seer in *Revelation*. In the new Jerusalem he saw no Temple for its Temple was the sovereign Lord God and the Lamb.

These are the four great material images. But as the Christians combed the scriptures for possible allusions there were plenty they could find. One was the rock. Isaiah had the image, associated with the righteous king, of the shadow of a great rock in a thirsty land (32.2). Further the rock which Moses struck had given refreshing water, and Paul had already used this analogy of Jesus (1 *Cor.* 10.3). Another, not far removed, goes back to the gospels. The psalmist declared

> The stone which the builders rejected
> has become the chief corner-stone
> (*Ps.* 118.22)

This was an obvious passage to take up, and it was taken up (*Matt.* 21.42; *Mark* 12.10; *Luke* 20.17; *Acts* 4.11).

SCENES FROM THE LIFE OF JESUS

Although the main early representations of Jesus in art are symbolic there are some scenes from his life:

(a) Scenes from the birth narratives. One of the early representations appears in the catacomb of Priscilla and shows the three Magi bringing their gifts. By the fifth century representations are becoming more systematic and standardized. A gospel cover from Milan, datable to 402, shows the Annunciation, Nativity and Magi, as well as the Massacre of the Innocents.

(b) The baptism. This was a precious scene to Christians, for Jesus had experienced what they accepted. The baptism of Jesus with the dove descending can be seen, for example, on the S. Maria Antiqua sarcophagus.

(c) Scenes of teaching. Mostly Jesus as teacher is a symbolic scene rather than representing a particular episode in the gospels. Still it should be considered in some sense 'biographical', as there are plenty such episodes in the gospel. The image of Jesus as teacher generally shows him expounding the Torah and presenting the new Law. We see him in the catacombs seated on a dais; the box for the scroll is in front of him. In another scene from the catacombs he holds a scroll in his left hand and gestures with his right; on either side is an attentive listener; under his feet is a subject figure no doubt representing the old law. There is a beautiful figure of Jesus as teacher in a third-century statuette in the Museo delle Terme, Rome, where the type is derived from Orpheus. Jesus as teacher is a frequent figure on the sarcophagi. In this figure come together the actuality of his work, his title as Rabbi, and his assimilation to the Greek philosopher who appears frequently on pagan sarcophagi.

(d) Scenes of healing. Jesus as healer was a natural image: this too brought together his historic acts with his image as healer of body, mind and spirit, and, later, an assimilation to pagan healers such as Asclepius. The healing of the paralytic is found more than once in early frescoes. One, from Dura-Europos, now in Yale, shows him lying on his stretcher, but another in the catacomb of Calixtus shows him delightfully walking with his bed. A fragment of a sarcophagus in the National Museum, Rome, dating from about 300, shows the healing of the woman with the issue of blood, the paralytic, and the man born blind. A Constantinian sarcophagus in the same Museum, shows a beardless Jesus laying two fingers across the eyes of the man born blind. A sarcophagus in the Lateran shows the woman with the issue of blood. By the fifth century other scenes are appearing: an evocative carving in the Louvre shows a still beardless Jesus healing the Gadarene demoniac, with some delightful pigs which deserve a better fate. The blind man of Jericho is another scene which now comes in. A delightful mosaic scene in S. Apollinare Nuovo in Ravenna shows the paralytic being lowered from the roof, a small pleading figure beside the healing power of Jesus.

(e) Lazarus. A particular scene which recurs time and again both in the catacombs and on sarcophagi is the raising of Lazarus from the dead, a story told with realistic detail by John. It can be seen for example on a Constantinian sarcophagus in the National Museum in Rome.

(f) Other scenes. An excellent fresco from Dura, from the first part of the third century, shows the scene with the Samaritan woman at the well; this is appropriately in the baptistery: the Samaritan woman also appears in the catacombs. Another scene from Dura shows Jesus stretching out his hand to save Peter from the waves. One of the most excellent scenes is in low relief on a superb sarcophagus in the Lateran Museum showing Jesus confronting Peter with the cock. In the more systematic exposition on the Milan gospel-cover from 402 we have such scenes as the boy Jesus in the Temple, the miracle at Cana, the entry into Jerusalem, and the widow's mite. An Italian ivory in the Victoria and Albert Museum, datable to about 450, shows six miracles, the loaves and fishes, the healing of the blind man, the paralytic (carrying off his bed), the raising of Lazarus, the miracle at Cana, and the healing of a leper. A scene that becomes a favourite is the entry into Jerusalem; it is marvellously shown in the sixth-century illuminated manuscript in Rossano, where the palm-branches appear like an army of spears, the spread cloaks are purple and orange-red, and the donkey treads as proudly as Chesterton ever envisaged him.

(g) Scenes from the Passion. Scenes of sharing bread and wine round a common table appear from an early period, but perhaps represent the church's liturgy rather than the actual Last Supper, though of course they recall this. From about 400 however the Last Supper takes its place firmly in the life-cycle of Jesus as portrayed in art. The early cycles of pictures do not show Jesus in agony. There is a catacomb painting of him with the crown of thorns, but his face is calm. A fourth-century reliquary, now in Brescia, shows a sequence of the Passion narrative: the agony in the garden, the arrest, Peter's denial, Jesus before Caiaphas, Pilate washing his hands.

(h) Scenes from the resurrection. There are a number of representations from the late fourth century. A diptych from Milan shows the tomb as a Mausoleum with soldiers asleep in the top half, and the appearance of Christ risen below. In Munich we can see another scene with a mausoleum tomb, and Jesus both risen and ascending into heaven.

PAGAN IMAGES

Some of the artistic representations are borrowed from pagan art. This is not surprising, as the Jews had no tradition of representing the human figure.

(a) Orpheus. The Jews had in fact already seen in Orpheus, the great musician, an analogue of David, and the typical representation of Orpheus is curiously like Isaiah's vision of the wolf in amity with the lamb, the leopard with the kid, and the calf, bull and lion together. We see Orpheus in a Messianic context in the synagogue at Dura. David himself is the type of the good shepherd. So Orpheus becomes an analogue of Jesus. We can see the transformation in a series of paintings in the catacombs. In the first Orpheus is charming the animals; yet around are Old Testament scenes. The second shows Orpheus still; the Phrygian cap is unmistakable, but the listening animals are sheep. In the third the sheep are still there, but the seated musician has been replaced by the Good Shepherd, lamb on shoulder. Sometimes there is no transformation; Orpheus is a symbol in his own right. There is a beautiful example in the Byzantine Museum at Athens, another on an ivory pyxis in Bobbio, supposedly presented by Gregory to Columba. One of the most fascinating representations of Orpheus is in a fourth-century Roman house in Ptolemais in Cyrenaica. The context is not certainly Christian, but Christianity was prominent in the city. Orpheus is uniquely portrayed with a blue halo: the nearest parallel is the Good Shepherd on a contemporary pavement in Aquileia. Orpheus also influences another type, Adam charming the animals on an ivory diptych in Florence. Eusebius compares the Logos taming mankind with Orpheus charming the animals (*Laud. Const.* 14).

(b) Hermes, Apollo, Aristaeus. Hermes was easily christianized; he was the escort of souls to darkness or light; as the messenger of the gods he became a type of the Logos. Justin Martyr says 'In this we are one with you, in that we both regard the Logos, whom you call Hermes, as the messenger of God' (*Apology* 1.22). The same thought is found in Hippolytus and in the Pseudo-Clementine *Recognitions*. Apollo is a natural image for 'the young Prince of Glory': he also, in an image flanked by two griffins, affects the type of Daniel between the lions. The beardless Good Shepherd of the fifth-century mosaic in the Mausoleum of Galla Placidia in Ravenna is Apolline in type. In fact, Hermes carrying a calf, Apollo and the shepherd-god Aristaeus all contribute to the image of the Good Shepherd.

(c) Helios. Clement of Alexandria called Jesus the Sun of Righteousness, he who rides in his chariot far over everything (*Protrepticus* 11, 114, 2-3). So in the necropolis under St Peter's he was depicted as Helios the Sun-god riding across the sky.

(d) Heracles was the son of God who laboured for mankind, died in agony and was received into heaven. On the whole it is strange that the analogy with Jesus is not more frequent and explicit: perhaps it was too close to be comfortable. But Heracles appears in a Christian context in six pictures in the

The Early Church: Types and Symbols 109

new catacombs beyond the Porta Latina, and provides one of the types for Samson or David killing the lion. In fact in the silver plate from the Cyprus treasure in the Metropolitan Museum, New York, David is using Heracles' club. Heracles descended into the lower world to save Alcestis; he also faced and overcame temptation in a famous allegory; he took the form of a slave; he laboured for mankind; he passed through death to deity. He was an obvious type of Christ and it is slightly odd that he appears only in this one corner of the catacombs.

(e) Mithras. The mysteries of Mithras seemed to Christian interpreters to be a devil's parody of their own mysteries. Mithras was a Mediator and a Saviour, and the mysteries involved a common meal celebrated with what look extraordinarily like hot cross buns. Portrayals of Mithras do not in general affect the direct iconography of Jesus, but they affect the portrayal of some of the typological scenes, Moses striking water from the rock, for example, or David (or Samson) with the lion, which is sometimes gripped as the bull is gripped by Mithras.

(f) Horus. Isis was another of the eastern divinities who had her mysteries, one too who made universal claims. These claims had to be countered, and the figure of Isis with the divine child Horus on her knee became the type of Mary and the infant Jesus.

(g) Dionysus or Eros. Dionysus, because of the symbolism of the vine, and Eros, because in Plato he is the aspiration towards God, are natural types for Jesus, and the youthful, unbearded, idealized divine Jesus is usually taken from one or the other, as can be seen by close observation of the hairstyle.

(h) The bearded god. The great bearded God type is Zeus, and the chalice of Antioch which shows the shepherd-judge above the eagle, puts Christ on the throne of Zeus. At Gerasa a third-century head of Zeus in the basilica was actually re-used as a head of Christ. Theodorus Anagnostes tells a story of a fifth-century painter who portrayed Christ in the likeness of Zeus; the hand with which he painted was withered away but restored in answer to prayer. In fact the Byzantine bearded Christ can be traced back in direct line of descent to the Zeus Olympius of Phidias. But this analogue is richer still, for there were already assimilations of Asclepius, the healing god, and Sarapis, the new universal god of the Ptolemies, to Zeus. In fact they formed a kind of mystic trinity.

(i) The bearded philosopher. We have already noted that the bearded portrayal of Jesus was also affected partly by portraits of Epicurus, and partly by the philosopher who appears teaching on pagan sarcophagi.

(j) The Christian mosaic pavement at Hinton St Mary has Bellerophon killing the chimaera: this is a type of Christ's victory over evil. Perseus rescuing Andromeda from the sea-monster also gives rise to similar imagery (which later affects the portrayal of George -- or Michael – and the dragon).

(k) Odysseus. In Hippolytus *Refutation of All Heresies* (6. 13) Odysseus is compared to Christ in his capacity to resist the Temptation of the Sirens. (Clement of Alexandria uses Odysseus rather as the type of the believer.) In the catacombs the return of Odysseus is the return of Christ to claim his bride, the Church, and to destroy pride.

OTHER EARLY SYMBOLS IN ART

(a) The Orans. The Orans or figure in prayer stands with both hands raised shoulder high. He is often to be seen on Christian sarcophagi, sometimes coupled with the Shepherd. The Orans is often identified with the Christian soul, but seems rather to be a divine symbol, perhaps initially of the Spirit (whom Paul declares to pray alongside us). But on one of the best known sarcophagi, from S. Maria Antiqua in Rome, we have Jonah, the Orans, the Philosopher, the Good Shepherd, and the baptism of Christ: read one way they are all symbols of the Christian life, but another way they all represent Christ. The Orans is a new figure, not taken from pagan art. Grabar has shown a connection with pagan expressions of piety, but the examples are not identical.

(b) The anchor. The symbolism here is obvious, as in the later hymn 'Will your anchor hold?' Clement of Alexandria, noting that Seleucus, one of the Hellenistic monarchs, used it as a seal, thought it none the less appropriate to Christians. The anchor appears between two fishes in an epitaph in the Vatican. An additional reason for the use of the anchor-symbol was that its form approximated to that of a cross. This is clear in the inscription of Hesperus from the crypts of Lucina, dating from the early third century.

(c) The fish. The fish is a very ancient religious symbol. It was peculiarly appropriate to Christianity as several of the disciples were fishermen, and Jesus had invited them to become fishers of men. Fish was one of the foods which Jesus had shared with his followers, at the great Messianic banquet of the 5,000 and in the record of one of the post-resurrection appearances. Further the initial letters of Jesus Christ, God's Son, Saviour spelt out the Greek word for a fish: I Ch Th Y S. So in the epitaph of Abercius in the Lateran Museum, datable to 216 he says, 'there was handed to me everywhere as nourishment the Fish from the spring, the pure Fish of great size caught by the chaste Virgin.' This is Christ. Also from the third century (some have argued for the second) is the original of the epitaph of Pectorius, found in Autun. The meaning is a little uncertain in parts:

> Divine race of the heavenly Fish, preserve a holy
>   heart, taking among mortals an immortal spring
> of god sent waters, friend, refresh your soul
>   with the eternal waters of wisdom's rich giving.
> Receive the honey-sweet food of the Saviour of saints,
>   eat eagerly holding the Fish in your grasp.
> Let me be filled with the Fish, I yearn for it,
>   my Master, my Saviour.
>   May my mother sleep well, I implore you,
>   Light of the dead.
> Father Aschandios, dear to my heart, with my sweet
>   mother and brothers,
>   in the peace of the Fish remember your Pectorius.

The epitaph in the Vatican which shows the anchor between two fishes also bears the words ICHTHYS ZONTON, the Fish of the Living. In the catacomb of Calixtus a fish and a basket of loaves represent the food of life. The fish is another symbol Clement declares appropriate to a Christian's seal.

(d) The dove. The dove is a symbol of the Spirit, but the Spirit is called the Spirit of Christ, and may be a reminder of Christ. Further sometimes, as in a second-century gem in the Kircher Museum, the dove is shown with the olive branch, as in the story of Noah, and is in fact a reminder of salvation from disaster. This too Clement thought appropriate to a Christian seal.

(e) The cross. The cross in the form of a T appears in some early works of art, as in that same gem in the Kircher Museum. It is hard to know whether to make anything of the cross in the plaster at Herculaneum. It might have held a clamp to support a cupboard, but it equally might be a Christian symbol. If so it antedates 79. A + appears on the inscription of Rufina and Irene in the crypts of Lucina from the early third century. The cross was a pre-Christian symbol (derived from the sun-wheel), and naturally and easily adopted and adapted. The Montanists were regarded as defiantly aggressive when they inscribed crosses on the headstones of their graves. There is a glorious cross in a star-studded sky in the Mausoleum of Galla Placidia in Ravenna.

(d) A lyre. This was used as a seal by the dictator Polycrates. Despite this Clement thought it appropriate to the Christian: it spoke of the new harmony, which came through the Word.

(g) A ship sailing before the wind. Another appropriate symbol for the Christian to use. The mast and yardarm formed a cross, which made it especially appropriate. Sometimes this is linked with the myth of Odysseus and the Sirens: the soul, firm against the cross of the mast, resists temptation. Similarly the ship in the portrayals of Jonah is an independent symbol.

(h) The fisherman. Another of Clement's approved symbols. He associated it with the apostles; it is a reminder too, he says, of the children fished from the water. Here again the symbol really speaks of Christ as Saviour.

(i) The chi-rho symbol has a curious history. On his way to fight the battle of the Milvian Bridge Constantine had a vision of a rare but attested example of the halo-phenomenon, a cross superimposed on the sun, and the words came to him

'Triumph in this'. It was a vision sent from the ancestral god yet speaking of Christ, and Constantine syncretized the two, and eclipsed the pacifism of Christ with the militarism of the sun; his god was always a god of power, never of love. He put a form of cross and circle on his banners, and he did triumph. From this came the chi-rho ⊕ interpreted as a monogram of the first two letters of Christ in Greek. The symbol, while in one sense obviously and explicitly Christian, is also blurred. It is close to the ancient sun-wheel, especially when, as often, it is held within a circle or wreath. It is also close to other ancient symbols, notably the *crux ansata* of Egypt, the symbol of eternal life; the ankh was itself used by Coptic Christians. The chi-rho appears fascinatingly on a floor mosaic found at Hinton St Mary in Dorset behind a head which must be that of Jesus, though it is odd that it should appear on the floor.

(j) The athlete's palm. This symbolizes the victory over death, of Christ and those whom he saves. Thus palms surround the figure of Christ in the apse mosaic in S. Costanza, Rome.

(k) The peacock. The peacock, the bird of Hera-Juno in pagan imagery, was believed to have incorruptible flesh, and is taken over by the Christians as a symbol of immortality. One of the finest appearances is on a sixth-century sarcophagus in Ravenna, but it appears earlier on the ambiguously pagan-Christian ceiling-mosaic in S. Costanza, Rome.

(l) The pelican. The image of the pelican lacerating her breast so as to feed her young with her blood becomes an image of Jesus giving his life. Its use as a Christian symbol goes back to Jerome and Eucherius in the early fifth century.

(m) The phoenix. A natural symbol of resurrection, found in the catacomb of Priscilla.

CLEMENT OF ALEXANDRIA AND OTHER HYMNODISTS

Clement of Alexandria was born in about 150 either in Athens of Alexandria; interestingly he bears a Latin name and was perhaps a descendant of a freedman attached to the family of

T. Flavius Clemens, a relative of the Flavian emperors, and perhaps himself a convert to Christianity. Clement's career belonged to Alexandria, where he taught and wrote. He was still alive in AD 211 but dead by 216.

Appended to the manuscript of his work *The Tutor* appears a hymn in praise of Christ in lilting, marching anapaests, full of titles and symbols of Christ.

> Bit for untamed colts,
> Wing for sure-coursed birds,
> Sure helm for ships,
> Shepherd of the royal flocks,
> gather your children
> all together
> to praise in holiness
> to hymn without guile
> with blameless lips
> Christ who guides his children.
>
> King of the saints,
> almighty Word
> of the supreme Father,
> source of wisdom,
> support of our labours
> with never ending joy,
> Jesus Saviour
> of mankind,
> shepherd, ploughman,
> helm, bit,
> winging your holy
> flock through heaven,
> fisher of men
> who finds salvation,
> charming by bliss
> away from the Sea's malice
> the holy fish
> of the bitter wave.

Holy shepherd
of men who find the Word,
King, be leader
of your stainless children.
Tracks of the Christ,
road to heaven,
Eternal Word,
infinite Aeon,
everlasting light,
fount of mercy.

Guardian of righteousness,
glorious life
for them that praise God,
Christ Jesus,
milk from heaven,
pressed out
from the lovely breasts
that adorn your bride,
your Wisdom.
We are babes,
breast-fed
with tender lips,
filled
with the dewy breath
of the breast of the Word.
Let us sing together
unison praises
to Christ our King,
in sacred payment
for life and teaching.
Let us sing simply
of the child of power,
a choir of peace,
those born of Christ,
an obedient people.
Let us hymn together
the God of Peace.

The imagery is noteworthy. Its varied intensity recalls John's gospel, but, curiously, Clement does not draw particularly closely on that imagery. Some of the images, such as 'fisher of men', are drawn from scripture; this particular example is applied by Jesus to the disciples, not actually to himself. The idea of the 'tracks' or 'footsteps' comes from 1 *Peter* 2.21; the idea that we are babes at the breast from 1 *Corinthians* 3.2 and *Hebrews* 5.12-3; the milk of the Word from 1 *Peter* 2.2; the Peace from *Romans* 15.33 and *Hebrews* 13.20. But some of the images seem to be independent and do not have any obvious scriptural source. Clement may have received these from elsewhere. The synthesis is his own.

An older contemporary of Clement, Theophilus of Antioch, has an important disquisition on the names of God — Light, Logos, Mind, Spirit, Wisdom, Strength, Potency, Providence, Sovereignty, Lord, Judge, Father, Fire (*Ad Autol.* 1.3). Some of the imagery is directly applicable to Jesus, and all of it, even Father (*John* 14.9) is associated with him.

This interest in the names of Christ continued across the centuries. Isidore in the seventh century has a long account (7.2), in which he discusses various appellations: Only-Begotten Son of the Father, from his relationship to God; Christ from his anointing, which he rightly says is not a proper name, but the affirmation of a common power; Saviour, because of his saving work, implicit in the name Jesus; Emmanuel, 'God with us' in Hebrew, because he was in the flesh; God, as one in substance with the Father; Lord because creation is subject to him; God and man, as Word and flesh; Twiceborn, eternally from the Father, temporally from his mother; Only-begotten because of his uniqueness; First-born, because men become his brothers by adoption; *Homoousios* (of one substance) with the Father; *Homoiousios* (of like substance) since man is in the image of God; the Beginning; the End; the Face or Mouth of God; the Word, because through him the Father formed everything; Truth, because he does not fail; Life, because he created; Image, being like the Father; Figure, because he took the form of a slave and yet held the Father's likeness; Hand of God; Arm in whom all is held together; Virtue; Wisdom; Splendour; Light (*Lumen* and *Lux*); Sun; Orient; Spring; Alpha and Omega (an important symbol at all times, based as it is on *Rev.* 1.8,11; 21,6; 22,13); First and Last; Mediator; Paraclete or Advocate (1 *John* 2.1); Intercessor; Bridegroom (of the Church); Angel; the One who is sent; Man; Prophet; Priest; Shepherd; Master; Nazarene from his home; Nazarite from his purity; Bread; Vine; Flower as being chosen; Way, by which men come to God; Harbour; Mountain; Rock; Corner-stone; Stone of stumbling (1 *Cor.* 1.23); Lamb for his innocence; Sheep for his patience; Ram for his sovereignty; Kid for his likeness to sinful flesh; Calf for his sacrifice; Lion for kingship and courage; Snake for death and wisdom; Worm, for his resurrection; Eagle, because he soared to the stars.

Notker and Sedulius also treat the theme. Here is Notker's list:

> Messiah, Saviour, Emanuel, Sabaoth, Adonai,
> Only-begotten, Way, Life, Hand, Like-substanced,
> Beginning, First-born, Wisdom, Virtue,
> Alpha, the Head, the last letter Omega,
> Fount and Origin of God, Paraclete, Mediator,
> Lamb, Sheep, Calf, Snake, Ram, Lion, Worm,
> Mouth, Word, Splendour, Sun, Glory, Light, Likeness,
> Bread, Flower, Vine, Mountain, Door, Rock, Stone,
> Angel, Bridegroom, Shepherd, Prophet, Prince,
> Deathless, Sure, God, All-Ruler, Equal.

A Greek manuscript of the thirteenth century now in Paris actually brings the list to ninety-two without using all of Clement's. Notker's imagery is more dependent on the Old Testament than is Clement's; the somewhat surprising worm, for example, comes from *Psalm* 22.6 'I am a worm and no man', but see Isidore also.

CONCLUSION

The general conclusion of all this must be that during the formative period of the life of the Christian Church, there was a strong tendency to recall Jesus and his work through types and symbols. Yet through all this contact with the man himself as he appeared in his lifetime was never lost and might always be renewed through the written records.

BIBLIOGRAPHY

There is an excellent chapter in H. Daniel-Rops *Jesus in His Time* (ET London ²1956). An old book but scholarly and still valuable is F. W. Farrar *The Life of Christ as Represented in Art* (London 1901). For early Christian Art generally see another book, originally published in the same year, but constantly revised, W. Lowrie *Art in the Early Church* (New York 1965). Very important is A. Grabar's A. W. Mellon Lectures *Christian Iconography* (London 1969) with an excellent bibliography. H. Child and D. Colles *Christian Symbols* (London 1971), while containing interesting material, is unfortunately rather slight. See also W. F. Volbach *Early Christian Art* (London 1961); E. B. Smith *Early Christian Iconography* (Princeton 1918); M. Gough *The Origins of Christian Art* (London 1973); C. Diehl *Manuel d'art byzantin* (Paris ²1925-6); G. H. Ferguson *Signs and Symbols in Christian Art* (1954). For the catacombs see G. Wilpert *Le Pitture delle Catacombe Romane* (Rome 1903) and now J. Stevenson *The Catacombs* (London 1978), and for the sarcophagi J. Wilpert *I sarcofagi cristiani antichi* (Rome 1929) and F. Gerke *Die christlichen Sarkophage der vorkonstantinischen Zeit* (Berlin 1940). There is some excellent illustrative material in F. van der Meer and C. Mohrmann *Atlas of the Early Christian World* (ET London 1959). For the Turin Shroud see R. Hoard *The Testimony of the Shroud* (London 1978); I. Wilson *The Turin Shroud* (London 1978). A. Farrer *A Study in St. Mark* (Westminster 1951) was a pioneering interpretation of typology in the gospel. Allegorical interpretation including typology is treated in a masterful manner by R. P. C. Hanson in *Allegory and Event* (London 1959); other important treatments include W. J. Phythian-Adams *The Fulness of Israel* (Oxford 1938); L. Goppelt *Typos* (Darmstadt 1939); J. Daniélou *Sacramentum Futuri* (Paris 1940); A. G. Hebert *The Throne of David* (London 1941). Melito of Sardis has been superbly edited by S. G. Hall (Oxford 1979).

5
Christ and Culture

H. RICHARD NIEBUHR

H. Richard Niebuhr of Yale, theologian and ethical philosopher, is less widely known than his more volatile and vocal brother Reinhold. Less influential in his own day, it is possible that his work may prove to be more lasting. In 1949 he gave a series of lectures at Austin Presbyterian Theological Seminary, Texas on the Alumni Foundation; the lectures were published two years later. He took as his theme *Christ and Culture*, and in prefatory words identified this theme as 'the double wrestle of the Church with its Lord and with the cultural society with which it lives in symbiosis.' The issue is a perennial one and a complex one. There is no clear-cut division between the exponents of a Christian civilization and the non-Christian defenders of a wholly secularized society, and never has been.

Niebuhr goes back to the beginning, and takes the views of a sensitive Jewish scholar, Rabbi Klausner, on how Jesus' attitude to culture alienated the Jewish leaders of his own day. Jesus was a product of Jewish culture, and there is nothing which he taught which cannot, point for point, be paralleled from within pre-existent Jewish culture. Yet his total effect was disruptive and anarchic. For he separated his religious and ethical insights from the traditions of national life. 'He did not come to enlarge his nation's knowledge, art and culture, but to abolish even such culture as it possessed, bound up with religion', said Klausner. For civil justice he substituted nonresistance; he was indifferent to family life; he cut at the roots of economic effort by pointing to the life of flowers and birds. 'Jesus ignored everything concerned with material civilization: in this sense he does not belong to civilization.' The attitudes of Jesus were arguably more subtle, more involved, and even more 'realistic' than Klausner would suggest, but Klausner gives a fair picture of how he must have appeared to the Pharisees and Sadduccees.

For more than two and a half centuries Graeco-Roman civilization rejected Jesus Christ and the Christians. Niebuhr identifies the principal points in their indictment: first that, in Gibbon's words, Christians are 'animated by a contempt for present existence and by confidence in immortality', a charge to be reiterated later in different circumstances by Marx and Lenin; second, that Christians rely on God's grace instead of human effort; third, though less prominently, that Christ and his church are intolerant, whereas the Roman genius was one for assimilation. Other factors include some of Jesus' paradoxes: the stress on ceaseless forgiveness runs counter to the sense of justice and moral responsibility.

We may digress from Niebuhr to see how an intelligent pagan of the second century, Celsus, who wrote a book entitled *The True Word* (Logos) somewhere about AD 175, whose argument we can trace through Origen's extensive answer. He criticizes Jesus himself intensely. Jesus, he says, was illegitimately born. He was a mere carpenter by profession — and Christians continue to be drawn from the lower orders of society, woolworkers, cobblers, fullers, the vulgar and illiterate, even slaves. He had a special penchant for women, silly women, and children, which the Christians have continued. He kept bad company: nothing revolts Celsus more than the fact that Jesus and his followers did not, like other practitioners of mystery cults, call in the pure, clean, wise and righteous, but sinners, the anti-social, thieves and burglars, poisoners and desecrators. Jesus' teaching was a garbled version of the insights of Greek philosophy, his language coarse and unsophisticated. His miracles Celsus accepts as authentic, and treats them as part of the common stock of Egyptian wonder-workers. But Jesus was all too human; he tried to evade the cross, and when he was forced to undergo it could not endure his thirst 'which many an ordinary man will endure'. As to the resurrection, why did he not simply vanish from the cross? And why did he not show himself to those who had doubted, reviled and condemned him? No, the evidence for the resurrection rested on the testimony of a madwoman. It was of the same kind as the stories of Pythagoras or Zalmoxis or Orpheus or Heracles, and no more plausible because of ingenious details like the cry from the cross, the earthquake and the darkness, added by some fiction-writer (dramatist, says Celsus) to add verisimilitude to a narrative otherwise bald and unconvincing.

To return to Niebuhr. He next moves to the normal definition of the Christian as 'a follower of Jesus Christ'. But the approaches, among Christians, to Jesus are very varied. To some he is primarily a Teacher; to others it is what he was rather than what he taught which matters; to others again it is what he did in founding a new community. Yet Niebuhr insists that there is an original picture against which the other pictures may be judged, one who remains distinctive and 'can never be confused with a Socrates, a Plato or an Aristotle, a Gautama, a Confucius, or a Mohammed, or even with an Amos or Isaiah'. I remember J. S. Whale speaking of the Church and using the image of a hall of distorting mirrors, in one of which the picture is inflated till it bursts the frame of the mirror, and in another of which it is whittled away to almost nothing; yet they are all reflections of the same body. It is so with Jesus too. We may have in different mirrors a socialist Jesus and a capitalist Jesus, a pacifist Jesus and a militaristic Jesus, a blazingly angry Jesus and a milk-and-water gentle Jesus meek and mild, an ascetic Jesus and a hail-fellow-well-met Jesus, an ethical Jesus and an eschatological Jesus. We challenge them all by reference to the original. Even in our earliest records there is distortion. But behind a variety of distorted images it is possible to glimpse something of the original form. Niebuhr attempts to establish a common ground. The characteristics of Jesus include love, hope, obedience, faith, humility; none of these must be isolated at the expense of others; all must be interpreted in terms of the relation he believed himself to have with God.

The other ground of Niebuhr's thesis is culture. This must not be interpreted as the culture of a single society, nor can it be isolated, as Burckhardt tried to isolate it, from political and religious society. Culture is 'the artificial, secondary environment which man imposes on the natural'. Culture is first social. As Malinowski put it, 'The essential fact of culture is the organization of human beings into permanent groups.' Culture is the individual's social inheritance. Culture is, second, human achievement. A river is natural, a canal cultural. Third, culture is concerned with values, and predominantly with the good for man, with the temporal and material realization of values, and with the conservation of values. But, whatever theoretical constructs we may produce, all cultures are characterized by pluralism: values are many and complex.

Christ and culture, Niebuhr affirms, stand in dialogue. He proceeds to analyse the five main forms that this dialogue has taken as the opposition between Christ and culture, the recognition of a fundamental agreement between Christ and culture, a synthesis in which Christ stands above culture, an acceptance of polarity and tension in which Christ and culture stand in opposition to each other and yet both have ineluctable claims, and the conversionist solution in which Christ is seen as the converter of man within his culture and society. The remainder of Niebuhr's book consists in a close examination of these five approaches.

CHRIST AGAINST CULTURE

Niebuhr defines the first solution as 'the one that uncompromisingly affirms the sole authority of Christ over the Christian and resolutely rejects culture's claims to loyalty'. It is an attitude which can be discerned within the New Testament but which is never to be found absolutely. For example Jesus, in speaking to Jews, exalted his claims above those of the Torah; yet he asserted that he came to fulfil the Torah not to destroy it. The nearest to an absolute dichotomy is perhaps to be found in the first Letter of John. In this letter obedience to Jesus is central, and out of his command that his followers should love one another, and out of the very nature of God ('God is love') comes the Christian's way of life. This way of life is set in sharp contrast with 'the world', society outside the church, the region of darkness, dominated by the power of evil, marked by lies, hatred, murder, lust and pride. This world is perishing by its own contradictions; the Christian's loyalty must be directed to the imperishable truths of Christ. But the dichotomy is not in fact absolute, because the author sees Jesus as redeeming and transforming the world.

The same sort of mood is found among the Apostolic Fathers, the Christian writers of the next generation or so. They present Christianity 'as a way of life quite separate from culture'. Christians appear as a third race, standing apart from Jews and Gentiles, that is, effectively, from Jewish culture and from Graeco-Roman culture. Harnack in his *Mission and Expansion of Christianity* summed up early Christian beliefs:

1. Our people is older than the world.
2. The world was created for our sakes.
3. The world is carried on for our sakes; we delay the judgment of the world.
4. Everything in the world is subject to us and must serve us.
5. Everything in the world, the beginning and course and end of all history, is revealed to us and lies transparent to our eyes.
6. We shall take part in the judgment of the world and ourselves enjoy eternal bliss.

In a recurring image, based on Jesus' teaching, there are two ways, one of life and one of death, and there is a vast difference between them. One is the way of Jesus, the other the way of the world, one of virtue, the other of vice. There is no concept that within the old society some things might be relatively better; the contrast is rigidly drawn between the old society and the new. Yet even here the dichotomy is not absolute, since in the first Letter of Clement there is recognition that obedience is due to earthly rulers and that they receive their power from God.

The finest of the early exponents of 'Christ against culture', though he does not fit neatly into any narrow pigeonhole, is Tertullian. Tertullian has the centre of his faith firmly fixed upon Jesus. 'We worship God through Christ', he shouts in his great *Apology* (21). Christ came as authority and teacher in grace and godly learning, to be mankind's illuminator and guide, Son of God, fully human and filled with divinity. Tertullian gives him titles, Power of God, Spirit of God, Word, Wisdom, Reason, Son of God. The life of the Christian then is obedience of the commandments of Jesus, and Tertullian in interpreting this is literalistic, rigid and somewhat grim and negative.

'Tertullian's rejection of the claims of culture is correspondingly sharp', Niebuhr goes on, rightly and incisively. 'The conflict of the believer is not with nature but with culture, for it is in culture that sin chiefly resides. Tertullian comes very close to the thought that original sin is transmitted through society, and that if it were not for the vicious customs that surround a child from its birth and for its artificial training its soul would remain good.' That is well said. So Tertullian utterly rejected the religion of the Graeco-Roman world as idolatry, and wrote a whole treatise on the subject. But this did not mean rejecting an optional extra on the fringe of normal life. It meant rejecting normal cultural practices *in toto*, for religion permeated the whole of life, and Tertullian showed that education, the arts and crafts, commerce, political office, army service (here bloodshed was another barrier, for Tertullian saw pacifism as part of the Christian life) were all idolatrous. So were the festivals which were the only breaks in the normal working routine, since the Romans had no week-ends. And in any case, as he argued in another treatise, the spectacles offered for entertainment were brutal and corrupting, the theatre ministering to lust, the amphitheatre to sadism, and the circus (he might have said the same about twentieth-century football) to irrational excitement. All, he claimed, were idolatrous, in origin, title, equipment, place and practice.

Niebuhr's other example of this position is Leo Tolstoy. The crisis of his middle years was resolved when he came to accept the Jesus Christ of the New Testament as his sole authority. He had increasingly found himself 'threatened in his own life by the meaninglessness of existence and the tawdriness of all the values that his society esteemed'. But until he had accepted an alternative in the Lordship of Jesus, he could not escape from them. So he wrote in *What I Believe*: 'I understood and believed that Jesus is not only the Messiah, the Christ, but that he is really the Saviour of the world. I know that there is no other exit either for me or for all those who together with me are tormented in this life. I know that for all, and for me together with them, there is no way of escape except through fulfilling those commands of Christ which offer to all humanity the highest welfare of which I can conceive.' Tolstoy's new law had five articles: live at peace with all men; do not make the desire for sexual relations an amusement; never take an oath to anyone; do not meet violence with violence; love your enemies. By these standards every phase of culture stands under judgment. The state first. The revolutionaries try to replace one governmental system by another, but a Tolstoyan Christian says, 'I know nothing about the governmental organization, or how far it is good or bad, and for the same reason I do not want to support it.' The churches are anti-Christian organizations, proud, violent, self-assertive, inflexible, dead, joining with the state to produce violence, inequality, privilege and fraud, instruments of the devil. The economic system is based on robbery and maintained by violence. Even the world of art, science and scholarship is not immune: the New Testament is sceptical about the wisdom of those the world calls wise, because it does not deal in fundamentals. Further, art as it has been practised is class-based, and Tolstoy renounces even *Hamlet* and Beethoven's ninth symphony.

It is important to notice one difference between Tertullian and Tolstoy. Tertullian was looking forward, with indecent glee, to the Last Judgment. From this point of view he was not concerned whether the way of Jesus 'worked' in this world; he viewed it *sub specie aeternitatis*. But Tolstoy was offering a practical alternative here and now to the accepted mode of life.

In general Niebuhr sums up 'Christ against culture' as a necessary and inadequate position. It is a costly position to take up; it exposes those who hold it to derision, animosity and persecution. Its upholders are aiming to live up to their professions. By maintaining the lordship of Christ over against Caesar they have in fact helped to reform society in ways they did not intend. De Montalembert said of Benedict of Nursia: 'Historians have vied in praising his genius and clear-sightedness; they have supposed that he intended to regenerate Europe, to stop the dissolution of society, to prepare the reconstitution of political order, to re-establish public education, and to preserve literature and the arts.... I firmly believe that he never dreamt of regenerating anything but his own soul and those of his brethren, the monks.' That is right; yet Benedict touched society beyond his planning and his choosing. Just so the pacifist stand of Tertullian and Tolstoy, through Gandhi, has permeated the political consciousness, and now affects practical social reformers such as Martin Luther King, Cesar Chavez, Archbishop Helder Camara, Danilo Dolci and others, and even international concepts of peace-making and peace-keeping through the United Nations. Niebuhr says well, 'If Romans 13 is not balanced by 1 John, the church becomes an instrument of state, unable to point men to their transpolitical destiny and their suprapolitical loyalty; unable also to engage in political tasks, save as one more group of power-hungry or security-seeking men.'

But Niebuhr goes on to deny the possibility of sole dependence on Jesus Christ to the exclusion of culture. 'Christ claims no man purely as a natural being, but always as one who has become human in a culture.... If Christians do not come to Christ with the language, the thought patterns, the moral disciplines of Judaism, they come with those of Rome; if not with those of Rome, then with those of Germany, England, Russia, America, India, or China.' The writer of 1 *John* uses the categories of Hellenistic religious thought, Tertullian proclaims himself a Roman with every sentence, Tolstoy is to be understood only as a nineteenth-century Russian. Niebuhr explores the theological implications of this dilemma at some length; he says less than he might about the problems arising from Jesus' involvement with the culture of his own day, but a good deal about the interaction of reason and revelation, law and grace, and in particular about the relation of Jesus Christ to the Creator of nature and the

Christ and Culture 127

Governor of history. Many of those who hold this point of view have tended to be suspicious of nature and nature's God, to rely on inner spiritual guidance, and 'to divide the world into the material realm governed by a principle opposed to Christ and a spiritual realm guided by the spiritual God'. And this in turn leads to a denigration of the historical Jesus and the substitution of a spiritual Christ.

THE CHRIST OF CULTURE

'In every culture to which the Gospel comes there are men who hail Jesus as the Messiah of their society, the fulfiller of its hopes and aspirations, the perfecter of its true faith, the source of its holiest spirit. In the Christian community they seem to stand in direct opposition to the radicals, who reject the social institutions for Christ's sake; but they are far removed from those "cultured among the despisers" of Christian faith who reject Christ for the sake of their civilization.' With these eloquent words Niebuhr identifies his second group. They interpret culture through Christ; at the same time they understand Christ through culture. So they harmonize Christ and culture. They do not reject other-worldliness, but see it as continuous in time and character with life on earth. They belong to the category of 'once-born' and 'healthy-minded' Christians. Niebuhr does not quite accept the label 'liberalism' for this view, though on the whole it fits quite well, and prefers Karl Barth's 'Culture-Protestantism', though it is by no means a post-Reformation phenomenon.

The attitude is a very common one. It is perhaps the commonest of all basic attitudes within the Church, whether we think of the glorification of the pacifistic Jesus within military cultures (Clovis is said to have remarked on the crucifixion 'If my Franks had been there, we wouldn't have let them do it,' whereas the equivalent of his Franks were in fact available and Jesus refused to call on them), or of the export of European and American culture in the name of Christian mission (dear Anna Hinderer in Yorubaland could never quite distinguish between long skirts for girls and love of the neighbour). This makes Niebuhr's choice of illustration the more puzzling. From the ancient world he chooses the Gnostics.

The Christian Gnostics, men like Valentinus and Basilides, though the theology which triumphed dismissed them as heretics, undoubtedly thought of themselves as Christians. Indeed their thought is Christ-centred. F. C. Burkitt said of them that 'the figure of Jesus is essential, and without Jesus the systems would drop to pieces' (*Church and Gnosis* p. 8). More recently R. M. Grant has suggested that a would-be Gnostic, searching for security in a troubled and evil world, could hardly ignore the claims being made for Jesus by Christians, and that it is highly probable that in all the Gnostic systems Jesus either is the Saviour or provides the model for the Saviour-figure (*Gnosticism and Early Christianity* pp. 35-6). This is broadly true, but they interpret the figure of Jesus almost beyond recognition. For example, as we have seen, according to Valentinus, the Pleroma or fullness of the godhead embraces thirty Aeons or spiritual beings. The thirtieth and weakest, Wisdom, is responsible for the production of the world of matter, a kind of fall. Because this stands in need of redemption the Father produces a new pair of Aeons, Christ and Spirit, and all the Aeons unite to produce Jesus, in whom the Fullness is gathered together and the unity of the cosmos realized. He is the 'perfect fruit of the Pleroma'. The Gnosis is eventually brought to mankind by Jesus made one with Christ entering the human body of the human Jesus at his baptism, and according to some testimonies leaving before his death, though in *The Gospel of Truth* the death itself is an object of wonder and awe. In the Gnostic systems speculation about spiritual cosmology is more important than the facts of history.

Niebuhr regards the Gnostics as offering an interpretation of the person and work of Christ in terms of contemporary philosophy and science, astronomy and psychology, but his treatment of them is exceedingly sketchy, and they were a very odd illustration to choose. For in the first place they were not at all representative of the intellectual thought of their day, being largely found in Alexandria, where, as a character in Herondas put it, everything was to be found, and in Syria. Secondly, they did not accept their cultural environment. In the great *Hymn of the Pearl* our unredeemed humanity is described as 'impure, filthy clothes', to be doffed and escaped from. Thirdly, William James would certainly not have described them as once-born or healthy-minded.

In some ways the most obvious representative of this viewpoint in the ancient world is Constantine. His family were worshippers of the Unconquered Sun, and the vision he saw on the way to the Milvian Bridge, as we have noted, was a Christian symbol coming from his family-god. Throughout the following decade the Sun appeared on his coins from all the mints all over the empire. On one coin of his young Caesar, the sun is associated with the legend CLARITAS REIPVBLICAE, 'the glory of the state'. Jesus was already, as we have seen, the sun of righteousness. The old religion, political continuity, and the new religion are being held in a single cultural entity. On the great arch which still stands in Rome most of the pagan deities are eliminated, but the sun and moon remain; Constantine's victory is attributed noncommittally to 'divine' inspiration. In AD 321 Sunday was proclaimed as a day of rest; there was accommodation to Christianity, but the stated grounds were precisely that it was Sun-day. Constantinople was founded 'on the command of God' as a new capital to the Christian Empire; New Rome was one of its names. The emperor's statue stood there as Apollo-Helios with a radiate crown, fashioned, as he believed, from the nails of Christ's crucifixion. The essential continuity could hardly be more vividly expressed. The organization of the Christian Empire was not significantly changed. The city had its senate, like Rome; the senators were in fact a step lower in status, *clari* not *clarissimi*. It was governed not by a prefect but a proconsul. The citizens enjoyed their 'bread and circuses' at public expense. There was a Temple to the Fortune of the City. But no pagan rites were associated with the inauguration, and on the emperor's death he was interred among the cenotaphs of the twelve apostles of Christ, himself the thirteenth. Constantine in short did just what Niebuhr asserts of this group; he interpreted culture through Christ and understood Christ through culture.

Niebuhr takes as another illustration Peter Abélard. He rightly says that the problem of the relationship of Christ to culture became more rather than less acute with the development of so-called Christian civilization. This was why some groups of Christians retreated into an anti-cultural form of monasticism. Abélard by contrast offered a moral theory of the Atonement achieved by Jesus. Jesus was a great moral teacher who directed all that he did, his life, his acts, his doctrines, and his death towards our instruction. The Christian faith thus becomes 'a philosophic knowledge about reality, and an ethic for the improvement of life'. Jesus is offering an improved version of what Socrates and Plato (whom Abélard also interprets ethically) had to offer: 'they give evidence of an evangelic and apostolic perfection and come little or nothing short of the Christian religion. They are, in fact, joined to us by this common zeal for moral achievement.' In this attitude, Niebuhr suggests, all conflict between Christ and culture is gone. There is, however, a certain almost ironical ambiguity about Abélard, which Niebuhr misses. It is that the predominant factor in the culture of Abélard's own day was the Church, which according to Abélard had entirely misunderstood its Master, and Plato, although an object for study among the Paris intellectuals, was not obviously a major formative influence on the general culture of the day. To take a more extreme instance: if a twentieth-century British Christian were to suggest that Gautama the Buddha and Lao-tzu 'give evidence of an evangelic and apostolic perfection and come little or nothing short of the Christian religion' (and it would not be an appreciably more eccentric judgment than Abélard's), we should hardly place him in the 'Christ-equals-culture' category. There is a more direct line from fourth-century Athens to twelfth-century Paris than from sixth-century Asia to twentieth-century Britain, but a question-mark must remain.

Niebuhr's third illustration is taken from Culture-Protestantism properly so called — Karl Barth's term for what a Marxist might call 'the bourgeois Christianity of democratic and individualistic liberalism'. He instances John Locke's

The Reasonableness of Christianity, and Thomas Jefferson's exaltation of the (selected) moral teachings of Jesus, and rightly says that this attitude is prevalent among philosophers, statesmen, reformers, poets, novelists and indeed theologians in the nineteenth century. They see Jesus as the great enlightener, the one who directs all men within their culture to the attainment of a peaceful co-operative society achieved by moral training.

Niebuhr's best illustration here is Albrecht Ritschl, a particularly good example because Ritschl, unlike Jefferson or Kant, insisted on close attention to the New Testament evidence about Jesus. 'Ritschl's theology had two foundation stones: not revelation and reason, but Christ and culture.' Ritschl selected his evidence, though not as flagrantly or forcedly as did Jefferson. He played down the eschatological element in Jesus' teaching, but so did most contemporary theologians. Equally he did not pick out capitalism or nationalism or materialism as aspects of contemporary culture. But although he is selective he is quite fair, and his picture of Jesus is based on the gospels, and his concept of culture does depend on the actualities. The integrative point for him was the Kingdom of God. 'The Christian idea of the Kingdom of God' he wrote in *Justification and Reconciliation*, 'denotes the association of mankind — an association both extensively and intensively the most comprehensive possible — through the reciprocal moral action of its members, action which transcends all merely natural and particular considerations.' Ritschl was a highly representative figure; very much nineteenth-century and early twentieth-century theology took a similar approach. He has also been enormously influential. Walter Rauschenbusch's social gospel belongs to the same school, 'though with greater moral force and less theological depth'. So does the concentration of popular theology on the Fatherhood of God and the Brotherhood of Man.

Niebuhr has thus, though his earlier examples are dubious, rightly identified a major cultural attitude among Christians. Something not dissimilar is to be found today among some third-world theologians: E. B. Idowu for example has claimed that indigenous African culture offers an understanding of sacrifice which Europe and America lack; Kosuke Koyama entitled a highly original study *Waterbuffalo Theology*; the Chinese version of *John* 1.1 runs 'In the beginning was the Tao.' Niebuhr well stresses some of its strengths. Negatively the critics of this position often share the general attitude which they arraign. Positively, 'one cannot doubt that the acculturation of Jesus Christ has contributed greatly in history to the extension of his power over men.' If the blood of the martyrs is the seed of the church, there is other seed in the harmony of the Christian message with the highest vision of others. Jesus was relevant, temporally, socially and politically relevant, to his own day; his vision also transcended that particular culture and is applicable to other cultures. So this position makes effective the universal meaning of the gospel; it presents a Jesus who is Saviour of the world.

There is of course a danger. The Christ of culture becomes a chameleon, a bourgeois capitalist exponent of the Protestant ethic in the USA, a card-carrying comrade in the USSR. Here it is a matter of constant return to Jesus himself. Niebuhr shrewdly says: 'One is tempted to formulate this notion theologically, saying that the Spirit proceeds not only from the Son but from the Father also, and that with the aid of the knowledge of Christ it is possible to discriminate between the spirits of the times and the Spirit which is from God.' The Christ-of-culture theologians are invariably selective. They are the obverse of the previous group. Like them they separate reason from revelation, but unlike them they exalt reason at the expense of revelation. Whereas the others overestimated the offence arising from social values, these underestimate it. In the polarity between law and grace they incline to the side of law. This position too is one-sided.

CHRIST ABOVE CULTURE

The third position is a more difficult and subtle one, not always easy to distinguish from the second. Human beings like clearcut dichotomies. If Christ and culture are the two facts with which they are wrestling, the easiest solutions are to accept Christ and reject culture, accept culture and reject Christ — or to equate the two. Yet very many Christians, without being theologically articulate, do not disown their culture, but see Christ as challenging it with a higher vision. Their obedience to the God revealed in Jesus is exercised in their natural lives.

Niebuhr calls his third position synthesist. This is right in so far as a synthesis involves a bringing together of two distinct entities each with its own values, but confusing because it suggests the sort of accommodation or equation characteristic of the previous group. 'Christ Above Culture' is thus a clearer expression. According to this third view we may not say 'Either Christ or culture' because both are God-given; we must say 'Both Christ and culture' but not in such a way as to put them on a single plane. Among passages in the New Testament which express this view are Jesus's words in the Sermon on the Mount: 'Do not suppose that I have come to abolish the Law and the prophets; I did not come to abolish, but to complete. I tell you this: so long as heaven and earth endure, not a letter, not a stroke will disappear from the Law before all that it stands for is achieved. If any man therefore sets aside even the least of the Law's demands, and teaches others to do the same, he will have the lowest place in the Kingdom of Heaven, whereas anyone who keeps the Law, and teaches others so, will stand high in the Kingdom of Heaven. I tell you, unless you show yourselves far better men than the Pharisees and the doctors of the Law, you can never enter the Kingdom of Heaven' (*Matt.* 5.17-20). It is a highly ambiguous passage in its exaltation of the Torah, and at the same time the establishment of a higher standard, especially when we reflect that Jesus constantly broke through the technical interpretation of the commandment about Sabbath-observance, and is recorded as telling the people who were following him in crowds that they would have to hate their fathers and mothers if they wanted to follow him (*Luke* 14.26). Another obvious passage came when they were trying to trap Jesus by asking him, as he taught in the court of the Temple, whether it was lawful to pay taxes to the Romans.

The answer 'Yes' was unpopular, 'No' treasonable. He asked them to produce a denarius with the emperor's head on it. They did so, and this itself was a religious offence, since they were carrying a human image within the sacred precincts. They agreed it bore Caesar's image, and Jesus evaded the trap by saying 'Pay to Caesar what is due to Caesar, and pay God what is due to God' (*Matt.* 22,15-22). It was a clever answer, but the implication was also that the higher loyalty was to God, though Caesar was not without his claims. So too Paul told the Christians in Rome that the secular authorities received their authority from God (*Rom.* 13.1-10) though Paul was the last person to obey them uncritically or fail to acknowledge that God had a higher claim on him. In fact the general attitude of the Christians for two and a half centuries, well exemplified by the anonymous *Letter to Diognetus*, was to accept the normal obligations of citizenship, to outdo their contemporaries in the quality of their citizenship, but when the normal obligations ran counter to their obedience to Jesus to say a clear, uncompromising and prophetic 'No!'; this last was mostly over either idolatry or bloodshed.

Niebuhr's first representative exemplar of this approach is that very attractive man, Clement of Alexandria. In his little pamphlet *Salvation for the Rich*? Clement begins with a vigorous attack on servility towards the rich. That done he turns to the passage in the gospel where Jesus told a rich young man of upright life to sell all that he had. In the light of that, could there be any place within the Church for a man of means? It was no doubt an existential question in Alexandria. Clement is commonsensical. He cannot see any good in being without means of livelihood; destitution is a distraction from higher things; we cannot share if we have nothing to share. What we must do is avoid dependence on material possessions (a Stoic view) and use them responsibly. So Clement gives the literal command a spiritual meaning. Yet in the end he goes beyond this. The Christian life is a response to Jesus. 'For each of us he gave his life — the equivalent for all. This he demands of us in return, to give our lives for one another. And if we owe our lives to the brethren and have made such a mutual compact with the Saviour, why should we any more hoard and shut up worldly goods, which are beggarly, foreign to us, and transitory?' (37). So Stoic detachment and Christian love are to Clement not contradictory, but they are distinct; they lead to different actions, life among possessions which we do not allow to possess us, and life without possessions. These are to be seen as separate stages along the same road to salvation.

Clement had expressed a similar view over a wider field earlier in *The Tutor*. This presents a great many practical precepts for daily living. Much of it corresponds to and is derived from current Stoic handbooks on the subject. It tells his readers how to eat and drink, how to behave at parties, what to do about sleep and sex; it tells them about clothes, ornaments, cosmetics, hair-style, behaviour in and out of church, exercise, entertainment, home-life. Much of it is entertaining, like his injunction 'Don't talk with your mouth full; it sounds awful' or his reservation of cosmetics for use by a wife whose husband has a roving eye. It has properly been called a portrait of the Christian gentleman — and gentlewoman. But all these practical social injunctions are embedded within a deeper call to love and to righteousness as embodied in and conveyed by Jesus who is the Word. So here again the Christian's higher calling does not lead him to neglect social graces; these are a stage on the road, good but not enough of themselves.

In general Clement's approach may be seen in his teaching that to the Hebrews the Torah is a schoolmaster leading people to Christ, and in the same way to the Greeks philosophy serves the same purpose. Or, to put it differently, the Word (Logos), is both the Memra which was powerful in the Hebrew creation-story and spoke to the prophets, and the Logos behind the philosophy of Heraclitus, Plato and the Stoics, but is fully revealed only in Jesus. In this way Clement brings together the two great cultural strands available to him, the Jewish and the Greek, and sees both as incomplete without Christ, but as finding fulfilment in Christ.

Niebuhr's second illustration here comes from Thomas Aquinas. Thomas, as he says, 'represents a Christianity that has achieved or accepted full social responsibility for all the great institutions'. So Thomas asserts, 'Both Christ and culture', but his Christ is far above culture. Niebuhr illustrates this by Thomas's own life: 'He is a monk, faithful to the vows of poverty, celibacy, and obedience. With the radical Christians, he has rejected the secular world. But he is a monk in the church which has become the guardian of culture, the fosterer of learning, the judge of the nations, the protector of the family, the governor of social religion.' So in his system of thought 'he combined without confusing philosophy and theology, state and church, civic and Christian virtues, natural and divine laws, Christ and culture', producing a great structure of theoretical and practical wisdom.

If we take Thomas's ethical system we find that he brings together in a single mighty system the insights of Aristotle and of the New Testament. Ethics is a matter of discerning the end, the *telos*. Nature is rationally purposive, and the purpose implicit in our existence is to actualize our potentialities as intelligent, willing beings. This is in fact sheer Aristotelianism christianized. Thomas also follows Aristotle in seeing two distinct kinds of fulfilment, the practical and the contemplative, and the contemplative is higher, and its object is God. But Thomas goes beyond Aristotle in asserting that neither of these two ways offers perfect happiness which is to be had only by the free gift of God in and through Jesus Christ — and this happiness does not depend on the achievement of ethical holiness or philosophic wisdom, but is given to, in the eyes of Aristotelian wisdom, the most improbable people. Thomas values moral effort; he values self-discipline; he values ascetic obedience; he values the cardinal virtues of prudence, self-control, courage and justice; all these are necessary to life, and he does not underestimate the difficulty of achieving them. But over and above them is the spontaneous outpouring of love which comes when Jesus Christ takes hold of a man, becomes a part of him, and lifts him out of himself.

Another approach may be seen in Thomas's attitude to law. Law is essential to society, and laws imposed by rulers and ruling-classes for their own ends can be judged by natural law. Thomas does not seek to derive from the gospels the ordinary practice of human living. He seeks that in reason. But Jesus has commandments which transcend natural law. 'You shall not steal' is found in both reason and revelation. 'Sell all you have and give to the poor' comes from revelation alone.

So Thomas can defend the great institutions of society by nature and reason, and does not regard them as running contrary to revelation. Yet there are in Jesus truths which could not be discerned by nature and reason alone, and they are higher truths.

The view of 'Christ above culture' is an attractive one, and as handled by Thomas Aquinas a singularly impressive one; as Niebuhr says it is a necessary approach to the question and a necessary affirmation of a truth or truths. But it is difficult to see it as an absolute or final answer. There is an inevitable tendency in seeking a synthesis to make the relative absolute on one side, and the infinite finite on the other; some people would say that Thomas was wrong to seek his solution within the bounds of history. Certainly his own monumental construct is mediaeval and European. It has a limited attraction only for other climes and times. And any such approach tends to underestimate the defects inherent in all human societies.

CHRIST AND CULTURE IN PARADOX

This last point is emphasized by the dualists, a word here used not for those who set Christ against culture, but for those who see Christ and culture as both exercising valid claims in different fields. The dualist sees a dichotomy between the human and the divine, and Jesus Christ standing athwart it. Yet God is still God and man still man; grace in God and sin in man. So that all man's works are corrupt and all his culture askew; in politics power rules, in economics greed, and the rational defence of culture usually turns out to be a rationalizing of this. Yet we cannot renounce or escape it, for love is an impossible possibility. This is why the dualist is a dualist. Niebuhr says of him: 'He is under law, and yet not under law but grace; he is sinner, and yet righteous; he believes, as a doubter; he has assurance of salvation, yet walks along the knife-edge of insecurity. In Christ all things have become new, and yet everything remains as it was from the beginning. God has revealed Himself in Christ, but hidden Himself in His revelation; the believer knows the One in whom he has believed, yet walks by faith, not sight.'

Niebuhr rightly sees this attitude as a vital *motif* in Paul's thought; subsequent exponents of it appeal to Paul. There is no question of the centrality of Jesus Christ for Paul, Christ 'the power of God and the wisdom of God'. Paul believed himself to have had a personal revelation of the risen Jesus, and this transformed his life. For him thereafter the insights of the Torah and the insights of Greek philosophy were 'equally remote from the knowledge of the glory of God in the face of Jesus Christ'. But Paul did not, like the radicals of the first group, try to escape from society. He warned against its obliquities and excesses, but he did not retreat from it. Political authority was, he said, divinely constituted and valid within its own sphere. Economic institutions were taken for granted, whether money or slavery. Paul in fact gives a lot of practical advice, but he does not derive it from Jesus; it mostly reflects the Torah, or Stoicism, or common sense. And for Paul this practice has no virtue; virtue resides solely in the love that is in Christ. So that Paul effectively presents us with two ways of life, each valid within its own sphere, and both pressing on the Christian.

Niebuhr touches briefly upon Marcion, the second-century heretic, rightly interpreting him as a Paulinist rather than a Gnostic. But Marcion believed in two gods, a just but tyrannical god of creation and a loving and merciful god of redemption, and Marcion opts wholly for the second and allows the first no place for the Christian, who must withdraw as far as possible from the culture founded on nature from which Christ came to rescue us, and it seems that Niebuhr himself felt that he was misguided in introducing Marcion here.

The supreme representative of this type, though he is too complex to be neatly classified, is Martin Luther. Luther makes sharp distinctions between the temporal and spiritual, external and internal, body and soul, the reign of Christ and the world of works. 'There are two kingdoms, one the kingdom of God, the other the kingdom of the world. . . . God's kingdom is a kingdom of grace and mercy . . . but the kingdom of the world is a kingdom of wrath and severity. . . . Now he who would confuse these two kingdoms — as our false fanatics do — would put wrath into God's kingdom and mercy into the world's kingdom; and that is the same as putting the devil in heaven and God in hell' (*Works* 4, pp. 265-6). Luther does not make an absolute division between the two realms; they are distinct but related. Christ is Lord of both, but in a different way. Niebuhr puts this excellently.

> Christ deals with the fundamental problems of the moral life; he cleanses the springs of action; he creates and recreates the ultimate community in which all action takes place. But by the same token he does not directly govern the external actions or construct the immediate community in which man carries on his work. On the contrary he sets men free from the inner necessity of finding special vocations and founding special communities in which to attempt to acquire self-respect, and human and divine approval. He releases them from monasteries and the conventicles of the pious for service of their actual neighbors in the world through all the ordinary vocations of men.   (p. 174)

Thus the life in culture is the sphere in which Christ can be followed, and yet the rules to be observed are independent of Christian doctrine. So Luther justified political and military activities on their own terms, while ruling out the monastic life.

The strength of this position can be seen in an analogy. 'If we look to the revelation of God for knowledge of geology, we miss the revelation; but if we look to geology for faith in God, we miss both Him and the rocks.' So it is with politics. If we try to impose on politics a spirit of loving community which is totally dependent on the gift of God, we shall end up with a self-righteous autocracy; if we regard our political structures as the Kingdom of God on earth, we shall fail to discern God's Word, and at the same time be politically ineffectual. The Christian lives in two worlds in a state of joyful tension.

On the other hand the relegation of practical living to a world of relativities has tended to devalue it. If it is a sinful world under judgment, if we cannot apply the way of Christ here, does it matter very much how we practise? The actual result of course has been a cultural conservatism or moderate reformism: better the devil you know than the devil you don't! More seriously — and this is a criticism which Niebuhr fails to make — the dualist position fails to do justice to a good deal of Jesus' teaching which has clear social implications. Luther justified the military profession, but Jesus in a concrete practical situation said 'Put up your sword into its place: all those who take the sword shall perish by the sword.' Even more, for one to whom Jesus is Lord, it is impossible to deny him lordship of politics, which in the end is only corporate human life.

CHRIST THE TRANSFORMER OF CULTURE

So we come to the fifth and last of Niebuhr's five attitudes, the one which he calls conversionist. The conversionists distinguish firmly between God's work in Christ and man's work in culture. They do not withdraw from society; nor do they detract from Jesus' searching critique. They are more likely to speak of Jesus as Redeemer than as Lawgiver. They see all cultural activity as under judgment, and at the same time under God's sovereign rule. They are thus more optimistic about culture than the dualists. This optimism is fed by three theological convictions. The first is that creation, the work of God and his Word, is good, and when the Word became flesh he entered his own world. The second is that man's fall is moral and personal rather than physical and metaphysical, and its consequence is, in the strict sense, corruption, corruption of an originally and essentially good nature. The third is that God is the Lord of history, and to him all things are possible.

The *motif* is most clearly seen in the New Testament in the fourth gospel. There are undoubtedly ambiguities and contradictions in the gospel. There is a seemingly absolute dichotomy in the words 'That which is born of the flesh is flesh and that which is born of the Spirit is spirit' (*John* 3.6). And yet, as Niebuhr puts it, 'the physical, material, and temporal are never regarded as participating in evil in any peculiar way because they are not spiritual and eternal. On the contrary, natural birth, eating, drinking, wind, water and bread and wine are for this evangelist not only symbols to be employed in dealing with the realities of the life of the spirit but are pregnant with spiritual meaning.' The key words of the gospel are 'God sent his Son into the world, not to condemn the world, but that the world might be saved through him' (*John* 3.17). So in *John* the first miracle takes place at a wedding, it has to do with the need for drink (which has run out), and it is a transformation, of water into wine. *John* is the most mystical gospel, and at the same time the most politically conscious. Sir Edwyn Hoskyns once said: 'The theme of the Fourth Gospel is the nonhistorical that makes sense of history, the infinite that makes sense of time, God who makes sense of men and is therefore their Saviour' (*The Fourth Gospel* p. 120).

Niebuhr's chief representative of this mode of thought is Augustine of Hippo. He stands with Thomas Aquinas as the great exponent of a systematic solution which rejects alike anti-culturalism and accommodation, but his answer is not the same. Like Luther and others he is too large a figure to fit a narrow pigeonhole, but there is no doubt of the general force of his message. Niebuhr as usual has put the matter incisively: 'Christ is the transformer of culture for Augustine in the sense that he redirects, reinvigorates, and regenerates that life of man, expressed in all human works, which in present actuality is the perverted and corrupted exercise of a fundamentally good nature; which, moreover, in its depravity lies under the curse of transiency and death, not because it is intrinsically self-contradictory.' Augustine insists on the goodness of creation. He goes further. 'There cannot be a nature in which there is no good. Hence not even the nature of the devil himself is evil, in so far as it is nature, but it was made evil by being perverted' (*City of God* 19.13). Man was made good, and depends on the goodness that is God. The primal sin was to turn away from this, and it led inevitably to social disorder, so that even social virtues become splendid vices. But disorder cannot exist without an underlying order. There can be peace without war, but war cannot exist without some kind of peace (19.12-13). So that although Augustine puts his City of God in sharp contrast with the city of the world, and although his conclusion is not the transformation of the world but an eschatological vision of a spiritual society, all the presuppositions of his argument would lead us to expect him to point triumphantly to the conversion of the whole of life, social, political and practical and to proclaim 'the vision of universal concord and peace in a culture in which all human actions had been reordered by the gracious action of God in drawing all men to Himself, and in which all men were active in works directed toward and thus reflecting the love and glory of God.'

Niebuhr's other main illustration — he touches in this connection on Calvin, Wesley and Jonathan Edwards — is Frederick Denison Maurice. Maurice was a Johannine thinker. He came early to the conviction that Christ is Lord of mankind whether men believe it or not. Men are social by nature; they have no existence except in community; of this community Christ, recognized or not, is the centre. But man's unawareness of his true nature involves him in self-contradiction and corruption, and this appears not merely in secular life but in the Church itself. Yet Maurice clung firmly to his central conviction that Christ is King, and this made him a consistent conversionist. 'The conversion of mankind from self-centredness to Christ-centredness was for Maurice the universal and present divine possibility.' Eternity for Maurice is not the negation of time but the divine dimension of working. So 'the kingdom of God begins within, but it is to make itself manifest without.... At last it is to penetrate our whole social existence' (*The Lord's Prayer* p. 49).

It is significant that Niebuhr does not expose this view to the same searching critique he offers of the other views. He might for example have easily shown that Maurice's certainty of the conversionist solution, combined with his faith that

Christ and Culture 143

Christ is at work even in an unredeemed humanity, led him to posit the direction conversion must take, humanly speaking. Maurice was for example a Christian socialist. He may have been right in that, but the judgment involved was of a different kind from his other certainties. Further, although Augustine was wrong to evade the temporal implications of his insights and escape into a vision beyond space and time, Maurice was wrong to suppose that fulfilment would be found in a social perfection which man, redeemed or unredeemed, will never achieve. An MP who became a minister of the Church of Scotland declared that he was involved in every bit as much corruption and intrigue in ecclesiastical as in secular politics. If Christians cannot, even under Christ, order their own communities, it is hard to see how, even under Christ, they can order the world.

CONCLUSION

No one view contains the whole truth. All contain some truth, all contain some error, all have some basis in the New Testament, all have been held by utterly sincere Christians. Error has come generally either from straying away from the Jesus of the New Testament, sometimes to a Christ who is a construct of the believer's imagination, or from ignoring the actualities of social, cultural and political life. A simple example of the latter may be useful. If a man or a group is to be converted to Christ, they must *in some sense* be converted within their culture, since their language is a part of their culture, and even if they learn, say, Greek and Hebrew, these will never become a part of them in the way their original language is a part of them. If we turn to Jesus himself, we find that he neither rejects nor accepts the culture of his day; the first two views are clearly too one-sided. It is hard to see the fourth view as doing justice to the Jesus of the gospels; it is derived from Paul rather than from the evangelists. Probably therefore we may say that the third and fifth views are those which do most justice to the evidence: Jesus did historically both accept and go beyond the culture of his day. It is notable that both views also show a practical grasp of cultural reality; Clement, Augustine, Thomas and Maurice certainly in their different ways had that. Both regard the claims of Christ as transcendent, or, to put it differently, both see the words and ways of Jesus as applicable (not necessarily literally transferable) to periods and cultures other than his own. A rationalist critique may be impatient at this. Not necessarily: most of us assume enough of a common human condition to feel that the insights of people from other cultures are valid for us, or we would not still go to the plays of Euripides or, for matter of that, Wole Soyinka. But we have still to come to terms with the fact that many people across the centuries have responded to Jesus as both human and divine, Son of Man and Son of God: that itself is a datum of cultural history.

BIBLIOGRAPHY

The chapter is based closely on H. Richard Niebuhr *Christ and Culture* (New York 1951). Other references are to J. Klausner *Jesus of Nazareth*. The text of Celsus has been reconstructed in O. Glöckner *Celsi Alethes Logos* (Bonn 1924); Origen's answer is conveniently available in English in Henry Chadwick *Origen: Against Celsus*. For the Gnostics I have used principally H. Jonas *The Gnostic Religion* (ET Boston ^{2}1963). See also R. M. Grant *Gnosticism and Early Christianity* (New York ^{2}1966). The full text of 'The Hymn of the Pearl' is available in my *Greek and Roman Religion: A Source-Book* (Park Ridge, NJ 1979). I have written also on *Clement of Alexandria* (New York 1974).

6
Son of God

BYZANTIUM

The first great age of the exaltation of Jesus as Son of God to the effective exclusion of his humanity was the Byzantine era. The Christian Roman Empire inherited all the paraphernalia of its pagan predecessor. The emperor had been a semi-divine figure, himself the son of a god, with the expectation that if like other sons of gods, Hercules or Aesculapius for instance, he served mankind well, he would be co-opted into the heavenly senate. The blunt soldier Vespasian, feeling death coming over him, remarked 'Oh dear! I think I'm becoming a god.' He was normally not worshipped in his lifetime, except in conjunction with Rome, though honour might be paid to his *genius* (life-force) or his *numen* (sacred power), and in Egypt he had to be the divine monarch: the temperate Claudius deprecated this, but the governor publishing his letter said 'that you may marvel at the greatness of our god Caesar'. As the centre of gravity shifted eastwards the emperor came to look more and more like an oriental divine monarch. A Christian emperor could not be this, but he retained the pomp and circumstance. In the Council-chamber was a throne with the Gospels on it. As the Emperor approached his own throne he saw above him a mosaic of Jesus and the words 'King in Christ'. If he, Christ's vice-gerent on earth, was far exalted above his people, his Lord was exalted even further. And in the hieratic court of Byzantium the emperor was so exalted. Norman Baynes evoked the matter with a sure touch:

> Picture for a moment the arrival of a barbarian chieftain from steppe or desert in this Byzantine Court. He has been royally

entertained, under the vigilant care of imperial officials he has seen the wonders of the capital, and to-day he is to have audience with the Emperor. Through a dazzling maze of marble corridors, through chambers rich with mosaic and cloth of gold, through long lines of palace guards in white uniforms, amidst patricians, bishops, generals and senators, to the music of organs and church choirs he passes, supported by eunuchs, until at last oppressed with interminable splendour he falls prostrate in the presence of the silent, motionless, hieratic figure of the Lord of New Rome, the heir of Constantine, seated on the throne of the Caesars: before he can rise, Emperor and throne have been caught aloft, and with vestments changed since last he gazed the sovereign looks down upon him, surely as God regarding mortal men. Who is he, as he hears the roar of the golden lions that surround the throne or the song of the birds on the trees, who is he that he should decline the Emperor's behests? He stays not to think of the mechanism which causes the lions to roar or the birds to sing: he can scarce answer the questions of the logothete speaking for his imperial master: his allegiance is won: he will fight for the Roman Christ and his Empire.

(*The Byzantine Empire*, London 1925, ch. 4, pp. 72-3)

If that was the elevation of the King, what must be the elevation of the King of Kings! If that was the sovereignty of the Emperor, what was the sovereignty of Christ!

A simple comparison may be made of two successive illustrations in René Guerdan's book on *Byzantium*. The first is from an ivory, and shows the Emperor presiding over the games at the circus. Below, the chariots speed round the course; above he sits, aloof and aloft. The other is from a privately owned MS of the eleventh century. A vertical ladder stretches through the universe; souls are effortfully clambering; one is toppling from the heights. At the foot is a dragon waiting to catch those who slip. At the top is Christ, aloof and aloft, with a winged surround which recalls and is derived from the sun chariot of Ahura Mazda in Persian art.

The great controversy over image-worship which racked the empire is here of particular interest. The writings of the Iconoclasts have been destroyed. We can trace their arguments

Son of God

only through their opponents' answers. They were not rationalists. Their claim was that the ikon came between the worshipper and the Divine; it was an illegitimate and inferior intrusion, a blasphemous reduction of the Divine to a material emblem. The Iconodules followed Basil, 'Honouring the image leads to the prototype.' If you do not worship images you do not worship the Son of God, who is himself the Image of God.

Byzantine art is hieratic art. There is a discernible legacy from the Hellenistic Age. But it is broadly true to say that where Hellenistic art is, or appears to be, naturalistically human, Byzantine art is not concerned with lifelike impressions, but with evoking a feeling of awe. So representations tend to be two-dimensional, not because the artists were incapable of portraying a third dimension, but because they were not interested in doing so. Size and proportion vary to express the dignity of the figures, or to bring out emotions; witness the exaggerations and distortions of the Crucifixion at Hosios Loukas in Greece. So in the great *Dormition* at Sopocani in Yugoslavia Jesus towers above the scene, only the inclination of his head expressing grief. He is often portrayed enthroned, stiff, stark, immobile, unbending; we see him so with intricately curling robes, carried up by angels at Ochrid, or over the west door of S. Sophia in Constantinople (Istanbul) as Leo VI lies prostrated at his feet, or within the church towering above the two figures at his side, the empress Zoe and her husband Romanos — or Constantine Monomachos, her second husband, whose likeness she had substituted; or, later, in the Kariye Camii with the donor kneeling at his feet; or in Monreale in Sicily crowning the emperor William II without even looking at him. At Daphni on the outskirts of Athens the figure of Christ Pantocrator glares down from the dome, searing, terrifying. Talbot Rice wrote: 'This strange, awesome figure belongs to the oriental conception of Christ as the stern judge — the Jehovah of the Old Testament; it is far removed from the Western conception of Him as a suffering mortal.' The transfiguration becomes a totally superhuman scene. In a manuscript of the 1370s, now in Paris, we see it bathed in blue, the figures of

Christ hieratic, aloof, upright in a nimbus of blue light whose rays spread out, the two figures at his side on peaks of their own such as no mountain ever saw, bowing to him, the three disciples far below, in standard iconography, John pointing up, James turning away, and Peter in the centre shuddering head-first down the slope. There is a similar scene in a magnificent ikon in the Tretyakov Gallery in Moscow, from the school of Theophanes; here the radiance is white, in the form of an elongated star within a circle. The figures are habitually elongated to make them more impressive. We can see this in another famous ikon in the Tretyakov, this time by Dionysius, portraying the Crucifixion, or in another, anonymous, of the Deposition, where the body of Christ is taller than the cross itself. Such elongation, disproportion, and indifference to naturalism are characteristic of the most Byzantine of later painters, El Greco, though his scenes have a dynamic movement lacking in Byzantine iconography; witness, on both counts, *The Cleansing of the Temple* (National Gallery, London, and, still more, the version in San Gines, Madrid) or *The Baptism* in Hospital Tavera, Toledo. El Greco could paint marvellous portraits, but his pictures of Christ are for the most part inconceivable as portraits, they are bundles of superhuman energy.

Even when Byzantine art is gentler and humanized it tends to be stiff and hieratic. There is a miniature mosaic of Christ in the Museo Nazionale, Florence, dating perhaps from 1150. This has been taken as an example of the delicacy of which the Byzantines were capable: but the face is a mask, and the gesture ritualistic.

It must be remembered that these manifestations of the supernatural in the approach to Christ were the staple fare of the ordinary worshipper, the Bible of the illiterate, and the form in which the Bible found visual interpretation for literate and illiterate alike.

THE MEDIAEVAL WEST

When we look at the art of the mediaeval west we find a similar remoteness. Jesus is the divine Saviour and Judge. The most characteristic representations of him are either on the cross or enthroned in majesty.

The scene of the crucifixion was a means to worship, and an emphasis on the suffering Saviour emerged strongly in the eleventh century. Anselm, later Archbishop of Canterbury, voiced it well: 'Why, O my soul, were you not present to be transfixed with the sword of sharpest grief at the unendurable sight of your Saviour pierced with the lance, and the hands and feet of your Maker broken with nails?' The emphasis is not on human suffering but on divine suffering. In the great tenth-century mosaic in S. Clemente, Rome, Christ on the Cross appears in the middle of the Tree of Life, whose spiralling vine-tendrils enfold chalices. Birds perch on all four of the bars of the cross; below, harts lead a procession of birds, including peacocks, to drink of the Water of Life. (It should be said that the figures of Mary and John are later additions.) In the Gospel book of the Abbess Uota of Niedermünster (1002-25) Christ's cross stands between the symbolic figures of Life and Death. In the Regenberg Sacramentary done for King Henry II (1002-14), now in Munich, the figures of sun and moon give the scene cosmic significance. The same figures, together with earth (Terra) sustaining the cross like some Atlas, appear on the cover of the Codex Aureus Epternacensis from Trier. But even without these figures, crucifixes like the First Cross of the Abbess Matilda of Essen, or the Cross of Gisela of Hungary, or the silver Crucifix of Archbishop Bernward offer, amid the splendour of their jewelry, 'a taut symbol of divine immolation'.

Most striking is the Crucifix carved in wood (and painted) of Archbishop Gero of Cologne. It is poignant but unsentimental, brilliantly sculpted in its feeling of dead weight, and in its delineation of the planes of the body. This is not a suffering man to evoke pity, but a dead God to command adoration. It no doubt dates from the late tenth century. Almost a century later comes a very different work, yet designed to be the same. It comes from the Abbey of Helmstedt at Werden, and is cast in bronze. Here the head drops, but the slender elongated body is upright, and the ribs show through the skin; the expressionless face has a rare dignity —

'a noble evocation of Divine submission to death', says John Beckwith.

For the devotion kindled by the Passion we may look at some words of the English hermit-poet Richard Rolle in the first half of the fourteenth century:

> Than was thy body lyk to hevyn. For as hevyn is ful of sterris so was thy body ful of woundes; bot, Lord, thy woundes bene bettyr than sterris, for sterres shynen bot by nyght, and thy woundes bene ful of vertu day and nyght. All the sterris by nyght lygheten bot litel, and oon cloud may hide ham alle; bot oon of thy woundes, swete Jhesu, was and is inough to do away the cloudes of al synful men . . . Here, swete Jhesu, I besech the that these woundes be my meditacioun nyght and day, for in thy woundes is hool medicyne for euche desaise of soule.

So in Langland's *Piers Plowman* Reason is made to ask 'Who suffereth more than God?' and answer 'No person, I believe.' It was God suffering that men saw on the crucifix, and that is why German piety particularly, as in the fourteenth-century *Pietà* in the Rheinisches Landesmuseum in Bonn or in Matthias Grünewald's later *Crucifixion* the agony has contorted Christ out of humanity into suffering divinity.

Christ in Majesty appears in a variety of contexts. An ivory panel, once in the Abbey of Seitenstetten, now in New York, shows an Emperor, perhaps Otto I (962-73), offering a church (perhaps Magdeburg Cathedral) to Christ enthroned on high, who, gracious but unbending, turns to receive the gift. Another ivory shows Otto II, Theophano and the future Otto III offering adoration. A fascinating ivory relief from Trier shows Christ enthroned in a kind of four-leaf-clover, with the four evangelists around. In the Regenberg Sacramentary mentioned above he is framed in a mandorla, a very Byzantine figure attended by angels, as he condescends to crown Henry. He sits again in a mandorla with angels around him as the Emperor Conrad II and the Empress Gisela kneel at his feet in the Codex Aureus of Speyer (1045-6); no doubt he receives their homage, but he is totally unmoved by it. In an ivory relief from Liège he is in a mandorla with the four evangelists, receiving the adoration of Bishop Notker. In

Son of God 151

another relief in Cologne the mandorla is held by angels and studded with stars; he is blessing the saints Victor and Gereon, but it is a hieratic ritual and he does not look at them. On the cover of Uola's Gospel book already mentioned he sits in majesty among the symbols of the evangelists, surrounded and bedizened with precious stones. The image persists; from the 1090s in Toulouse we find Christ, beardless, well-fleshed, but still impassive, seated in his mandorla surrounded by the symbols of the evangelists. This is in stone, but some of the decoration suggests that it may have been copied from a bronze original. Even in a manuscript painting of the Ascension from a Sacramentary in Limoges the mandorla is there, and we have the impression that he has stood up and is bursting from the mandorla, rather than that he is about to settle within it. The symbols of the sun and moon appear here too. In an enamel plaque for a book cover from Limoges (now in Lyons) Christ is enthroned on a rainbow, against a dark-blue sky powdered with stars, and the mandorla is picked out by formalized clouds.

Many of these were relatively private matters. The place where Christ in Majesty must have struck the ordinary worshipper was in the tympanum of the doorway (normally the west) of the great Abbey and Cathedral Churches, with or without the Last Judgment. Thus in the third Abbey Church of Cluny, as we know from an eighteenth-century engraving, he appeared colossal, seated on what looks uncommonly like a Ghanaian royal stool, in a mandorla held by angels, with cherubim flying around. This must date from about 1110. At Moissac in the next decade he sits in majesty above the scene of the Last Judgment; this is especially interesting for Islamic elements in the decoration. Emile Mâle said of this that 'examples are numerous, but none surpasses in beauty the tympanum at Moissac, which is comparable even to the text.' At Autun a little later, the magnificent tympanum of Gislebertus shows the same scene. So too at Vézelay, where the Christ in Triumph with his set face and swirling, spiralling drapery has been described as 'the most emotional and most intellectual of all the Romanesque sculpture of Burgundy. There are many other Benedictine examples. Further to the north in France much the same pattern prevails. At Bourges the west front is covered with a proliferation of sculpture; there are no fewer than five portals, the central one portraying Christ presiding over the Last Judgment. At Chartres the central portal bears Christ in Majesty on the tympanum, flanked to the right by the Incarnation and to the left by the Ascension. These are theological reminders. The crucifixion scenes and the scenes of enthronement alike invoke the *rex tremendae maiestatis* of Thomas of Celano's *Dies irae*, already quoted and continuing:

> King of awesome majesty,
> freely saving those to be saved,
> spring of righteousness, save me.
>
> Merciful Jesus, remember
> I am the cause of your journey:
> do not abandon me on that day.
>
> In seeking me you sat in weariness;
> you suffered the cross to redeem me;
> do not let that effort go for nothing.
>
> Justly vengeful judge,
> grant pardon as a gift
> before the day of reckoning.
>
> I groan as already condemned;
> guilt brings a blush to my cheeks;
> spare your suppliant, God.

This is the Jesus whom the Middle Ages adored, and feared.

THE MYSTICAL EXPERIENCE OF CHRIST

Despite some interpreters it does not seem that the experience of mystics from different religious traditions is essentially different, though the form of the experience may be determined by their previous religious affiliation, as is naturally their subsequent interpretation. The experience of the ultimate in the form of a Trinity seems confined to those whose theology

Son of God

it fits (not merely Christians, but some in antiquity to whom Zeus-Sarapis-Asclepius formed a Trinity in Unity). Christian mystics have naturally sometimes experienced the ultimate in the form of Jesus: usually also this has meant an experience of Jesus in the form of the ultimate, that is exalted and divine.

The Lady Julian of Norwich records sixteen revelations. They took off from her contemplation of the crucifix, but went far beyond the earthly life of Christ. In the first she saw fresh blood trickling from the crown of thorns; she had a revelation of the Trinity and of the glory and humility of Mary; she saw Jesus hold out to her a little thing, the size of a hazel-nut, which was all that is made, existing because God loves it — made it, loves it, sustains it (a Trinitarian experience); she grasped the greatness and goodness of God. The second revelation showed the face of Christ on the crucifix changing colour, and involved an imaginary journey down to the sea-bed, safe in God's presence. The third involved the Unity of the Trinity, the whole Godhead concentrated into a single point. (Teresa de Jesus had a similar experience of 'God in a point' in the Seventh Habitation of the Soul.) The fourth showed Christ's body bleeding on the crucifix, to wash away sin. The fifth, still using the crucifix, involved a recognition that temptation by the devil is overcome by Christ's suffering. In the sixth she received thanks from the suffering Christ for her own suffering, and an experience of heavenly bliss. This was continued into the seventh, which also included an experience of desolation and dryness. The eighth showed the figure on the crucifix going through the agony of dying; there was at the same time a sensation of a cold wind; she had an acute awareness of Christ's thirst; she understood that Mary and others who love Christ share in the agony; she could not take her eyes from the crucifix. In the ninth Christ spoke first of his suffering, and then swept her up to an experience of heaven. In the tenth she contemplated the wound in his side, and was led to see his broken heart. The eleventh was an experience of Mary, starting from her figure at the foot of the cross. The twelfth was a revelation of Christ in glory. The thirteenth involved a meditation on sin in which she heard Jesus saying to her that sin was necessary, but everything would be all right ('Sin is behovely, but all shall be well, and all shall be well, and all manner of thing shall be well'). The fourteenth was a revelation from Jesus about prayer. The fifteenth was about the promise of future deliverance. The sixteenth was an experience of her own soul as a city, in which Jesus sat as king, handsome, tall and glorious, God and Man, his Godhead ruling all that is. Julian was deeply persuaded that these revelations came from Jesus in person.

We can take another example from the Spanish mystic Luis de Leon. He describes the state when mystics are overmastered by a power greater than themselves in terms of possession by Christ. Christ 'occupies them wholly'. Christ 'looks out from their eyes, speaks from their tongues, works through their senses.' 'Christ's very Spirit comes and is united with the soul – no, rather it is infused throughout its being, as though he were the soul of its soul indeed. And thus, infused and absorbed by the soul, this Spirit takes possession of its faculties and powers.' Already it is clear that Christ may be a term for the ultimate as experienced by the Christian, and Luis is in fact liable to use vaguer language. 'God, when He is united with the soul, penetrates it wholly and enters into its secret chambers till He is made one with its inmost being', or again, the divine Word so penetrates the soul that in very truth the soul not only has God dwelling within it, but is actually God.'

Again Meister Eckhart experienced the ultimate as the birth in man of the Son or Word. He repeats this time and again. 'When the soul is free from time and place, the Father sends His Son into the soul.' 'When the Father begets His Son in me, I am that very same Son.' 'He makes me His only-begotten Son without any difference.' Eckhart insisted on this even to the detriment of the historical birth of Jesus: 'It is more worthy of God that He should be born spiritually of every virgin (that is, of every good soul), than that He should have been born physically of Mary.'

Protestant mystics use the same language. So Boehme says that 'the Son of God, the eternal Word of the Father, must become man, and be born in you, if you will know God'. So William Law declares that if we follow the desire for God when it stirs in us, it will lead us to the birth of Jesus not in a stable at Bethlehem in Judaea, but to his birth in the dark centre of our own fallen soul. He sees Christ as a universal principle, manifested indeed in the historic Jesus, but, more profoundly, 'the life and light and holiness of every creature that is holy'. The German mystics, Sebastian Franck and his follower Valentine Weigel, see Christ as the Son who from all eternity put on human nature and who was from all eternity the complete and perfect image of God, a divine humanity incarnate wherever men experience union with God. Caspar Schwenckfeld actually rejected the traditional doctrine of Christ's two natures, and held that he was altogether divine; his body was formed of spiritual flesh. In the exalted life of that spiritual body he imparts his own divinity to those who open their inmost selves to him.

THE REFORMATION

The Reformation was in part a reaction against the Renaissance; it was a turning from man to God. It was deeply rooted in scripture, but because it was deeply rooted in the whole Bible (or most of it: Luther considered *James* 'an epistle of straw') it did not concentrate on the gospels, and Luther's thinking was deeply rooted in Paul's *Epistle to the Romans*. His theology was Christocentric; its prime point was justification by faith in Christ. The famous Ninety-Five Theses, while they start from Christ's call to repentance and end with an exhortation to follow him, contain little about Jesus, except the assertion of the merits of his person and his cross. The constant emphasis of Luther's preaching was upon God in Christ and Christ as the Revealer of God, upon the saving work of God in Christ. He concentrated primarily on the Nativity and the Crucifixion, the birth and the death. For the God who is awesome and terrifying in storm and earthquake is also, Luther insisted, merciful; but we cannot know that except in Christ, the Lord of Life, abandoned at his birth to an outhouse among the animals, and at his death to derision and anguish, and yet annihilating our offences. Luther interpreted the gospel-story through *Romans*. He might say epigrammatically 'This Man is God; this God is Man', but his point was that the act of salvation, though coming through a man, had come from God. Luther's theology, expressed with equal succinctness, is *'Christus Gottessohn ist unser Heiland'* ('Christ, God's Son, is our Saviour'). J. S. Whale once said, 'The christology of the Lutheran Church strongly emphasizes the *majesty* of Christ's humanity.'

The Calvinist tradition laid more stress on the reality of Christ's humanity, and Calvin was at constant pains to insist that Jesus was fully God and fully man: 'So much and more was it necessary that he who was to be our Mediator should be true God and man' (*Inst.* 2.12.1). He insisted both on the unity and on the distinction between the two natures. Calvin would not separate God from Christ. But equally he suggested that the two natures must be distinct or we shall introduce a change in and diminution of the divinity by becoming man. He used the eyes as an illustration of the combination of unity and distinction: 'Each eye can have its vision separately; but when we are looking at anything . . . our vision, which in itself is divided, joins up and unites in order to give itself as a whole to the object that is put before it.' His authoritative view appears in the second edition of The *Institutes*.

> But this which is said, that the Word was made flesh, ought not to be understood as though it were converted into flesh or confusedly mingled therewith; but only that it took from the womb of the Virgin a human body, to be a temple in which he dwelt. And he who was the Son of God was made the Son of Man, not by confusion of substance but by unity of person: that is, he so joined and united his divinity with the humanity that he had taken, that each of the two natures retained its properties; and nevertheless Jesus Christ has not two distinct persons, but only one.   (2.14.1)

But despite Calvin's care for a balanced view his greater emphasis is on the divinity. 'Jesus Christ then was adorned with this excellence according to the flesh . . . of being the

Son of God: but we must not, however, imagine the unity of his person as a confused mixture which robs the deity of what belongs to it' (2.14.7). 'Although he united his infinite essence with our nature, nevertheless that was without being enclosed or imprisoned; for he came down from heaven miraculously, in such sort that he still dwelt there; and he was also carried miraculously in the womb of the Virgin, and conversed, and was crucified in such a matter that at the same time, according to his divinity, he was still filling all the world as before' (2.13.4). Again, in the commentary on *Luke* 2.40, 'Although in unity of person he was God and man together ... it does not therefore follow that all that belonged to our divinity was communicated to the human nature, but that so far as was needed for our salvation the Son of God kept his divine power as though hidden.' Calvin was in fact in something of a dilemma. He was concerned with salvation, with reconciliation to God. He was certain that reconciliation came through Christ, and the merit of the offering made by Christ could hardly avail save through his divinity. So though Calvin stressed the work of Jesus as mediator, and sometimes seemed to accord him a power of independent action, as in the sermon on *Ephesians* 6.19-24 ('Our Lord Jesus Christ did not have the office of enlightening us in the faith and of reforming our hearts today only inasmuch as he is our mediator and inasmuch as he is a minister of God, but because he has that also of himself'), in general his Predestinarian theology granted Christ merit because of the determinate purposes of God. It is not too much to say with Max Dominicé that 'this humanity of the Christ has value for him only by its union with the divine nature'.

THE EARLY-TWENTIETH-CENTURY RATIONALISTS

It is a matter of some irony that one effect of late-nineteenth and early-twentieth-century rationalism was actually to increase the supernaturalism of approach. H. G. Wood in his critique *Did Christ Really Live?* put it well: 'Christ-myth theories find favour with rationalists who regard religion as illusion, and with mystical idealists who regard every entanglement of religion with historic fact as a degradation of a pure spiritual faith. Those who wish to destroy religion and those who wish to refine it unite in the endeavour to prove Jesus to be a fictitious creation.'

The most interesting exponent of this school was John Mackinnon Robertson (1856-1933), one of the more remarkable figures of British history, who should be rescued from oblivion, a man largely self-educated, a militant free-thinker and disciple of Bradlaugh, a journalist by profession, a parliamentarian and Privy Councillor beside, a man whose learning ranged wide and deep, and who among other things wrote the standard history of free thought, became a major Shakespearian scholar and literary critic and made important contributions to the social sciences, and a man of the highest integrity whose bluntness offended some but whose charm and candour attracted more. Robertson's two major studies, *Christianity and Mythology* (1900) and *Pagan Christs* (1903), show that the Biblical account of Jesus conforms closely to myths drawn from all over the world. Thus the dying and re-arising Saviour-God is exemplified from the ancient Near East in Adonis, Attis, Heracles, Osiris and Dionysus; parallels are taken from the Khonds and Aztecs, and from various totemistic tribes; a line of descent is drawn from Mesopotamia through Judaic belief and practice. The evidence from Mexico is drawn out in some detail. There are extended discussions of parallel events recorded of Jesus with the lives of Krishna, the Buddha and Mithras. What we are left with is supernatural myth and ritual drama.

A variant on this was provided by a German Pastor from Bremen, Albert Kalthoff, who wrote in 1903 *Das Christusproblem, Grundlinien zu einer Sozialtheologie*, which he elaborated and tidied up the following year in *Die Enstehung des Christentums. Neue Beiträge zum Christusproblem*, which Joseph McCabe translated as *The Rise of Christianity*. Kalthoff's thesis was that Christianity was a radical lower-class social-revolutionary movement, for which the Roman Empire was ready (his account of such movements in Greek philosophy, Judaism and the Roman Empire is produced with learning and understanding); that we cannot take the gospels as a historical record of a historical person, so much of them being unhistorical, contradictory or fantastic; that the triumph of the Christian organization over the other religious-social bodies was due to the figure of Christ, 'the Christ-god . . . the one who is to come, for whom the world must prepare'. The well-known Social Democrat Karl Kautsky presented a similar view.

The most influential work from this general standpoint came from Arthur Drews (1865-1935), professor at Karlsruhe, in his book *Die Christusmythe* (*The Christ-Myth*) (1909-11). Drews was a monist, a disciple of von Hartmann, who believed in a wholly immanent God, present in every man, in all nature and all history. Belief in the historical actuality of a human in whom God was uniquely incarnated ran counter to this. So Drews argued against the historicity of Jesus. He starts his examination of the New Testament, in correct chronology, with Paul, without whom the Christian movement would have disappeared in the sand, and concludes: 'The fact is therefore settled, that Paul knew nothing of an historical Jesus; and that even if he had known anything of him, this Jesus in any case plays no part for him, and exercised no influence over the development of his religious view of the world. . . . Paul knew absolutely nothing of Jesus as an historical personality' (ET p. 207). He goes on to argue (rightly!) that the synoptic gospels are not historical biographies, but dogmatic treatises presenting a humanized God. He suggests that Jesus was already a cult-figure in Jewish sects, and became later taken up in forms of Gnosticism.

This movement had its greatest influence in the fifteen years before the first World War.

THE MISSIONARY PREACHING

There was a strong tendency for the Roman Catholic missionaries, who went out in the Age of Discovery with a great passion for the saving of souls, to proclaim Christ as a divine figure. They were facing a people they regarded as superstitious; they countered the superstitions by an affirmation of what they saw as true religion. Here is Francis Xavier's account of a service on the coast of Coromandel:

> I give out the First Commandment, which they repeat, and then we say all together, Jesus Christ, Son of God, grant us grace to love thee above all things. When we have asked for this grace, we recite the Pater Noster together, and then cry with one accord, Holy Mary, Mother of Jesus Christ, obtain for us grace from thy Son to enable us to keep the First Commandment. Next we say an Ave Maria, and proceed in the same manner through each of the remaining nine Commandments. And just as we say twelve Paters and Aves in honour of the twelve articles of the Creed, so we say ten Paters and Aves in honour of the ten Commandments, asking God to give us grace to keep them well.

We can see the process with great clarity in Latin America. Some of the *conquistadores*, notably Pizarro, made no pretence to any concern with religion; all he wanted was gold. More generally, the conquests had as one aim the propagation of the Christian, or, more strictly, the Catholic faith, since there were those who saw the new conversions as offsetting those lost to Luther's Protestantism. But the practice of the *conquistadores* did not suggest a great regard for Jesus as an exemplar of human life; Latourette wrote bluntly 'The methods of conquest were in sharp contradiction to the principles of Jesus, and in their loose relations with the women of the land the *conquistadores* departed widely from the injunctions of the religion which they represented' (III 109). At the same time the mass-conversions do not suggest any deep understanding on the part of the converted. Peter of Ghent wrote on 27 June 1529: 'I and the brother who was with me baptized in this province of Mexico upwards of 200,000 persons – so many in fact that I cannot give an accurate estimate of the number. Often we baptized in a single day 14,000 people, sometimes 10,000, sometimes 8,000.' Bishop Julian Garces of Tlaxcala baptized and confirmed 300 a week. Zumarraga in 1531 said that the Franciscans alone had baptized over a million in twelve years; other writers suggest a total of up to about 10 million converts. It was partly that the Indians were ready to go over from the cruelty of the Aztecs to an acceptance of the Spanish way of life, partly that they were enrolling in the service of a more powerful God. It is hard to know how deep it went. In two ways behaviour was changed radically: human sacrifice was eliminated, and monogamy replaced polygamy. But many pagan customs remained covertly or even overtly in the churches. The veneration paid to the crucifix was not different in kind from the veneration paid to their previous idols, and sometimes the ancient images were set discreetly behind the crucifix itself.

In general missionaries, whether Catholic or Protestant, as they went out into the third world, presented a supernatural Jesus, the Son of God, the Saviour of the World. As an example of this we may take a passage from *A Half Century among the Siamese and the Lao* by an American pioneer missionary in Northern Thailand, Dr Daniel McGilvary (1828-1911), cited by Kosuke Koyama in his *Waterbuffalo Theology*.

> Why do we worship Jehovah-Jesus? Because he is our sovereign Lord. The Buddha groaned under his own load of guilt, and was oppressed by the sad and universal consequences of sin among men. The Christ challenged his enemies to convince him of sin, and his enemies to this day have confessed that they find no sin in him. . . . Our Jehovah-Jesus, as our Scriptures teach, is the only self-existent being in the universe, and himself the cause of all other beings. An infinite Spirit and invisible, he manifested himself to the world by descending from heaven, becoming man, taking on our nature in unison with his holy nature, but with no taint of sin. He did this out of infinite love and pity for our race after it had sinned. He saw there was no other able to save, and he became our Saviour. . . .
>
> We pressed home the thought, new to them, that there must be a maker of the world and of all creatures in it. We told them the old, old story of the infinite love of God, our Father, and of Christ, his Son, who suffered and died to save us, and of pardon freely promised to all who believe in him. This is the final argument that wins these people.   (pp. 181-2, 328)

This of course was written for his own people not the Thai. Yet it reveals his preaching. And we can note two major factors: first, it is about God and the Son of God; second, it makes no attempt to come to terms with the local culture, except to reject it.

As an example of a nineteenth-century response to Jesus we may look at Ramakrishna, born in Bengal on 18 February 1836 to devout Hindu parents. From an early age Ramakrishna was subject to trances which might last many days. He was an ecstatic and a visionary. For ten years he was the devoted priest of the goddess Kali. He explored all the planes of religious experience known to Hinduism, and then went on to Islam and to Christianity. In 1874 he had a vision of Jesus Christ; this was connected with a picture of the Madonna and Child, and the fact that a Muslim friend had been reading the New Testament to him. From the date of his vision he believed that Jesus (with the Buddha, Krishna and a few others) was an incarnation of God, kept a picture of him and burned incense to it twice a day.

Or in Africa we may reflect how in Yorubaland David Kukoji of Ibadan hearing David Hinderer preach Jesus as the Son of God, mighty in power, promptly thought of him as another *orisa*, that is one of the subsidiary deities, ministers of the supreme and sovereign God Olodumare. This was before his conversion. Samuel Ajayi Crowther, greatest of the nineteenth-century converts, Bishop on the Niger from 1864, used repeatedly in his encounter with those of other faiths to speak to Jesus as Judge. We have a fascinating record of his encounter with the Emir of Ilorin on 4 January 1872. The passages he read to the Emir, in English and Yoruba, were *Luke* 1.28-35 (the Annunciation), *John* 14.6 ('I am the Way, the Truth and the Life'), *Matthew* 28.18-20 (the post-resurrection commission to the disciples). Discussion moved on to Jesus as Judge, and Crowther cited three texts (*Matt.* 25.31-4; *Acts* 1.7; *Luke* 12.39-40), all about the looked-for Second Coming of Jesus at an unknown moment.

From the first in Africa Christians have had to relate their preaching to the indigenous situation. African Christian thinkers have rightly been complaining that expatriate missionaries were often indifferent or prejudiced about that. Even so we can see certain emphases. To take one obvious example, to a people oppressed by fear of spirits, Jesus as the one whom the spirits obey comes as a Saviour and Liberator.

There have been in the past twenty years or so, a number of attempts, both by expatriates and Africans, to seek out a distinctively African theology. Thus Bengt Sundkler wrote that in Africa, 'Christ, the King, proves Himself to be the Life and the Fullness with power to liberate from sickness and death and devil.' Traditional African thinking is mythical. It follows that the Christian preaching in Africa must be concerned with the great cosmological issues of the Beginning and the End, and of the unity of life. So a Zulu priest, Michael Mzobe, showed in an Easter sermon Jesus appearing as the Second Adam who overcomes Satan, Sin and Death, and bringing peace to the First Adam. Sundkler quotes a fascinating essay by a Zulu theological student. According to this student the missionaries were right to preach the Christ who 'went to the dead to show them who He was, and came up from the dead to show himself to the living ones', but in so doing they missed the boat, because they missed the African belief in the living dead, who might have been linked with the Christian doctrine of angels. The *caveat* is interesting and important; equally interesting and important is that this young African regards the descent into Sheol as central to the presentation of Christ. So in the Douala antiphonal hymn;

> Christ ascended on to the Cross;
> Christ descended into the Grave;
> Christ overcame the Power of Death.
>   Yes, he overcame him.
>   Did he overcome him?
>   Yes, he overcame him.
>   Did he overcome him?
>   Yes, he overcame him.
>   Did he overcome him?
> Christ overcame the Power of Death.
>   Yes, he overcame him.
>   Did he overcome him?

> Yes, he overcame him.
> Did he overcome him?
> Yes, he overcame him.
> Did he overcome him?
> Christ overcame the Power of Death.
> Yes, he overcame him.

Two more examples may be taken from African theologians. Harry Sawyerr of Sierra Leone was the first African theologian to do anything really substantial in this field. His *Creative Evangelism* was a brief, pioneering study. Sawyerr is trying to build on the points which African traditional religion and Christian theology have in common, and stresses the themes of God and Creation, the spirit-world, the great family, immortality and worship. An obvious problem about this approach is that Jesus of Nazareth is not one of the common factors, though the eternal Word of God may be. But Sawyerr lays great stress on the Eucharist as the keypoint transforming the African background into Christian understanding and practice. Sawyerr is himself a deeply committed Christian: the inevitable tendency of his system is to reduce the historical Jesus and stress the divine Son of God.

The most subtle essay in the interpretation of African beliefs in Christian terms is a study by John Mbiti. Mbiti takes off from his own people, the Akamba of Kenya, and shows how eschatology not merely forms the most significant point of contact between traditional beliefs and Christian faith, but is central to the Christian faith of the Akamba converts. For example, there are 211 hymns in the Kikamiba hymnal, and nearly half of them have a substantial eschatological reference. Mbiti is fascinating on some of the problems in handling eschatological concepts. For example the Akamba have a two-dimensional concept of Time, with a dynamic present and an ever-increasing past, which makes difficult the concept of an end or goal. Mbiti says, with some wit, that Christian eschatology means newness, and it is a newness in Christ. Again there are four ways of saying 'Jesus will come' in Kikamba, and all four are used in the Kikamba Bible. One means that he will come after a few months, one after a few hours, one that he will certainly come but the date is not fixed, one that he is outside the door waiting. Mbiti stresses the vital importance of the Resurrection: 'The Resurrection of Jesus makes the entire existence of the faithful absolutely Christocentric.'

To turn over the pages of *EACC Hymnal*, published by the East Asia Christian Conference, is in general to hear the note of triumphalism sounded. A hymn from China (182) invokes Jesus as 'God the love that saved mankind'. One hymn by the finest of these writers, D. T. Niles, calls glory upon Jesus as Word of the Father, Lord of the world, Priest of his people, and Judge; Jesus was 'humbled as man' but the emphasis is on adoration (191). Another from the same hand uses the praise-cry 'Namo' (190). In another the cry is 'Saranam' ('refuge'); Jesus is Saviour, Lord, Rock, Refuge (163). A superb Urdu hymn invokes him as the Bread of Life, the Door, the Light, the Shepherd, the Resurrection and the Life (121). A hymn from the Marathi by another fine writer, Narayan Vaman Tilak, calls on him as 'Wisdom, Joy and Liberty' (145). In one from Thailand he is 'Jesus, our Lord and King' (173). Another by D. T. Niles has the haunting refrain:

> Jai Jai Yesu, Jai Jai Yesu
> Conqueror over my soul – Lord!
> Won, Thou must win;
> Enter within,
> Save me from sin.
> Jai Jai Yesu, Jai Jai Yesu.

This ends with the thought of the Second Coming (130). The majority of these impressive hymns ring with the sound of glory.

BIBLIOGRAPHY

Byzantium
After centuries of neglect, the study and appreciation of Byzantium has come into its own. There is no better short account than N. H. Baynes

166 *Son of God*

The Byzantine Empire (London 1925) from which the quotation comes. A more recent summary is D. Talbot Rice *The Byzantines* (London 1962). For the religion see H. C. Beck *Kirche und theologische Literatur im byzantischen Reich* (Munich 1959), and, in English, N. Zernov *Eastern Christendom* (London 1961) and J. Meyendorff *Byzantine Theology* (London 1974). For the art two books by D. Talbot Rice, *The Art of Byzantium* (London 1959) and *Byzantine Art* (Harmondsworth 1961). Also A. Grabar *Byzantine Painting* (London 1953). For the Russian material see M. W. Alpatov *Art Treasures of Russia* (ET London n.d.); for El Greco conveniently J. Lassaigne *El Greco* (ET London 1973), superbly illustrated.

The Mediaeval West
It is hard to imagine a better book than John Beckwith *Early Mediaeval Art* (London 1964). For the great churches of Burgundy see R. Oursel *Bourgogne Romane* (1968). Joan Evans *Art in Mediaeval France 987-1498* (London 1948) puts the whole thing in context: see also A. Gardner *Mediaeval Sculpture in France* (Cambridge 1931); E. Mâle *Religious Art* (ET London 1949). The best general books on the Middle Ages known to me are F. Heer *The Mediaeval World* (ET London 1962) and G. G. Coulton *Mediaeval Panorama* (Cambridge 1938).

Mysticism
My own *An Illustrated Encyclopaedia of Mysticism and the Mystery-Religions* (London 1976) offers a conspectus and a survey: also a bibliography. There is no better one-volume account than Evelyn Underhill *Mysticism* (many edns). F. von Hügel *The Mystical Element of Religion* is a palmary study of Catherine of Genoa (London 1927). A sensible book is S. Spencer *Mysticism in World Religion* (London 1966). Several of the texts are available in the Penguin Classics. I hold the general unity of mystical experience as against e. g. R. C. Zaehner.

The Reformation
I have learned a great deal from working with Dr. Francis Clark and his four booklets on the Reformation for the Open University course A201 *Renaissance and Reformation*, Units 20-7, are a model of scholarly and fairminded exposition. For a general work J. S. Whale *The Protestant Tradition* (Cambridge 1959). For Luther, R. H. Bainton *Here I Stand* (1950: many editions); useful documents in E. G. Rupp and B. Drewery *Martin Luther* (London 1970), J. Dillenberger *Martin Luther* (New York 1961) and B. L. Woolf (tr) *Reformation Writings of Martin Luther* (1953-6). For Calvin I know nothing better than F. Wendel *Calvin*

(ET London 1963, pb 1965). Key works are available in English in The Library of Christian Classics vols 20-2 (London 1954-61). Of direct relevance to the purpose of this study are M. Dominicé *L'Humanité de Jésus d'après Calvin* (Paris 1933) and E. Emmen *De Christologie van Calvijn* (Amsterdam 1935).

Rationalism
The major books are identified in the text.

The Missionary Preaching
The great and indispensable work is K. S. Latourette *A History of the Expansion of Christianity* (7 vols 1938-47). Smaller in scale, but judicious is S. Neill *Christian Missions* (Harmondsworth 1964). For Latin America there is the important C.S. Braden *Religious Aspects of the Conquest of Mexico* (Durham, NC 1930). The sixteenth-century work G. de Mendieta *Historia Eclesiastica Indiana* (Mexico 1870) is to all intents and purposes a primary source. W. H. Prescott's famous *History of the Conquest of Mexico* and *History of the Conquest of Peru* remain useful. For Africa there is the incredibly dull and incredibly learned C. P. Groves *The Planting of Christianity in Africa* 4 vols (London 1948-58). The literature is immense: Neill has a good selective bibliography and Latourette a more comprehensive one, now somewhat outdated. For Ramakrishna see *The Gospel of Sri Ramakrishna*. There is an outstanding recent study of Crowther in P. R. McKenzie *Interreligious Encounters in West Africa* (Leicester 1976). For the new African theology see among others: B. G. M. Sundkler *The Christian Ministry in Africa* (London 1960); J. V. Taylor *The Primal Vision* (London 1963); S. G. Williamson *Akan Religion and the Christian Faith* (1965); E. B. Idowu *Towards an Indigenous Church* (London and Ibadan 1965); A. Hastings *Church and Mission in Modern Africa* (London 1967); C. G. Baeta (ed.) *Christianity in Tropical Africa* (London 1968); H. Bürkle (ed.) *Theologie und Kirche in Afrika* (Stuttgart 1968); H. Sawyerr *Creative Evangelism: Towards a new Christian Encounter with Africa* (London 1968); D. B. Barrett (ed.) *African Initiatives in Religion* (Nairobi 1969); J. S. Mbiti *New Testament Eschatology in an African Background* (London 1971 rep. 1978); A. Shorter *African Christian Theology: Adaptation or Incarnation* (London 1975).

7
Son of Man

INTRODUCTION

'The face of Christ', wrote Photius in the ninth century, 'is differently portrayed by the Romans, the Greeks, the Indians, the Ethiopians, for each affirms that Our Lord appears to them in this particular guise.' Daniel-Rops, writing as a Christian, comments on this passage in words which are still vital to our understanding of the subsequent response to Jesus: 'A Christ with a Chinese or Negroid face can outrage only those who fail to understand the Christian testimony. Christ was a Jew by race and it is probable that he had the physical characteristics of the Chosen People, but this birth, which came out of the mysterious testing of Israel, was not thereby limited; the real message of Christ's life was in his death. He died for all men, and it is to the whole family of humanity that he belongs. Every man from that time on has sought to find himself in him' (*Jesus in His Time* p. 239).

ISLAM

Muhammad rescued the Arab tribes from a religious state which it would be improper to call polytheism and was at best polydaemonism, a belief in a multiplicity of spirits, into an austere monotheism.

The natural consequence of this rigid monotheism was the rejection of belief in Jesus as Son of God and of the Christian Trinitarian doctrine. This recurs through the Qur'an. 'They say "God has taken to Him a son." Glory be to Him! No!' (2.110) 'God is only One god. Glory be to Him — that He should have a son!' (4.169). 'It is not for God to take to Him a son' (19.36). 'They say "The All-merciful has taken to himself a son." You have certainly advanced something hideous! The heavens are almost torn apart by it and the earth split in two, and the mountains almost fall down with a crash because they have attributed to the All-merciful a son; and it is not fitting for the All-merciful to take a son' (19.91-3). 'Believe in God and His Messengers, and do not say "Three" ' (4.168). 'They are unbelievers who say "God is the Third of Three" ' (5.77). 'Say "He is God, One, God, the Everlasting Refuge, who has not begotten, and has not been begotten, and there is none equal to him." ' (112). This last brief Sura is called the Cleansing; it scours away the errors of polytheists and Christians alike.

Jesus then is to Islam a human being, known by his proper name 'Isa, the Arabic being derived from the Syriac Yeshu' and ultimately from the Hebrew Yeshua. But he is treated with considerable respect and honour, and pious Muslims speak of "Isa, on whom be peace'. He is designated as a prophet, the culminating figure, before Muhammad, in a line of prophets. Moses brought the Torah, Jesus the Gospel, Muhammad the supreme revelation of the Qur'an. Jesus is called Son of Mary (Ibn Maryam) in the Qur'an. Some Muslim scholars interpret this to be a further insistence on his normal humanity, especially as matrilineal descent was known in Arab communities; others say that it is associated with a miraculous birth from a virgin mother. It is an interesting title, since it occurs only once in the New Testament (*Mark* 6.3), but it is found in the Syriac and Arabic Infancy Gospels, which suggests that it was taken over from local Christian sources. Other titles accorded Jesus in the Qur'an are the Messiah (Al-Masih), interpreted either as a messenger of God or as a generally honorific title, Servant (*'abd*), which has a clearly human reference, Prophet (*nabi*), Messenger or Apostle (*rasul*), Word (*kalima*), but as a word from God, not as the Word of God.

Jesus is identified in the Qur'an particularly as a healer of the sick. He is assigned other supernatural powers; the story from the Infancy Gospels of his making clay birds and breathing life into them is treated as fact. One of the most interesting of the Qur'an stories tells of the disciples asking for a table from heaven. Jesus' immediate response is 'Show piety to God if you are believers.' He goes on to pray God to 'send down to us a table from heaven, to be to us a festival, to the first and to the last of us, and to be a sign from You, and provide for us, for You are the best of providers', and of God's promise to do so (5.112-14). It is not quite clear how this originated: it may be an elaboration of the prayer 'Give us this day our daily bread' or an embellishment to the story of the Feeding of the Five Thousand or of the Last Supper. Islamic tradition in general assimilated it to the second of these; Baidawi told how a red table of food descended on two clouds, with cooked fish, salt, vinegar and garnishings, and five loaves; Jesus declared this to be food from heaven, brought into being by the power of God. Modern Muslim scholars reject these embellishments, and rationalize. The disciples had food but no table; they asked Jesus to pray for a table from heaven. The Qur'an does not claim that God did so; it is suggested that Jesus' answer was that they should fear God and not make requests of this sort.

Primarily, Jesus in the Qur'an is the bringer of the *Injil*, Gospel or Good News. He is the one who confirms the Torah and offers guidance and light. The Gospel is conceived as a Holy Book; there is in Islam an intense belief in the Book, and the Holy Books of Judaism, Christianity and Islam are seen in a culminating succession; Jews, Christians and perhaps Zoroastrians were treated differently from pagans because they were the people of a Book. Later Muslim writers suggest that the Christians corrupted the interpretation (Ibn Khaldun) and even the text (Biruni) of the Gospel; they have found it hard to understand why there should be four gospels, when God entrusted to the prophet Jesus a single Gospel, and why Jesus did not dictate the Gospel himself. The concentration on teaching is understandable. Muhammad, like Jesus, deplored the demand for signs and neglect of teaching.

The Qur'an does not, of course, profess to give a systematic account of the teaching of Jesus; that was already in the gospels. But there are a large number of references to the teaching, direct or indirect. Muhammad had steeped his mind in the Jewish and Christian scriptures, and there are many quotations from or allusions to the sayings of Jesus. One of the most interesting comes from Sura 61.6 'Jesus, son of Mary, said: "O children of Israel, I am God's messenger to you, confirming the Torah which was before me, and announcing the good tidings of the messenger who will come after me, bearing the name Ahmad." ' There is a variant on this recorded by Ubayy ben Ka'b, one of Muhammad's secretaries, 'O children of Israel, I am God's messenger to you, and I announce to you a prophet whose community will be the last community and by which God will put the seal on the prophets and messengers.' Both versions are taken to refer to Muhammad. They are probably based on Jesus' promise of the Spirit, and Ibn Ishaq explicitly refers this to Muhammad, with a fantastic wordplay on the Prophet's name and the Manaḥḥemana, life-giver, comforter or Paraclete.

There are a few actual sayings or episodes which do not occur in the gospels, though they have their parallels. Here is one: 'I have come to you with a sign from your Lord: I shall create for you from clay the form of a bird and I shall breathe into it and it will become a bird by the permission of God, and I shall heal the blind and the leprous, and bring the dead to life by the permission of God, and I shall announce to you what you may eat, and what you may store up in your houses; truly in that is a sign for you if you are believers. Confirming what is before me of the Torah, and to make allowable for you some things which have been forbidden to you, I have brought you a sign from your Lord, so act piously towards God and obey me. Truly God is my Lord and your Lord, so serve Him; this is a straight path.' (3.43/40). The phrase 'my Lord and your Lord' is characteristic of Jesus in the Qur'an; it recalls the New Testament 'my God and your God' (*John* 20.17). Another very interesting story runs: 'So when Jesus perceived unbelief on their part he said, "Who are my helpers for God?" The apostles replied, "We are the helpers of God, we have believed in God; testify that we are among those who submit. O our Lord, we believe in what You have sent down, and have followed the Messenger; so write us down among the witnesses" ' (3.45/52). Those who submit are precisely the Muslims. The passage shows clearly the Muslim attitude over the relation of Jesus to God. This is spelled out again in a saying in which Jesus repudiates any claim to divinity. 'Glory be to You! It is not for me to say what I have no right to say. If I did say it, You know; You know what is in my soul, but I do not know what is in Your soul; truly it is You who know what cannot be seen. I said nothing to them but what You commanded me: "Serve God, my Lord and your Lord." I was a witness over them as long as I remained among them, but when you took me to yourself, it was You who watched over them, for You are witness over all. If You punish them — well, they are Your servants. If You forgive them — well, You are the Sublime, the Wise.' (5.116-18). So here. 'See, I am the servant of God; he has given me the Book and made me a prophet; he has made me blessed wherever I am, and has charged me with the Prayer and the Almsgiving as long as I live; He has made me dutiful towards my mother; He has not made me a tyrant, wretched. And peace is upon me the day of my birth and the day of my death, and the day of my being raised up alive' (19.31-4). The last phrase does not necessarily refer to Easter, but (perhaps) to the final resurrection of Muslim belief: similar words are applied to John the Baptist (19.15).

One or two stories and sayings of Jesus come from other Muslim sources. One of the most delightful tells of a pariah dog run over by a cart. A knot of bystanders gathered round and spoke of what a repulsive creature it was. Suddenly a voice said 'Pearls have not the whiteness of its teeth.' One of the crowd said to the newcomer: 'You must be Jesus; only Jesus could see any good in a dead dog.' Here Jesus appears as the compassionate human. Most of the sayings are connected with teaching. 'He who is greedy for riches is like a man drinking water from the sea. The more he drinks, the more he increases the thirst, and he goes on drinking until he dies.' 'Son of man, when I give you riches and power, you transfer all your aspirations and care from me to the riches and power. But when I make you poor, you grow weary with sadness and anxiety. Where will you find the loveliness of my name, and when will you bring to maturity reverence for me?' There is an amusing parable comparing the world to an old woman who has killed off a large number of husbands: Jesus' comment was that the later ones were very stupid to allow passion to triumph over discretion. Another similar story is probably to be regarded as a parable. Three travellers found a treasure. One decided to poison the others and keep it to himself. When he returned the other two, having plotted together, killed him — and then ate the poisoned food. 'Woe to him who seeks the world in the world.' One of the most interesting of the sayings was attributed to Jesus by the great Mogul Akbar and inscribed over the gate of a mosque at Sikri, west of Agra: 'Jesus, on whom be peace, had said: "The world is but a bridge, over which you must pass, but must not linger to build your dwelling." ' This is close to a saying of the Greek Epictetus, and is unlikely to be authentic; however, it shows what Muslims thought of Jesus as teaching.

References to the death of Jesus in the Qur'an are difficult to interpret, and I can here only give a brief view of a long and learned debate. Some passages seem clearly to affirm the full humanity and mortality of Jesus. It is unbelief to say that God is the Messiah, and it is unbelief to say that God could not wish to destroy the Messiah, son of Mary, and his mother, and those who are on the earth together, since God is the sovereign Lord of all (5.19/17). 'The Messiah, son of Mary, is nothing but a messenger before whose time the messengers have passed away' (5.79/75); the implication is that he too passed away. In one saying already quoted Jesus speaks unequivocally of the day of his death (19.34/33). In another God tells Jesus that he is going to bring his term to an end, and take him to Himself (3.48/55); elsewhere the language is used of death. There is, however, one passage which seems to take a different view. The Jews claim 'We killed the Messiah, Jesus, son of Mary, the messenger of God.' But they did not kill him and did not crucify him, but he was counterfeited for them (4.154-7/155-9). The natural reading of that is that it comes from a Docetic source, but that does not determine its meaning for Islam. In one popular Muslim version Judas (or some other) was crucified in place of Jesus.

Another view is that Jesus was crucified but did not die on the cross, but was rescued, concealed, and died later: according to the Ahmadiyya he died in Kashmir. Yet another view is that the Jews tried unsuccessfully to kill Jesus; he died indeed, but it was by the determinate will of God through the instrumency of the Romans; and his death was a death only of the body, as with the martyrs of Islam and all true servants of God. What is important is that Islam rejects altogether Christian soteriology associated with the death of Jesus. An outstanding contemporary scholar, Dr Kamel Hussein, has written 'I contend that the Apostles on that day had no idea of the Divine significance of Crucifixion or that it had been decreed from eternity. They had no idea of redemption, Atonement, or the role of Jesus Christ as Saviour. All this (I hope I am not wrong here) was defined and explained clearly by that most remarkable of men, St Paul' (*Mohammedanism* p. 69; *City of Wrong* p. 224).

The Muslim attitude to Jesus arises from Muslim theological presuppositions. Muslim monotheism means that Jesus cannot be regarded as divine, Son of God, or God, but that he is seen in the context of religious belief. So he is seen as human, but his life — especially his birth and death — is clothed with a supernatural aura. Primarily he is prophet, teacher, messenger of God.

FRANCIS OF ASSISI

Francesco Bernadone, son of a rich clothier, did more than any other single person to bring back into Christendom a warmly human Jesus. His beginnings were unpromising: carefree and extravagant, though always charming and generous, he might have become a second Alcibiades. But in 1205-6 at the age of 24 he had a succession of four mystical experiences which changed his life. To him they were encounters with Jesus Christ. The first was a voice, directing him back to Assisi at the cost of some personal pride. The second directed him to poverty, and led him to share his goods with the needy and kiss the hand of a leper. The third took place while he was praying in a ruined church; he heard a voice from the figure on the Cross saying, 'Francis, go and repair my church which, as you see, is falling down.' Christ was his Lord, but Christ was also his friend. He brooded on the sufferings of Jesus and said, 'I weep for the Passion of my Lord Jesus Christ, for whom I ought not to be ashamed to go mourning aloud throughout the whole world.' But he also felt himself to be living close to the man who was found at weddings and dinner-parties, who taught through laughter, who enjoyed the flowers and the birds around him, whose enemies complained that he enjoyed life too much, and who promised his friends joy. So was Francis torn between laughter and tears.

The fourth and decisive experience was on 24 February 1206, when the gospel for the day told of Jesus sending out his apostles, and Francis heard through the words a personal call to himself. He pledged himself to imitate Christ and to obey his commands, in humility, simplicity, poverty and prayer. Many years after his death Pier Pettignano, one of his followers, had a vision of a procession led by Jesus' mother Mary, followed by apostles, saints and martyrs, all with their eyes on the ground trying to discern the footprints of Jesus so as to walk in them. At the end of the elaborate, triumphal gathering came Francis, with brown robe and bare feet, swinging happily along in the actual footprints.

From Francis's own commitment a gathering of friends began to surround him. The growing community needed a Rule. Francis drew up a Rule under ten heads: effectively, they were taken straight from the words of Jesus. He took the Rule to Rome. The cardinals received it coldly; it was impossibly stringent. The Cardinal of S. Sabina, Francis's one supporter, suggested that to say this was to imply that Christ did not know what he was talking about. The rule was authorized.

There is no need to go through the sequence of success and crisis which followed. But two other episodes should be recalled. One was at Greccio in 1223. As Christmas drew near Francis was meditating on Jesus's earthly life. He called a friend to 'make a memorial of that child who was born in

Bethlehem, and in some sort behold with bodily eyes his infant hardships, how he lay in a manger on the hay, with the ox and ass standing by'. So came the first Christmas crib, and it was as if the straw really was warming the baby, and even the animals seemed to breathe warmth on to him. So came the cult of the *bambino*, Jesus having emptied himself, not clinging to equality with God, and becoming a helpless human baby like other helpless human babies.

In the following year on Holy Cross Day, 14 September, Francis was in prayer. 'O my Lord, Jesus Christ, two graces do I pray you to grant me before I die, that while I live I may feel in my body and in my soul, so far as is possible, that sorrow, dear Lord, which you suffered in the hour of your most bitter passion; the second, that I may feel in my heart, so far as may be possible, that great love, Son of God, by which you were kindled willingly to endure for us sinners such great agony.' As he prayed a blinding light surrounded him, visible for some distance, so that some muleteers actually thought that they had overslept and set out on their journey. This lasted an hour; when it faded he found wounds like those of Christ on his hands, feet and side. One thing is quite clear: Francis was no exhibitionist about it, and did his best to conceal the marks. They are well-authenticated, and it is not impossible to believe a power of identification of himself with Jesus which actually affected his body.

In the aftermath of Francis came Giotto. Giotto is often treated as a precursor of the Renaissance. The traditions he inherited were mediaeval and Byzantine. What directed him to a greater naturalism in handling his religious subjects was not, as is usually said, a residual Hellenism. It is true that something of the sort can be seen in the sculpture of Nicola Pisano with his human Christ on the pulpit at Siena. But, although Giotto, himself from Florence, could learn something of the styles of Rome through Torriti and Cavallini, the fact is that it was at Assisi that he met them, and not enough has been made of the impact on him of Francis's warm humanity. His earliest work of real importance was done in Assisi somewhere around 1300 (the date, like most of the facts of Giotto's life, is controversial). Here he began his two revolutions. The first was to reject (as Giunta Pisano, Coppo and others had begun to do) the characteristic absence of a third dimension in mediaeval and Byzantine painting, and to find the effective means of expressing depth, solidity, volume, relief, plasticity in paint; he was able to do this without becoming obsessed with the mathematical details of perspective as some of the early Renaissance painters were liable to be. The second was to free himself from dependence on ornaments, attributes and symbols and to tell a direct story directly, with human (and, as befitted a follower of Francis, animal) participants in natural surroundings. So we have a flesh-and-blood Francis, who stoops gently but firmly towards the birds as he speaks to them, but whose head is tossed back, a shade defiantly, as he preaches before Honorius III, whose face is filled with anxious concentration as he leans forward chin in hand, and some of whose court are plainly hostile.

In the Cappella degli Scrovegni, the Arena chapel at Padua, Giotto, given sole and full responsibility, carried on with an even firmer mastery to apply the same plastic human realism to the life of Christ. The west wall is filled with the Last Judgment. The side walls and the sanctuary arch bear thirty-eight scenes from the lives of Mary and of Jesus. At the beginning of the series we see Joachim, husband of Mary's mother Anne, expelled from the Temple, whose marbled sanctuary is set on a diagonal, giving both depth and direction to the thrust away. We pass through various legendary episodes, noting the boldness with which a concave apse is contrasted with a concave group of figures outside, and noting also that even when the scene is mythical or miraculous the people are real. So we come to Jesus, as a baby in swaddling-clothes being admired by a delightful donkey; held firmly by his mother as he is honoured by the kings; free from swaddling-clothes and reaching out realistically to his mother as he is presented in the Temple; riding on his mother's lap to Egypt on the back of a proud donkey; framed by a mighty apse, as, now older, he speaks before the doctors, ignoring his parents. We see him grown, being baptized by John, human yet with a mysterious power which creates at this moment a gap between himself and others; dining at Cana as a very corpulent drinker samples the wine; a figure of explosive energy raising Lazarus as the others show a variety of astonished or incredulous responses; riding into Jerusalem (the donkey this time is almost smug); driving out the money-changers, not with El Greco's flailing whip, but by the power of his anger; seated at the Last Supper, looking across the table with sad resolution to one of the other disciples, who is watching him intently, as he passes the sop without looking to Judas; washing the disciples' feet; mantled in Judas' cloak as the embrace betrays him, concentrating all his love and sorrow on the betrayer, oblivious of the waving pikes and whirling figures around; before Caiaphas, a detached figure expressing at once accusation and pardon, disdain and compassion; scourged; bearing the cross; crucified; dead; risen; ascended. Even in the great Last Judgment the figure of Jesus, isolated in an aureole, remains human. Salvini says of this, 'The Christ in his pink robe is magnificent, huge in the centre of the multi-coloured circle, but conserving, in spite of his gigantic dimensions, his human measure; the same human and moral greatness of the person who acted out the New Testament stories. It is the same figure who disappeared softly from the sight of Mary Magdalen in the *Noli me tangere*, and now reappears in all his power in the double gesture, of imperious condemnation and of merciful welcome.'

THE HUMANITY OF JESUS IN THE MYSTICS

We have seen that in general mystical experience tended towards the exaltation of Jesus as a cosmic figure. But this is not entirely so. For in the first place many of the Christian mystics insist on starting from the close study and understanding of the human life of Jesus. The very title *The Imitation of Christ* suggests something such; the first paragraph includes the injunction 'so let our prime endeavour be to meditate upon the life of Jesus Christ' (1.1); regular Bible reading is one means to this end (1.5). So too Walter Hilton in *The Ladder of Perfection* says that the first degree of contemplation consists in knowledge of God and of spiritual matters, and is reached through reason, through the teachings of others and through Bible study (1.4). The practice of contemplation is not possible without continual recollection of the humanity and Passion of Jesus Christ, and the pursuit of all virtues (1.92). Again, to love our fellows we must imitate Christ, and bring our actions up against the test of his earthly life (1.70). The *Theologia Germanica* speaks similarly (18; 30; 45). Teresa de Jesus and Henry Suso were among those profound contemplatives who discovered that, as Evelyn Underhill put it, 'deliberate meditation upon the humanity of Christ, difficult and uncongenial as this concrete devotion sometimes is to the mystical temperament, was a necessity if they were to retain a healthy and well-balanced inner life.' She goes on well: 'Further, these mystics see in the historic life of Christ an epitome — or, if you will, an exhibition — of the essentials of all spiritual life. There they see dramatized not only the cosmic process of the Divine Wisdom, but also the inward experience of every soul on her way to union with that Absolute "to which the whole Creation moves". This is why the expressions which they use to describe the evolution of the mystical consciousness from the birth of the divine in the spark of the soul to its final unification with the Absolute Life — are so constantly chosen from the Drama of Faith.' (*Mysticism* pp. 120-1)

Particular emphasis is placed upon the contemplation of Christ's passion. We have seen how Julian of Norwich began her mystical experiences from the contemplation of the crucifix. In the middle of her account of her revelations she has an extended discussion, which is a part of those revelations, suggesting three ways of looking at Christ's passion. The first is to concentrate on the pain and to identify oneself with it. The second is to concentrate on the love which led him to suffer. The third is to concentrate on the joy and happiness which he experienced in and through his suffering (pp. 21-3). Teresa de Jesus, while indicating that there are other subjects for meditation than the Passion of Christ, takes the binding of Jesus to the pillar as one of the most profitable (*Life* ch. 13). Thomas Traherne has a magnificent meditation on the Cross, 'the abyss of wonders, the centre of desires, the school of virtues, the house of wisdom, the throne of love, the theatre of joys, and the place of sorrows'. 'There we may see a Man loving all the world, and God dying for mankind' (*Centuries* 1.58-60). Catherine of Genoa's conversion on 22 March 1473 came from a vision of Christ carrying a cross dripping with blood.

But besides dwelling on the historic Jesus the mystic is enjoined to the Practice of the Presence of Christ. The Jesus who is so experienced is encountered in his humanity. *The Imitation of Christ* speaks naturally and easily of this:

The Familiar Friendship of Jesus

When Jesus is present, all is good and nothing seems difficult. But when Jesus is not present, all is harsh. When Jesus is not speaking within, external consolation is worthless; but if Jesus speaks one single word, there is a great sense of comfort. Did not Mary Magdalen jump straight up from her place of tears when Martha said to her 'The Master is here and is calling for you'? Happy hour, when Jesus calls from tears to spiritual joy. How dry and hard you are without Jesus! How foolish and vain if you set your heart on anything besides Jesus! Is not this a greater loss than to lose the whole world? What can the world offer without Jesus? To be without Jesus is a hell weighing on you; to be with Jesus is a paradise of delight. Once Jesus is with you, no enemy can harm you. The man who finds Jesus finds a good treasure, a good above all good. The man who loses Jesus, loses a great deal, more than the whole world. The man who lives without Jesus is a pauper; the man who is well with Jesus is a millionaire.

It requires great skill to know how to talk with Jesus, and great wisdom to know how to hold him. Be humble and a peacemaker, and Jesus will be with you. Be devout and quiet, and Jesus will stay with you. You can quickly drive Jesus away and lose his favour if you want to turn aside to outward things. And once you have driven him away and lost him, with whom will you take refuge? Whom will you ask to be your friend? Without a friend you cannot live a good life, and if Jesus is not above all others your friend, you will be desperately sad and desolate. So you are acting like an idiot if you confide or take pleasure in anyone else instead. It is preferable to have the whole world against us rather than Jesus offended with us. So out of all you hold dear, let Jesus be uniquely and specially loved.

    Love everyone for Jesus; love Jesus for himself. Jesus Christ alone is uniquely to be loved; he alone is found good and loyal above all friends. (2.8)

It is a long passage, but a telling and characteristic one.

Teresa de Jesus recommends similarly the practice of the presence of Christ. 'We should occupy ourselves, if we can, by gazing at Him who is gazing at us, and should keep Him company, and talk with Him, and pray to Him, and humble ourselves and delight in Him, and remind ourselves that we do not deserve to be there' (*Life* ch. 13). Even at the height of her ecstasy she felt the invisible presence not as the unconditional Absolute but as Christ in his humanity. 'In the prayer of union and of quiet, the presence of God may be experienced', she said, 'but in a vision the soul distinctly sees that Jesus Christ, the Virgin's son, is present' (*Life* ch. 27: the whole chapter is relevant). Teresa with all her high mystical experience was delightfully down-to-earth. On one occasion she was complaining to her Lord of the pain she was suffering, and heard a voice: 'But that's how I treat my friends.' 'Yes', she snapped back, 'and that's why you have so few of them!'

There is another aspect of mystical experience which is peculiarly difficult to evaluate. This is the use of the language of love, which is a common feature of mystical expression, in Christian mysticism often based on or linked with *The Song of Songs*. Such love seems to be physically felt: Bernini was not wrong to use sexual symbolism in his statue of Teresa in ecstasy, or to portray her as if in orgasm. It is easy to dismiss Thérèse de l'enfant-Jésus, Thérèse of Lisieux, when she describes herself as Jesus' doll or little flower or girl-friend: they seem intolerably coy and arch expressions of adolescent day-dreaming, but they are in fact a simple girl's account of what she was experiencing. 'The Rosy Sequence', a Latin poem, not by Bernard of Clairvaux but reflecting his mystical experience, shows something of the attitude. It has been excerpted in a number of well-loved hymns: here it is in a cruder precision.

> The thought of Jesus is sweet,
> it gives the heart true joy.
> Sweeter than honey or any thing
> else is his presence.
>
> There is no more musical song,
> nothing more joyful to hear,
> no thought sweeter
> than Jesus, son of God.
>
> Jesus, hope of the repentant,
> kind to those who ask,
> good to those who seek,
> what to those who find!
>
> Jesus, delight of hearts,
> spring of truth, light of minds,
> surpassing every joy
> and every longing.
>
> Tongue cannot tell,
> writing cannot express,
> he who knows can believe
> what it is to love Jesus.
>
> I will seek Jesus in bed,
> when the door of my heart is shut;
> in private and in public
> I will seek him with careful love.
>
> With Mary at daybreak
> I will seek Jesus in the tomb;
> with my heart's earnest cry,
> with mind not eye will I seek him.
>
> Jesus has returned to his Father,
> he has entered his heavenly kingdom;
> **My** heart has passed away from me,
> and gone after Jesus.

> Let us now escort Jesus
> with hymns, praises and prayer
> that he will grant us with him
> to enjoy a home in heaven.

In that sequence, from the first stanza, there is a constant sense of the presence of Jesus. It is not an experience of a suprapersonal divine force, but of the still living historical man whom Mary looked for in the tomb.

RENAISSANCE HUMANISM

The word 'humanism' has changed its meaning. The humanists of the Renaissance were not so called because they fostered the human as opposed to the divine, but because they engaged in humane studies, that is the studies which appealed to the essential and unique part of a human being, his reason. To do this they returned to classical antiquity, its literature, philosophy and art. In so doing they were in intention serving the Church and the Christian faith. But the actual result was not wholly in accordance with their intentions. For contact with the intellectually free speculations of the Greeks led to fresh advances in scientific understanding and a questioning of established dogma. And Graeco-Roman literature and especially art exalted the human personality and the human body in a way alien to the thought of the Middle Ages.

How this applied to Christ we may see in Michelangelo's *Last Judgment* in the Sistine Chapel. His Christ, larger than life, does not sit enthroned, isolated by a formal mandorla, unmoved, an image of supernatural awe. He is a young athlete, with rippling muscles on his well-formed body. He has a mandorla, but it is a great burst of light as he is carried into the scene on a cloud through the centre of the whirling circle of humanity, with the small, helpless, horrified, shrinking figure of Mary at his side. He is no longer frontal and impassive. He is half-rising for action, his arms raised to ward off pleas of sentiment, his face, handsome and human, but set and implacable. It is as frightening in its way as Daphni, but that spoke of the wrath of the Son of God. Here men are judged by Man.

A similarly human approach can be seen in other paintings. Haloes, like mandorlas, are eliminated. Michelangelo's *Holy Family*, a tondo in the Uffizi, is a brilliantly sharp evocation of a father, mother and child at play; his *Entombment* (unfinished) in the National Gallery, London, shows a very dead human body. Leonardo's *Last Supper*, sadly ravaged by time, eliminates all the symbolic artifices, which had come to spell out the theological meaning, and records the human responses to a theological event. Something similar is true of Raphael's *Transfiguration* in the Vatican. Something supernatural is undoubtedly going on at the top of the picture, only the Transfigured Christ is not still and hieratic, but a human receiving a profound spiritual experience, and the scene is set against the bustling human activity at the foot of the hill. Perugino's *The Charge to Peter* in the Sistine shows a human encounter set against an Italian square with a church and two monumental arches in the background; they may be symbolical but they are also natural.

Once the human image of Jesus is established it tends to continue. Something like a halo may sometimes return in the form of an aura of light, but the face remains human. We may see this, for example, in some of the pictures of Suffering, in Velasquez's *Christ at the Column* (in the National Gallery, London) where the attendant angel does not diminish the impact of human pain, or in the agonized martyr of Guido Reni's significantly titled *Ecce Homo* in Dresden.

Above all there is Rembrandt (1606-69). Protestant in his own theology, and working in Protestant Holland, he stripped away all priestly iconographic traditions and dogmas and went back to the gospels. Rembrandt in his younger days tended to give the figure of Christ a superhuman quality; we can see this in the 1632 etching of *The Raising of Lazarus* where he stands, dominant, larger than life, with a theatrical gesture which seems to have produced an explosion of light, or in the 1629 painting of *Christ at Emmaus* (in Musée Jacquemart-André, Paris), where again his figure seems larger than life, and again there is an explosion of light on the far side of him, silhouetting his figure as he leans back from one of the travellers who is already at his feet, and illuminating the startled face of the other. But later Rembrandt avoided this visual sense of glory. He took up one aspect of Luther's teaching: 'To know Christ, that he has become man, and has abased himself so deeply that he looked like the most despised and unworthy of men, afflicted and chastised by God (*Isaiah* 53), and all that for our sake — this is the right golden art of Christians and their highest wisdom.'

Rembrandt's later Christ is incognito. He is insignificant, yet he is the one on whom everything depends. At a glance he seems to be weak and powerless; as we look further the strength of the others seems affectation, and he is revealed as alone firm. He does not dominate the doctors in the Temple; his figure does not stand out from the picture -- until you compare his questioning face with the smugness, hostility, boredom and inadequacy around him. As he confronts the woman taken in adultery he lacks the venerability, the learning, the subtlety, the material power of those around him, even, in a worldly sense, the strength of personality; it is a little while before you realize that he has a compassion which transcends all these; the others are either concerned with their own cleverness in trapping him or with the abstractions of law, he is concerned with the woman. In *The Agony in the Garden* or *Christ Awaking the Apostles* you are at first conscious of his weakness. The 1655 *Ecce Homo* is dominated by the impersonal symbols of justice, the governor's palace and the tribunal, and secondly by Pilate with his turban; but take away that turban and staff of office, and who is judging whom? There is a wonderful sketch of *The Raising of the Cross* in Rotterdam, dominated by the centurion in command; yet we know that this centurion will say, 'This was a son of God.' In the Munich *Entombment* the helpless broken body is manipulated by those around; only it is they who are left helpless, and the face is strong in death. As in a drawing he walks to Emmaus there is nothing to distinguish him from any other traveller; only (in the Louvre painting) at the table, as ordinary hands hold an ordinary loaf, does radiance burst from behind the ordinary face.

Rembrandt's Christ always brings to me a short story by Turgeniev:

> I saw myself, in dream, a youth, almost a boy, in a low-pitched wooden church. The slim wax candles gleamed, spots of red, before the old pictures of the saints.
>
> A ring of coloured light encircled each tiny flame. Dark and dim it was in the church.... But there stood before me many people. All fair-haired, peasant heads. From time to time they began swaying, falling, rising again, like the ripe ears of wheat, when the wind of summer passes in slow undulation over them.
>
> All at once some man came up from behind and stood beside me.
>
> I did not turn towards him; but at once I felt that this man was Christ.
>
> Emotion, curiosity, awe overmastered me suddenly. I made an effort . . . and looked at my neighbour.
>
> A face like every one's, a face like all men's faces. The eyes looked a little upwards, quietly and intently. The lips closed, but not compressed; the upper lip, as it were, resting on the lower; a small beard parted in two. The hands folded and still. And the clothes on him like every one's.
>
> 'What sort of Christ is this?' I thought. 'Such an ordinary, ordinary man! It can't be!'
>
> I turned away. But I had hardly turned my eyes away from this ordinary man when I felt again that it really was none other than Christ standing beside me.
>
> Again I made an effort over myself.... And again the same face, like all men's faces, the same everyday though unknown features.
>
> And suddenly my heart sank, and I came to myself. Only then I realised that just such a face — a face like all men's faces — is the face of Christ.

UNITARIANISM

Unitarianism within Christianity (the word, in the form *unitarius*, dates from 1600, but the teaching is older), dates effec-

Son of Man

tively from the early sixteenth century, and is a product of Renaissance humanism. The effect of the Renaissance was to strengthen Platonism; a Platonist finds it hard to accord his loyalty and devotion to any material manifestation; Platonism favoured a general religious approach, but, whatever its exponents wished, did not in fact favour Christianity's claims to a special revelation in Jesus. A second effect was greatly to enlarge the scope of speculation, if only through contact with that highly inquisitive people the Greeks.

Erasmus was the father of the new modes of thought. He was alienated from scholastic controversies; his publication of the Greek New Testament in 1516 had a liberating effect, especially as he omitted 1 *John* 5.7, which had, or was deemed to have, significance for the doctrine of the Trinity. In 1527 Martin Cellarius published a work entitled *The Works of God (De Operibus Dei)* in which he seemed to say that Jesus was no different from any other who accepted God as Father. The first great opponent of Trinitarianism was Michael Servetus (1511-53). He created a considerable stir by his youthful *The Errors of the Trinity (De Trinitatis Erroribus Libri VII)*. In the year of his death (by burning for heresy) he elaborated this in the anonymous *The Restoration of Christianity (Christianismi Restitutio)*, in which he denied the doctrine of the Trinity and the divinity of Christ, without however denying the Logos-doctrine. Servetus died but his influence remained and spread, not least through refugees from persecution. In the Low Countries many Anabaptists tended to return to the doctrines of Arius. In 1542 David Joris of Delft wrote in his *Wonder-Book* that there is 'one God, sole and indivisible, and that it is contrary to the operation of God throughout creation to admit a God in three persons'.

The next important figure was Faustus Socinus, Fausto Paolo Sozzini (1539-1604). He came from Siena; his uncle, a friend of Melanchthon and Calvin, had shown individual ideas. Young Socinus was only 23 when he published an exposition of John's Gospel, in which he denied the essential divinity of Christ, though he accorded him adoration and regarded him as more than mere man though not fully God.

Socinus was thus in an ambiguous position. He stood firmly on the historical authenticity of the New Testament; he held that Jesus was fully and truly a mortal man; he used a doctrine of offices, that Jesus had the offices of prophet, priest and king, but he in fact stressed the prophetic ministry; he denied that Jesus' death was an atoning sacrifice, and saw it rather as a revelation of God's will to forgive and as a moral influence on those who contemplated it. But he also believed that Jesus was sent by God, was unique in his holiness, and was glorified by God in his resurrection. Essentially to Socinus Jesus was a man who achieved his own victory over sin; to this was added a resurrection which made that victory a source of salvation to others.

The next important movement in this connection was Deism. It emerged, primarily in Britain, in the seventeenth century as a product of Renaissance thought, and flourished in the rationalist climate of the eighteenth, being widely influential in France. We can trace something of the mood which led to deism in Lord Herbert of Cherbury (1583-1648) whose remarkable book *Truth, and its Distinction from Revelation, Probability, Possibility and Falsehood* (*De Veritate*) suggested five primary principles in religion, marked by priority, independence, universality, certainty, practical necessity, and immediate cogency, namely (i) that God exists (ii) that He ought to be worshipped (iii) that virtue is true worship (iv) that repentance for sin is a duty (v) that there will be rewards and punishments after death. Herbert was neither denying nor asserting the divinity of Jesus, but his approach made it irrelevant. Another forerunner of the Deists was John Locke (1632-1704). His advocacy of toleration of religious opinion (which, however, he withheld from atheists and Roman Catholics, deeming them politically dangerous) was important in creating a climate of thought where new ideas could flourish. In 1695 he published *The Reasonableness of Christianity as Delivered in the Scriptures*; the book was important for its assertion of Reason as the ultimate critical authority. Further, Locke insisted that the one essential article of Christian faith is that Jesus is Messiah.

It was in the year after Locke's work that the first blast of real Deism was sounded by John Toland in his *Christianity not mysterious, showing that there is nothing in the Gospel contrary to Reason nor above it, and that no Christian Doctrine can properly be called a Mystery*. The collocation of titles was deliberate: Toland was climbing on Locke's bandwagon. He regarded the mysteries of Christianity as contrary to reason, and the products of priestcraft and paganism. It was Bishop Stillingfleet who regarded Toland's work as a marriage of Locke with Unitarianism. Toland's leading successor was perhaps Matthew Tindal (1655-1733) whose *Christianity as old as the Creation, or the Gospel a Republication of the Religion of Nature*, published in 1730, argued that for all rational beings 'there's a law of nature or reason, absolutely perfect, eternal, and unchangeable, and that the design of the Gospel was not to add to, or take from this law.' Toland and Tindal did not so much face Jesus and find him human, as — in their basic thinking — ignore Jesus, and have no grounds for finding him other than human. Collins and Woolston in the meantime had looked more directly at Jesus. Collins followed Locke in seeing no other claims in the Gospels than that Jesus is Messiah, and stripped away supernatural arguments from prophecy; Woolston stripped away the miracles by allegorical interpretation. Woolston argued that if you accepted the miracles you were landed with something more like a subhuman than superhuman Jesus, and imagined him drunk with his mother at Cana, telling fortunes like any gipsy, and arraigned before the magistrates for damaging a herd of pigs.

Deism weakened Christian dogma without putting anything in its place to excite loyalty. An abstract Creator was less magnetic than the figure of Jesus, whether divine or human. Joseph Priestley (1733-1804) was a distinguished scientist and Fellow of the Royal Society. He entered the Dissenting ministry, and won a reputation for a strongly argued unorthodoxy. 1774 was for him a remarkable year, combining the discovery of oxygen with the opening of a place for Unitarian worship in Essex Street off the Strand. In 1791 he was a founder-member of the Unitarian Society. Priestley had an intense personal loyalty to Jesus, whom he believed to be Messiah, but not divine, infallible or impeccable; he took a straightforward humanitarian view of Jesus and revered his teachings as a basis for life. His work was taken up by Thomas Belsham (1750-1829), who presented Jesus as 'a man constituted in all respects like other men, subject to the same infirmities, the same ignorance, prejudices and frailties', chosen by God to introduce a new moral order.

Meantime Priestley, who had revolutionary sympathies, visited the United States, where liberal interpretations of the Christian faith were beginning to flourish, and Priestley's own writings were already circulating. Here the leading force was William Ellery Channing (1780-1842). Oddly, he embraced the title Unitarian, but was not characteristically Unitarian in his beliefs, accepting the pre-existence and the miracles of Christ. He in fact stressed 'one sublime idea' — 'the greatness of the soul, its divinity, the union with God by spiritual likeness' — a reemergent Platonism, this — 'its receptivity of his Spirit, its self-forming power, its destination to ineffable glory, its immortality'. The general effect of the Unitarian movement was to concentrate attention on the teachings of Jesus, and on his human personality. As such it has been widely influential, especially, but not solely, in Britain and America.

RATIONALISM

We have noted the ironical fact that one of the rationalist positions stressed the supernatural Christ at the expense of the historical Jesus. The general effect of rationalism however was naturally to treat the figure of Jesus as historical, and to treat all those reported events which do not accord with normal human experience as accretions. F.C. Conybeare, himself a member of the Rationalist Press Association, radically criticized Robertson in his own book significantly entitled *The Historical Christ*.

Here the influence of David Hume (1711-76) is inescapable. His chapter 'Of Miracles' in *An Inquiry Concerning Human*

Understanding argued from a doctrine of probability; probability depends on the principle of the Uniformity of Nature. If we carry out 150 experiments and 100 point in one direction and 50 in another, we have no great expectation of the result of a further experiment. If 99 point one way and only 1 the other (the figures are Hume's) our expectation is proportionately larger, and we begin to wonder whether there was something wrong with the exception. Hume claimed that a miracle was a violation of the laws of nature, an alleged event which ran counter to an absolute uniformity of experience, and that in such cases delusion or deception was infinitely more probable than the actuality of such an event.

> When anyone tells me that he saw a dead man restored to life, I immediately consider with myself whether it be more probable that this person should either deceive or be deceived, or that the fact which he relates should really have happened. I weigh the one miracle against the other; and according to the superiority which I discover, I pronounce my decision, and always reject the greater miracle. If the falsehood of his testimony would be more miraculous than the event which he relates, then, and not till then, can he pretend to command my belief or opinion.

It is clear that in fact to Hume the questions 'Is Nature uniform?' and 'Do miracles occur?' are the same question asked positively and negatively. But the particular laws of uniformity he and his followers choose are too limiting of our scientific understanding. Hume would rule out *a priori* the stigmata of Francis of Assisi; yet when a victim of the Nazis was hypnotized by medical psychologists in an attempt to heal his broken mind, and projected back into his prison-camp experiences, the deep weals of the ropes which had bound him appeared on wrists and ankles, and the two experiences do not seem necessarily dissimilar. Again there is too much evidence of the healing of organic disease, let alone psychosomatic illness, through some form of 'thought-force' (to use a question-begging term), for us to rule out *a priori* the possibility of what are often called 'healing-miracles'. Logically Hume's principles would have led him to disbelieve in the first four-minute mile or the first men on the moon because it had never happened before. T. H. Huxley once remarked that Hume's argument against miracles turned on the fallacy that induction can give certainty in the strict sense (*Life* II 262). None the less, Hume's treatise was highly influential in leading rationalists to take a view of Jesus which eliminated the miraculous and left the human.

Probably the most influential book which followed this critique was *Das Leben Jesu* (*The Life of Jesus*) by David Friedrich Strauss (1808-74), which appeared in 1835-6. Strauss's aim was to eliminate the supernatural elements in the story — everything before the baptism, the miracles (some of which he dismisses under the flippant heading 'Sea-Stories and Fish-Stories'), and most of *John*, for example. But the positive aim was to disentangle the historic Jesus, an eschatological prophet. Nearly thirty years later he returned to his theme in *Das Leben Jesu für das deutsche Volk bearbeitet* (*The Life of Jesus for the German People*). This is much more of a liberal approach, and is reflecting the climate of the second half of the century. It appeared in 1864, the year after Ernest Renan's *La Vie de Jésus*. Renan offered a vividly human Jesus. A critic described the central figure as the Christ of the Fourth Gospel, without his metaphysical halo. Renan himself said, 'I had a fifth gospel before my eyes, mutilated in parts, but still legible, and taking it for my guide I saw behind the narratives of Matthew and Mark, instead of an ideal Being of whom it might be maintained that he had never existed, a glorious human countenance full of life and movement.' Renan was a literary artist, and for this reason his book was more widely read than most. Even more impressive was the work of Karl Theodor Keim (1825-78) whose *Die Geschichte Jesu von Nazareth* appeared between 1867 and 1872. He rejected all that was supernatural or miraculous including the Resurrection, and denied the historicity of *John*. He saw Jesus as a human: 'Jesus fled because he desired to preserve himself for God and man, to secure the continuance of his ministry to Israel, to defeat as long as possible the dark designs of his enemies, to carry his cause to Jerusalem, and there, while acting, as it was his duty to do, with prudence and foresight in his relations with men, to recognize clearly, by the Divine silence or the Divine action, what the Divine purpose really was, which could not be recognized in a moment. He acts like a man who knows the duty both of examination and action, who knows his own worth and what is due to him and his obligations towards God and man' (2nd edn. pp. 228-9). Jesus' consciousness of his vocation was strengthened by success and disappointment. His views changed and developed. He held to an 'obsolete belief' of the imminence of the Day of Judgment. Yet his self-deception at this point 'steeled his human courage and roused him to a passion of self-sacrifice with the hope of saving from the Judgement whatever might still be saved', so that the very delusion proved advantageous in transforming the lives and souls of men.

Scientific advances also favoured the rationalist approach. Thomas Henry Huxley coined the word 'agnosticism' for his approach. Over much of his life he respected the human Jesus while believing that his picture had been overlaid with accretions by the Church; latterly he began to doubt even the central figure. A good example of scientific agnosticism is provided by a now forgotten book, enormously influential in its own day. It was published in Brussels in 1900, by Comte Camille de Renesse, under the title *Jésus-Christ: Ses Apôtres et ses Disciples au XX Siècle*. By the following year it had reached its 54th impression, and a translation into Spanish had gone through 22 impressions. For the Count Jesus was a human, anti-clerical teacher of peace, charity and love. He described himself as 'son of man'; sometimes, but rarely, as 'son of God', just as he considered every man as a son of God; never as God the Son. The true Christ is the preacher, the precursor of Freethought, who dreamed of a universal religion without dogmas, ostentation or clergy; the counterfeit is the purveyor of miracles. The true Christ is one who died for love of humanity; the counterfeit is the one the disciples were anxious to resurrect. The true Christ is he who accepted a drink from the woman of Samaria, sat at table with publicans and sinners, received Mary Magdalen and uplifted the woman taken in adultery; the counterfeit the weapon of fanatics and exterminator of heretics. The true

Christ lived in the open air in simple clothing; the counterfeit is enthroned in elaborate robes in sumptuous cathedrals. The true Christ imposed no dogma; the counterfeit is involved with creeds and sacraments.

In English the most influential of all the rationalist treatments was that of H. G. Wells (1866-1946) in *The Outline of History* (1920). This is an engagingly open, tolerant treatment.

> We shall tell what men have believed about Jesus of Nazareth, but him we shall treat as being what he appeared to be, a man, just as a painter must needs paint him as a man. The documents that testify to his acts and teachings we shall treat as ordinary human documents. If the light of divinity shine through our recital, we will neither help nor hinder it. . . . About Jesus we have to write not theology but history, and our concern is not with the spiritual and theological significance of his life, but with its effects upon the political and everyday life of men. (p. 356).

Wells regards the early narratives as accretions, and treats the miracles similarly. We are left 'with the figure of a being, very human, very earnest and passionate, capable of swift anger, and teaching a new and simple and profound doctrine — namely, the universal loving Fatherhood of God and the coming of the Kingdom of Heaven.' (p. 357)

PUBLIC-SCHOOL AND UNIVERSITY RELIGION

Before we leave the responses of the West there is one other phenomenon of the nineteenth and twentieth centuries to note. We may most readily illustrate it from Britain, where the class-structure has been particularly strong, and the majority of national leaders for a century and more have passed through the independent (or 'public') schools and the Oxford and Cambridge colleges, in which for much of the period chapel attendance was compulsory. The Jesus who appeared from chapel-religion was middle-class, at least by adoption; the masters and chaplains saw him in ways relevant to their clientèle. A Cambridge chaplain described him as 'a Cambridge man, and of course a Jesus man, and one of the

Son of Man

eight'; it was whimsically in character, a flagrant form of the culture-Protestantism of H. Richard Niebuhr's second group. Jesus was presented not as a supernatural figure, but as an example to follow. One of the favourite confirmation hymns, written by J. E. Bode (1816-76) ends

> O give me grace to follow,
> My Master and my Friend.

Another favourite, written by a headmaster, Frank Fletcher, conveys the mood well.

> O Son of Man, our hero strong and tender,
> Whose servants are the brave in all the earth,
> Our living sacrifice to Thee we render,
> Who sharest all our sorrows, all our mirth.
>
> O feet so strong to climb the path of duty,
> O lips divine that taught the words of truth,
> Kind eyes that marked the lilies in their beauty,
> And hearts that kindled at the zeal of youth.
>
> Lover of children, boyhood's inspiration,
> Of all mankind the Servant and the King:
> O Lord of joy and hope and consolation,
> To Thee our fears and joys and hopes we bring.
>
> Not in our failures only and our sadness
> We seek Thy presence, Comforter and Friend;
> O rich man's Guest, be with us in our gladness,
> O poor man's Mate, our lowliest tasks attend.

Even those 'valiant hearts' who gathered proudly, rank on rank, to war, were reminded that 'Christ, our Redeemer, passed the self-same way', as if there were a real parallel between Calvary and the Somme.

In the first part of this century there was a major attempt by a number of people, often with strong literary or historical interests, to present Jesus as he was historically. In England the most influential of these was probably T. R. Glover's *The Jesus of History*. Glover was an Ancient Historian, widely learned, and a mellifluous writer; in theology he was a somewhat spiky Baptist. Ironically, the book, which had such a wide influence within the Student Christian Movement in Britain, was originally presented as lectures in India in 1916. There was nothing unorthodox about Glover's book, although it came in for some criticism: it concentrated on one approach to Jesus, made historical sense of his life, and brought him to life for thousands of readers. In 1918 there appeared in novel form the anonymous *By an Unknown Disciple*, an attractively vivid retelling of the gospel-story; it ends on Mary's story of her experience of the risen Jesus in the garden, and the Unknown Disciple having an open-ended mystical experience. Middleton Murry, a literary critic of great sensibility, wrote *The Life of Jesus* in 1926. In his preface he said 'For much of my life has been spent in the effort to understand men of genius. And Jesus was above all else a man of genius. Of course there are many to whom he was above all a supernatural being – a God. I cannot share that belief because I do not know what it means.' But, as he went on to say, orthodoxy believes in the man as well as the God, and can well look at Jesus from that point of view. And Murry, while rationalizing the miraculous, was sensitive to spiritual values.

To these, among many others which might be mentioned, we may add two books by the great American pastor and preacher, Harry Emerson Fosdick. Fosdick, like Glover, was not unorthodox, but was anxious to bring his readers (and hearers) face to face with Jesus as he was. The earlier book, *The Manhood of the Master*, was written for American students and issued in Britain in 1914 by the Student Christian Movement Press. Fosdick describes the book as an endeavour to understand and appreciate the quality of Jesus' character, 'to see the Man Christ Jesus Himself as he lives in the pages of the gospels'. So, with daily readings for a week on each topic, he passes through the Master's Joy, Magnanimity, Indignation, Loyalty, Endurance, Sincerity, Self-Restraint, Fearlessness, Affection, Scale of Values and Spirit to his final section 'The Fulness of Christ'. His later book, thirty-five years after, *The Man from Nazareth*, begins from the insistence that Jesus was a real man and not a myth, and suggests how he appeared to the crowds, the scribes and Pharisees, the self-complacent, the religious and moral outcasts, women and children, the first disciples, the militant nationalists, and Jews with a worldwide outlook. The two books together give a persuasive picture of a historical person.

GANDHI

An interesting study of the impact of Jesus on a member of a different faith can be found in Mahatma Gandhi. Gandhi was and remained a Hindu. *The Bhagavad Gita* was his 'Bible', but he noted that his interpretation of *The Gita* had been criticized by orthodox scholars as being unduly influenced by the Sermon on the Mount. In his autobiography he called *The Gita* 'the supreme book for the knowledge of truth'. In 1925, speaking to Christian missionaries in India, he said that Hinduism filled his whole being, that in time of trouble he turned to *The Gita*, and found there a solace which he missed even from the Sermon on the Mount. Two years later he wrote in *Young India* (22 December 1927): 'I have not been able to see any difference between the Sermon on the Mount and the *Bhagavad Gita*. What the Sermon describes in a graphic manner, the *Bhagavad Gita* reduces to a scientific formula.... Today, supposing I was deprived of the Gita, and forgot all its contents but had a copy of the Sermon, I should derive the same joy from it as I do from the Gita.'

Gandhi's first confrontation with Christ and his teaching took place in London in 1888-9 when a Bible salesman persuaded him to read the Old and New Testaments. The Old Testament either bored or repelled him and he left off after the Pentateuch, but the Sermon on the Mount spoke to him from the first. It was (as he was later ashamed to confess) only in London that he first read (in Arnold's English version) *The Bhagavad Gita*: the two remained a united part of him. The next Christian work to influence him was Tolstoy's *The Kingdom of God is Within You*. This is an exposition of Christianity in terms of the Sermon on the Mount as a contemporary way of life involving revolutionary nonviolence. Third came contact with Trappists in South Africa, which deeply affected his own ashrams in their combination of the spiritual and practical, and the adoption of a day of silence. The next major Christian influence was Ruskin's *Unto This Last*, an exposition of Jesus' Parable of the Vineyard (*Matthew* 20.1-14). Gandhi interpreted the book to mean:

1. That the good of the individual is contained in the good of all.
2. That a lawyer's work has the same value as the barber's in as much as all have the right of earning their livelihood from their work.
3. That a life of labour, i.e. the life of the tiller of the soil and the handicraftsman, is the life worth living.

Finally there was his contact with individual Christians, above all C. F. Andrews, whom he met first in South Africa, whom he called 'simple like a child, upright as a die and shy to a degree', and whose personal devotion to Jesus Christ shone from him.

Stanley Jones, the American missionary, tells a good story of his first meeting with Gandhi. He asked him directly: 'How can we make Christianity naturalized in India, not a foreign thing, identified with a foreign government and a foreign people, but a part of the national life of India and contributing its power to India's uplift? What would you, as one of the Hindu leaders of India, tell me, a Christian, to do in order to make this possible?' Gandhi's answer was clear and direct: 'First, I would suggest that all of you Christians, missionaries and all, must begin to live more like Jesus Christ. Second, Practise your religion without adulterating it or toning it down. Third, Emphasize love and make it your working force, for love is central in Christianity. Fourth, Study the non-Christian religions more sympathetically to find the good that is in them in order to have a more sympathetic approach to the people.'

What impressed Gandhi about Jesus was primarily his teaching. He wrote, 'Jesus to me was one of the greatest teachers humanity has ever had. I believe that he belongs not solely to Christianity, but to the entire world, to all races and people.' On another occasion he described him as a supreme artist, because he saw and expressed Truth (*Young India*

13.11.24), putting Muhammad alongside him in this. But the Sermon on the Mount in particular was more precious to Gandhi than anything in the Qur'an, and he charged the Christians with negating it not merely by their behaviour but by their beliefs. It spoke to him of non-violence, forgiveness, simplicity of life. Alongside this he valued Jesus as a person, his life and his suffering. 'Though I cannot claim to be a Christian in the sectarian sense, the example of Jesus' suffering is a factor in the composition of my undying faith in non-violence which rules all my actions worldly and temporal. And I know there are hundreds of Christians who believe likewise. Jesus lived and died in vain if he did not teach us to regulate the whole of life by the eternal Law of Love.'

FROM THE FAR EAST

Just before the Second World War the Society for the Propagation of the Gospel published two small booklets, *The Life of Christ* (by Chinese Artists) and *Son of Man* (pictures and carvings by Indian, African and Chinese Artists). The titles both imply an emphasis on the humanity of Jesus, and the pictures portray him as human indeed (apart from an objectionably intrusive halo), not as a Jew of the early Roman Empire but rather as a Chinese (Indian or African) of indeterminate date but familiar artistic tradition. The Chinese scenes are set in the framework of a Chinese landscape, with Taoist symbolism (the Chinese version of *John* 1.1 is 'In the beginning was the Tao', and Jesus did declare himself the Way). So in many of the pictures we can see the interaction of conical mountains (the male principle, *yang*) and mist or cloud (the female, *yin*). Trees are marked with constellation holes representing union or harmony; this last is prominent in a number of pictures, the Baptism, the Feeding of the Five Thousand, the Entry into Jerusalem, Gethsemane. The swirling intertwining of tree-branches reveals the Tao. All these features are present in 'There was no room for them in the inn', with clear symbolism. So the interaction of the divine and the human is symbolically there, but the pictures, even when they represent miracles, are firmly and clearly human.

The problem, and the opportunity, are valuably discussed in Kosuke Koyama's *Waterbuffalo Theology* (London 1974). Koyama's concern is theological: it is the preachment of a Saviour. He tells how in his ministry in Thailand he used Luther's 'theology of assault' in presenting the story of Jesus and the Syro-Phoenician woman. The attempt was disastrous; he left his hearers with the feeling that the Christian faith depended on some kind of neurosis. So he looked again at the story and started from the woman's warmly human concern for her daughter. 'The beginning of faith must contain some universally valid and relevant factor which can erase religious, cultural and political demarcations. Otherwise, how can a Gentile woman sincerely come to Jesus Christ, an Israelite? Otherwise, how can the peoples of Hong Kong, Tokyo, Bangkok and Djakarta come to Jesus Christ, a Palestinian Jew?' (p. 75). The problem thus becomes acute, and he spells it out in an open letter to the already-mentioned long-dead missionary Dr Daniel McGilvary. To present Jesus to any people means presenting him as he was, in a particular culture at a particular point of history, that is as a Palestinian Jew of the late-Hellenistic, early-Roman period. But to do that may be an irrelevance; it may even be a stumbling-block (such as a British woman-anthropologist found in trying to contribute the story of Hamlet to a story-telling session in Africa: after all what should a widow do other than marry her deceased husband's brother as rapidly as possible?). To present a Jesus who is totally adapted to another culture is to take all the stuffing, all the flesh and blood out of him. Both offer what Koyama calls a 'dim' Christ, and he speculates whether the sharp edge of the love of Christ does not appear blurred in the Christian communities of northern Thailand, doubly blurred by the agents of West and East. Yet to remove any cultural context would be to present a theological abstraction; it would be (as Augustine might say) to present the Word, but not the Word made flesh. Koyama's tentative answer is in terms of a culinary metaphor, to find the points where Aristotelian pepper and Buddhist salt blend into an acceptable flavouring, and he does not pretend that it is easy. But this raises the question whether Aristotelian pepper is needed at all, though there must be something besides the Buddhist salt, perhaps Hellenistic-Judaic mustard. At all events, the reaction to Jesus in East Asia must arise from a confrontation with the historically human Jesus, presented in a way understandable within a different human culture. This conclusion is the more important, because it comes from one whose ultimate concern is with Jesus Christ as Lord. In *No Handle on the Cross* (1977) Koyama wrote that the way for Asia is through a crucified mind, guided by the One who died and who has risen.

We can trace something similar in Dr Kitamori's *Theology of the Pain of God* which appeared opportunely just after the end of the war in 1946. Dr Kitamori is a Japanese theologian deeply influenced by Luther. He is concerned with what he calls 'the love rooted in the pain of God'. He sees three orders of love in God: the natural love, pouring out immediately on his creation; the will to love those who are the objects of his wrath, so that he is in a sense fighting himself, and the love is at the same time a pain; and the love which embraces the fallen, which is rooted in and mediated by that pain. He links this with two Japanese principles – *tsutsumu*, which is involvement, natural love, but which is superficial without *tsuraso*, the basic principle of Japanese tragedy, suffering and death that another may live. In the Japanese film *Gate of Hell* a woman married to an easy-going husband attracts the love of a ruthless soldier, who swears to kill her husband and have her. She changes beds with her husband, dies herself, and thereby transforms both her husband and her murderer. It is a Buddhist film in inspiration, but profoundly Christian at the same time. And – this is the point – the love rooted in the pain of God is revealed supremely in the teaching, work and life of Jesus Christ. So, here again, we have a theologian whose concerns are with the divine, but claims that the divine truth can best be realized in the presentation of the human life of Jesus.

Among the hymns in *EACC Hymnal* a few come to terms with the human life of Jesus. Outstanding among these is a

Japanese hymn by Gumpei Yamamaro, who uses Jesus' profession as carpenter ('With His calloused working hands was salvation wrought') to bring the workers of Japan ('Toiler, trader, peasant, farmer') to face the challenge of Jesus (177). Another of this writer's hymns dwells vividly on the historic crucifixion, with the Roman soldiers, the priests, the crowd (122). D. T. Niles has a fine hymn similarly putting the birth into the firm historic setting of the census.

> On a day when men were counted,
> God became the Son of Man
> (177).

A Filipino hymn adapted by Niles is a dedication of the singers' lives to Christ Incarnate; here the human life is painted in the broadest outline, walking streets, knowing heat, shade, tiredness, rest, fighting with wrong, offering love and service.

AFRICA

Something similar has been happening in Africa. The movement was in one aspect negative. Bolaji Idowu has told how shocked he was by a Mission film, portraying Jesus as speaking with an American accent. He wondered why he was shocked, and realized that he was conditioned to imagining Jesus as speaking with an English accent! From that point Idowu pressed for an indigenous church, free from the suzerainty of Canterbury, Rome, or anywhere else irrelevant.

Idowu accepts the absolute Lordship of Jesus Christ. His answer might be simply put, that Jesus is Son of God, universal Lord who belongs in every land and nation; his answer is the triumphalist answer. A second answer was the effective rejection of the Christian claims as the shadow of western imperialism. Dr Azikiwe, the first President of independent Nigeria, while he was campaigning for independence, paralleled his political National Council of Nigeria and the Cameroons with a National Church of Nigeria and the Cameroons, proclaiming an African God, denouncing imported religions from

Canterbury, Rome and Mecca, and presenting a creed containing such clauses as 'I believe in the God of Africa.... I believe in Herbert Macauley, his son.' Herbert Macauley was a noted early campaigner for independence. That Azikiwe substituted him for Jesus suggests that his response to Jesus was as a purely human figure. I have never forgotten an evening in the University of Ibadan. For the first time the Dramatic Society presented three plays, written, produced and acted by students. Two of the three had to do with the rejection of Christianity for tribal religion. The sophisticated young authors did not believe in tribal religion and had no intention of going back to village life. They rejected Christianity as a human institution; they had not accepted Scientific Humanism or Marxism; they went to village religion, not because they believed in it, but because it was African. A Basuto student in Britain asked pointedly 'Is the identification of the Christian Church with social and political patterns not the fundamental cause of the complacency of the Western Churches today?' That is effectively to say that the Jesus accepted in the Western Churches, and too often exported to Africa, was a human product of their own society. This particular student went on shrewdly and searchingly 'Is the Africanization of the Church not a serious danger to be avoided at all costs?'

In general the answer has been to interpret Jesus in African terms. An outstanding example will be found in George Ademola's Presidential Address to the thirteenth assembly of the Christian Council of Nigeria at Kaduna in 1962. Dr Ademola was unfortunately ill, and his address was read in a truncated form. His theme was 'The Light of Christ as it Shines through his Church in Nigeria'. He started from the actual words and work of Jesus, and continually referred to his work of healing, to the feeding of the Five Thousand, to the call to the disciples, to the record catch of fish, to his teaching about Light, about Mammon, to the Upper Room and Gethsemane and the Calvary. Ademola's faith was rooted in the historical Jesus. But he was aware also of a problem:

> Here in Nigeria we cannot hope to convince our people of the relevance and immediacy of their need of Christ; if we preach

> Christ divorced from daily life. Our fishermen and our farmers, our clerks and shop assistants and bus conductors — and the thousands of youngsters leaving school who aspire to these and other occupations and find no openings for them — ask for Christ's Light to be shed on their own paths into the future. They need the assurance that Christ the Carpenter is aware of the difficulties faced by his fellow-craftsmen here and now. How do we hope to direct the rays of the Light of the World to guide their feet?

The words could have been spoken in any country, except that in Nigeria the work of farmer or carpenter is closer to that of their ancient Palestinian counterparts than is true in the spreading acres and mechanical workshops of the west. Ademola went on to interpret the message of Christ in terms of the normal activities of Nigerian life.

Dr S. U. Erivwo, one of the ablest young Nigerian Christian scholars, wrote an important article in *The Nigerian Christian* for February 1978 entitled 'The Jewishness of Jesus'. Unfortunately only the first part of this article has appeared. Dr Erivwo's thesis is, first, that the Christian takes Jesus as his example; second that Jesus was a Jew, living and dressing as a Jew, speaking Aramaic, and illustrating his teaching from his own contemporary culture; third, that much of this environment is alien and unfamiliar in an African context, and that for the African to embrace it is to make of him a split personality; fourth, that, equally, traditional culture uncritically used may not meld effectively with the Christian faith — Dr Erivwo is highly critical of such bodies as the Christian Ogboni Society (later the Reformed Ogboni Society) as being anything but Christian. It is a pity that, as in the best serial stories, we are left hanging on the words 'Having given so many examples of the wrong way to attempt to deepen our Christian roots, in our traditional culture, what is the right way to do it?' but one suspects that Dr Erivwo was going on to call, at least from the Christian teacher whom he was addressing, for a thorough understanding of the historic life of Jesus in its own context, a deep grasp of the essential aspects of his teaching and work, and a transfer of inessentials to the indigenous culture, leaving essentials intact.

In art the transformation was beginning to take place before the war. In the book *Son of Man* referred to earlier, three representations of Jesus from Africa stand out. One is an utterly wonderful, wholly African *Madonna and Child* by the black South African Ernest Macoba; the mask-like faces, slit eyes, flared nostrils, full lips form a powerful conception finely patterned. A painted panel by an anonymous artist shows *The Kiss of Judas*. Both figures are purely African; the figure of Christ is firm and upright; Judas stoops towards him, reaching out with full lips, his money bag in his hand. There is an impressive *Calvary* by Job Kekama, a pupil of Ernest Macoba. Here the figures of Mary and John are expressions of African faith, and there are African huts in the background. All three designs are marred somewhat by intrusive haloes, but otherwise are triumphally successful.

In 1956 the SPCK published *And Was Made Man*, a life of Jesus in pictures by students of the Makerere College Art School. K. M. Trowell in introducing it wrote: 'I do not think we shall fully preach Christianity in Africa until we too speak to men's eyes as well as to their ears, and tell the story of Christ in a language which all can understand. We can show Him not historically in foreign dress, but as a man amongst men as we know them here, for Christianity belongs to every race and time as is beyond all such considerations.' This is the work of students. It is not uniformly successful. Sometimes imagination has gone astray: in *The Transfiguration* Jesus is a neat black college student in white ducks and a blazer. Sometimes technique is inadequate to match the imagination. But the maquette of *The Burial of Christ*, as his stiff body is carried by four grieving disciples, is a minor masterpiece.

In Nigeria initiative was taken by a Roman Catholic missionary Father Carroll in encouraging local craftsmen to return to their indigenous skills and traditions and to place them at the service of the Church. Lamidi Fakeye, a brilliant craftsman, carved a series of panels for the doors of the Catholic chapel at the University of Ibadan, depicting the life of Jesus in a Nigerian setting; at the Annunciation, for example, Mary is discovered pounding yams, and Pilate is a typical Oba, a local chief or king. These doors compare very favourably with some garish, derivatively modernistic murals by a European artist within the same building; they are a masterwork by any standards. Nor was it only in the visual arts. At much the same time at Oye, among the Ekiti a nativity play was performed showing the nativity scenes in an Ekiti context.

Hans-Ruedi Weber and Bethuel Kiplayat have been fostering similar developments in East Africa. They secured the collaboration of the Tanzanian artist Elimo Njau for a Bible study workshop for artists in October 1978. Those who came included two from Ethiopia (including Gebre Kristos Desta, one of the best-known Ethiopian artists), four from Kenya, two each from Uganda, Tanzania, Madagascar and Zambia (including Emmanuel Nsama, director of the art school of the Christian Literature Centre in Mindolo). The whole concept, linking careful, thorough and informed Bible study to the African artists' portrayal of scenes in the African idiom, was something vitally new and important. There was, for example, a study in depth of the accounts of Jesus' Last Supper with his disciples, and a singling out of key dramatic gestures which led the artists to concentrate on the washing of feet, breaking of bread, and offering of wine.

LIBERATION THEOLOGY

By contrast with the theology which had been often preached to them by missionaries, the liberation theologians of Latin America in the second half of the twentieth century rediscovered a human revolutionary Jesus.

Gustavo Gutierrez may be taken as representative. In his influential book *A Theology of Liberation* he has little to say about Jesus until halfway through. He begins from a consideration of theology, first as wisdom or spirituality, and then as rational knowledge, but, without denying or eroding these other two functions, himself lays more stress on theology as critical reflection on historical praxis; for Latin America this means the historical praxis of liberation. Then follows an examination of the concepts of liberation and development, and particularly the change from *desarrollismo* ('developmentalism') or reformism to social revolution. Jesus is thus seen in the light of the present historical situation, and here he is introduced as liberator. 'In the Bible, Christ is presented as the one who brings us liberation. Christ the Savior liberates man from sin, which is the ultimate root of all disruption of friendship and of all injustice and oppression. Christ makes men truly free, that is to say, he enables man to live in communion with him; and this is the basis for all human brotherhood.' (p. 37)

Gutierrez's basic problem is 'What relation is there between salvation and the historical process of the liberation of man?' He claims that in our time social praxis is beginning to reach maturity; people are not content to be ruled by an élite, but want to share in political decisions. Human reason has become political reason. And in politics conflict cannot be avoided. Political action involves totality, radicalness and conflict; it involves the very meaning of Christianity. He goes on to examine, and reject, some traditional Church answers, the view that the Christian's political task lies in support of the Church (a political conservatism), and the view that it lies in an application of Christian principles within the old order (a political liberalism). Neither accepts a change to radically new social forms. From these emerged what he calls the distinction of planes (the analysis is Catholic and owes nothing to Luther), differentiating between the twofold mission of the Church, evangelization and the inspiration of the temporal sphere, and offering a similar differentiation between the office of priest and layman. But this model also ran into a crisis, a crisis of some ambiguity. Partly it arose because it became increasingly difficult to uphold the dichotomy. Partly there was the increasing recognition of secularization, of a worldly world — but no movement for withdrawal. The antitheses between natural and supernatural, temporal and spiritual, profane and sacred, were broken. A new unity, one single call to salvation, was being rediscovered, not metaphysically, but within history. The Latin American Church thus had to come to terms with the process of liberation in Latin America, and Gutierrez describes this at some length.

When he turns to the necessary theology to undergird the new movement he offers a Biblical theology based on the Creation story as the first salvific act, and on the Exodus, the liberation from Egypt.

Gutierrez's approach is thus theological. But it is doubtful whether the basis of his thought is Christological. Rather he faces the person of Jesus out of the careful but agonized working-out of his own historical situation. As we have noted, Jesus plays little part in this primary analysis. It is natural that there is some concentration on Jesus as a historic figure in a historic situation.

It will not do to overstate this. First, Gutierrez is a theologian; he believes in the Ultimate, and he believes that what one might call the permanent purposes of God are revealed in Jesus Christ. He uses the name Christ more than Jesus; he accepts the Pauline view of Christ's presence in creation, his pre-existence. Further, he declares that in Jesus we see the Incarnation of the Son of God. Christ is the temple of God. But he goes on to affirm that the Christian is likewise a temple of God, and that every man is a temple of God.

Gutierrez's primary stress is on the liberating action of Christ, 'made man in this history and not in a history marginal to the real life of man'. He rejects entirely the 'iconization' of the life of Jesus, the Jesus of hieratic, stereotyped gestures, all representing theological themes. 'To approach the man Jesus of Nazareth, in whom God was made flesh, to penetrate not only in his teaching, but also in his life, what it is that gives his word an immediate, concrete context, is a task which more and more needs to be undertaken.' (p. 226) Jesus was not apolitical; he died at the hands of the political authorities; he was near to the Zealots in their concern for liberation, far from them in the narrowness of their nationalism. Our love for Christ is shown in our love for our neighbour, and that, in hard concrete terms, means to participate in the struggle for the liberation of those oppressed by others. Christ is not a private individual; he is representative of all men. Gutierrez quotes with approbation a line from Cesar Vallejo's poem 'Los dados eternos': 'My God, if you had been a man, you would know how to be God.' To Gutierrez it is precisely because God has been a man that he does know how to be God. His equation is a subtle one, but in his vision the human face of Christ is foremost.

As a postscript to this examination of Gutierrez it is useful to note the remarkable movement to non-violent action taking place in Latin American Catholicism. Sometimes it has arisen out of sheer helplessness on the part of the oppressed. They went to non-violent action simply because the oppressors had all the arms. But then they turned to their Bibles and found that their actions were in accord with the New Testament as violent protest would not have been. Except perhaps for Dom Helder Camara, the movement came originally from the grassroots. But it has increasingly had episcopal support, and a meeting of Latin American bishops at Bogota in 1978 made a remarkable statement which included these words: 'Persevering nonviolent action is nourished by the conviction of the absolute value of the human being. To this conviction Christian faith brings an important contribution. We believe in the person and the works of Jesus, the nonviolent activist *par excellence*.' That is more simplistic than Gutierrez, and it undoubtedly shows the human face of Jesus.

Black theology has taken a similar stand. There is some ambiguity. Sabelo Ntwasa has said that Black theology calls the Black churchmen to start defining the Christ-event for themselves. He sees Christ as a fighting God not a passive God. In one sense this is to reject the historic Christ, to redefine him as the God of the guerrillas; in another sense it is to see him in a new incarnation, as an African freedom-fighter. James Cone, a far profounder theologian, insists on the necessity of starting from the historic Jesus. In an exceptionally interesting paper in *The Nigerian Christian* for December 1977 Dr E. B. Gbonigi exalted the revolutionary Jesus, seeing him as an angry young man in face of Roman violence and oppression, but himself committed to non-violence, the inspiration of Mahatma Gandhi, and Howard Thurman and Martin Luther King, the one who is born to set his people free, both in their individual lives and — in the end, through changing life-style — socially and politically.

One of the most remarkable recent statements of this last view comes from Juan Mateos, a Spanish Jesuit scholar teaching at the Oriental Pontifical Institute in Rome. It is taken from a new Spanish edition of the New Testament, and appeared in English in *Sojourners* for July 1977. It is learned, and deeply rooted in the New Testament account of the historical Jesus. His call was to liberation, without violence, into the new human community. 'Jesus's final word was that we should live and die as he had lived and died, creating the new society of disciples and standing up against the evil in the world. Since this was beyond human strength, he gave us his own life. . . . The cross of Jesus is the radical condemnation of an unjust world. You have to stay with the one crucified on it or stand with the crucifiers. There is no middle way.'

BIBLIOGRAPHY

Islam
Some use is made of passages from Islamic sources in R. Hofmann *Das Leben Jesu nach den Apocryphen* (Leipzig 1851). The material from the Qur'an is admirably treated in Geoffrey Parrinder *Jesus in the Qur'an* (London 1965 rep. 1976).

Francis
The literature is immense. The primary sources are discussed in J. R. H. Moorman *The Sources for the Life of S. Francis of Assisi* (Manchester 1940). P. Sabatier *Vie de S. François* (1893) is still standard. Father Cuthbert *S. Francis of Assisi* (London 1912) is as sound as any; G. K. Chesterton *St Francis of Assisi* (London 1923) is factually unreliable but full of brilliant insights. J. R. H. Moorman *St Francis of Assisi* (London 1950) is very good in a small compass. The standard work on Giotto is by Carlo Carrà (ET 1925). Unfortunately we lack a major study in English. But see J. White *Italian Art and Architecture 1250-1400* (London 1966). The influence of Francis is accepted in a small book *Giotto* by Camillo Semenzato (ET London 1964). The Arena chapel is presented in colour in R. Salvini *Giotto: Cappella degli Scrovegni* (Florence 1970).

Mysticism
See notes on the previous chapter.

Renaissance Humanism
The books are legion. The art is conveniently discussed in P. and L. Murray *The Art of the Renaissance* (London 1963) and L. Murray *The High Renaissance* (London 1967). M. Salinger *Michelangelo: The Last Judgment* (London n.d.) is beautifully illustrated. Among more general books see A. Chastel *The Age of Humanism 1480-1530* (London 1963). Rembrandt is best studied through pictures in O. S. Rachleff *Rembrandt's Life of Christ* (New York n.d.). There is an important theological study in W. A. Visser 't Hooft *Rembrandt and the Gospel* (London 1978).

Unitarianism
I have largely followed the excellent article by J. Estlin Carpenter in Hastings *ERE*. The best account of the Deists known to me is still that in Sir Leslie Stephen's *English Thought in the Eighteenth Century* (London 1876). For Channing see J. W. Chadwick *William Ellery Channing* (Boston 1903).

Rationalism
The books are indicated in the text.

Public School and University Religion
So here.

Gandhi
The basic book is his *An Autobiography or the Story of My Experiments with Truth* (Ahmedabad 1945). See also C. F. Andrews (ed.) *Mahatma Gandhi: His Own Story* (London 1930). The lives of Gandhi in English are mostly not very good. For Gandhi and Christ see E. Stanley Jones *Mahatma Gandhi: An Interpretation* (London 1948); also Donald Groom 'Gandhi and Christianity' in D. Collins and C. Hodgetts (eds) *Gandhi* (London n.d.).

From the Far East
This is only a small indication of what might be said: the books I have used directly appear in the text.

Africa
E. B. Idowu *Towards an Indigenous Church* (London and Ibadan 1965). Michael Marioghae and I explored some of the issues in *Nigeria under*

the Cross (London 1965). Dr Ademola's address is taken from *Kaduna 1962* (n.p. n.d., probably Ibadan 1962). Hans-Ruedi Weber wrote an account of his workshop in the WCC *Education Newsletter* no 3 (1978) 10-11.

Liberation theology
See G. Gutierrez *A Theology of Liberation* (ET London 1974). For Black theology Basil Moore (ed.) *Black Theology* (London 1973). These are of course only a representative selection.

8
Summing-Up

DOGMA AND EXPERIENCE

To give a historical account of different ages and areas which have emphasized the divinity or humanity of Jesus is simply to record facts. To interpret these facts is to become dangerously subjective. Obviously, a Christian is far more likely to regard Jesus as divine than are any others. Yet the likelihood is relative not absolute. There have been plenty within the churches to take a different view. The Arians were Christians; and there have been plenty of Unitarians and Quakers, for instance, with a deep devotion to the figure of Jesus, who were at the same time unwilling to call him God. But apart from the sects there has been a variety of views within what one might call the central organizations of the Church. As we look at the broad historical movements we can see some ages, notably those we call the Dark and Middle Ages, which have seemed to demand a revealed divinity, others to which the appeal of an ideal human has been more magnetic. This is broadly true of post-Renaissance Europe. Within these longer periods we can trace the pendulum swinging. Today the emphasis is on the human Jesus. In the 1970s a mild sensation was caused in Britain by a book called *The Myth of God Incarnate*. It was a curious episode, for there was nothing very new in the book, nothing which had not been said more incisively and clearly by rationalists over the previous century. The sensation arose partly because it is an age for sensationalism, though theological controversy could hit the headlines equally in the less sophisticated world of a century before. It was partly that this was written by Christian believers, and that the contributors included two of the leading theological professors in the country. At many stages in church history they would have been excommunicated. But even apart from this more blatant challenge there are many worshippers in the pews who either do not believe in the divinity of Jesus, or do not believe in it as it was understood at Nicaea or Chalcedon. If the Middle Ages was the Age of Faith, ours is in some ways the Age of Unfaith. If they were predisposed to believe in divinity, we are predisposed not to do so. Our predisposition is not necessarily better or truer, and it may not last into the twenty-first century.

Something similar seems to have happened in the mission field. The missionaries went out from a culture in which religion had ceased to be equated with the whole of life into cultures where religion and life were coextensive. They regarded the religions they encountered as superstitious, which they often were, though they sometimes dismissed them too cavalierly. They confronted what they regarded as false religions with what they regarded as the true religion. But it had to be presented as a religion, with overwhelming, overriding, exclusive claims. The irony was that the missionaries, heroically as they gave themselves to the often slow work of conversion in Asia and Africa, in some ways found more satisfaction than they could have done at home, precisely because their message could be more uncompromising. But as Africans and Asians came to share in western education and to seek an independent political order, if they did not renounce Christianity as a symbol of western imperialism they began to look more closely at the human life of Jesus and to come to terms with him as a person.

But there is something else which needs to be said. While it is true that a Christian is far more likely to regard Jesus as divine than are any others, this may be a misleading way of putting it. It is possible to say that he regards Jesus as divine because he is a Christian. It is also possible that he is a Christian because he regards Jesus as divine. This is not to say that he is right to do so, only that some are brought up Christians, some achieve Christianity (so to say), and some (not many these days) have Christianity thrust upon them, and even those who are brought up Christians, are supposed to accord a thorough scrutiny to their inherited beliefs before becoming full church members. To put it differently, there are probably more enthusiasts for cricket among the members of cricket clubs than among others, but it would be erroneous to suppose that they were enthusiasts because they were club-members, not the other way round.

Similarly, rationalists and Muslims are less likely to accept the divinity of Jesus than others. With most Muslims it is probably true to say that they have first accepted Islam, and from that predetermined standpoint cannot accept the divinity of Jesus; which is not to say that they are wrong. The western rationalists of the late-nineteenth and early-twentieth centuries in general had faced and rejected the claims of Christianity. In so far as the names 'rationalist' and 'free-thinker' connote the use of reason and openness of thought, this was the approach they brought with them; in so far as they connote an anti-religious conclusion, this was the decided result of their confrontation with Jesus. The older freethinkers, who on the whole showed more clarity and charity than their Christian opponents, were often in revolt against a corrupt Church. Foote and Wheeler called their book *Crimes of Christianity*. One of Bradlaugh's *Doubts in Dialogue*, written in 1884, ends, 'Is it not cant and hypocrisy to preach peace and goodwill on Christmas day when your navy and army at home and in India cost more than £45,000,000 a year and you in Britain alone have spent in war during the last 20 years more than £2,000,000,000?' Often, directly or indirectly, they challenged the churches in the name of Christ. They took the teaching of Jesus, the humanity of Jesus, more seriously than many churchmen.

This leads to one caveat. I have heard free-thinkers say, 'Of course Jesus is the greatest man who ever lived.' This is an extravagant statement, perhaps made as some kind of concession to the opinion of others. It is surely difficult to believe at one and the same time that Jesus is the greatest man who ever lived and that he was totally deluded about the things he held as central, the existence of a Father-God, the care of that God for his world, the call to live a life of love as a response to and reflection of the love of God to us, and the relationship of God to himself.

Of course the capacity of mankind to make idols in our own image and project them on the infinite is unlimited. The Jesus of John Vorster and the Jesus of Nelson Mandela might be hard to recognize as the same person. The hieratic figure of the Byzantines and the Balliol man of nineteenth-century upper-crust religion in Britain are not easy to identify with one another. Usually in such cases we find that, like Mark Pattison's charladies, the disputants are arguing from different premises. But there is a test; it is to bring the image alongside the historic Jesus as he may be discerned through the gospels. Within the Christian Church there have traditionally been three seats of authority. One has been the Bible, one the Church, and one the Inner Light. None is infallible. The Bible was written by human agents, and contains internal contradictions. The Church has done things of which it is now ashamed. The light within us may be a will o' the wisp, as with the young man who heard the Holy Spirit tell him to go shopping, only to find that it was early-closing day. There is for the Christian one ultimate authority — Jesus Christ.

The experience of two thousand years of Christianity has been that it is impossible to do justice to Jesus Christ without accepting his full humanity, and yet at the same time that it is impossible to do justice to Jesus Christ and hold that he was a mere human, executed at the age of 33, dead and buried, and that was the end of him. In some of the studies we have made where there is an emphasis on the humanity or the divinity it is an emphasis merely. Any Byzantine would have insisted that Jesus was fully man, but, existentially, the dominating thought of him was as a divine figure. Francis of Assisi or Rembrandt would have insisted that Jesus was the son of God, but, existentially, they thought of him in his humanity. The two views which were ruled out in Christian experience were Docetism on the one hand and on the other either atheism or a denial that Jesus stood in some special relationship to God. If Jesus were mere man or mere myth there would have been no church. This is what Rudolf Otto called the *mysterium tremendum atque fascinans* which he saw as the heart of all religion. Jesus is both awesome and winsome — and mysterious.

THE EVANGELICALS

No group of Christians held a juster balance than the evangelical movement of the latter part of the eighteenth century in Britain. There were two main groups, the Wesleyans and the Evangelicals properly so-called, who tended to a moderate Calvinism. They had their theological differences, but both groups were centred on the person of Jesus. There is a touching story of an interview between Charles Simeon (1759-1836), the brilliant young leader of the Evangelical Revival, and John Wesley (1703-91). The date was 20 December 1784, so that Wesley was over 80, and Simeon a mere 25. But Simeon, never personally arrogant, was confident in his own faith, and suspicious of Wesley's Arminianism, with its belief in free will (against Calvin's predestinarianism) and that Christ died for all (and not just for the elect). A verse of the day put the matter with grotesque precision:

> I'd rather be a Calvinist
> And wear a smiling face
> Than for to be a Methodist
> And always fall from grace.

And now for the confrontation:

> A young minister, about three or four years after he was ordained, had an opportunity of conversing familiarly with the great and venerable leader of the Arminians in this kingdom, and, wishing to improve the occasion, he addressed him nearly in the following words: 'Sir, I understand that you are called an Arminian; and I have been sometimes called a Calvinist; and therefore I suppose we are to draw daggers. But before I consent to begin the combat, with your permission I will ask you a few questions.' Permission being very readily and kindly granted, the young minister proceeded to ask; 'Pray, Sir, do you feel yourself a depraved creature, so depraved that you would never have thought of turning to God, if God had not first put it into your heart?' 'Yes,' says the veteran, 'I do indeed.' 'And do you utterly despair of recommending yourself to God by anything you can do; and look for salvation solely through the blood and righteousness of Christ?'

'Yes, solely through Christ.' 'But, Sir, supposing you were at first saved by Christ, are you not somehow or other to save yourself afterwards by your own works?' 'No, I must be saved by Christ from first to last.' 'Allowing, then, that you were first turned by the grace of God, are you not in some way or other to keep yourself by your own power?' 'No.' 'What then, are you to be upheld every hour and every moment by God, as much as an infant in its mother's arms?' 'Yes, altogether.' 'And is all your hope in the grace and mercy of God to preserve you unto His heavenly kingdom?' 'Yes, I have no hope but in Him.' 'Then, Sir, with your leave I will put up my dagger again; for this is all my Calvinism; this is my election, my justification by faith, my final perseverance: it is in substance all that I hold, and as I hold it; and therefore, if you please, instead of searching out terms and phrases to be a ground of contention between us, we will cordially unite in those things wherein we agree.'

It is a conversation which does credit to them both; Wesley in his *Journal* pays tribute to the younger man's earnestness and fervour of spirit.

The Wesleyans and Evangelicals were alike in rebellion against an indifferent church, against clergy arraigned, as they were by the Reverend Dr William Luke Phillips, for 'Immoral Conduct; Professional Ignorance; inattention to Duty; and lastly, attachment to the World', against pluralism and absenteeism, against political appointments and jobbery in the church, against what Gibbon called 'the fat slumbers of the Church'. They were against the corruptions of the day, the drinking, gambling, prize-fighting, bull-baiting, coarseness, violence and whoring of all classes ('Tryed one woman', wrote the Reverend John Thomlinson in his diary for April 1718, 'and did not like her.') They were against the cool, rationalistic, latitudinarian deism which was unable to meet the needs of the labourers in the villages, of the rootless drifters to the towns, of the sprawling suburbs of East London, of the mining villages and emergent industrial cities. Montesquieu in about 1730 wrote: 'There is no religion in England. If anyone mentions religion people begin to laugh.' The answer given by the rebels was a return to Jesus Christ.

Summing-Up

John Wesley was a son of the Rectory, though his grandparents had been Dissenters. His father, a High-Churchman, had a personal and individual faith and an intense belief in Christ as Saviour. His dying words to John might almost have been spoken by George Fox: 'The inward witness, son, the inward witness, that is the proof, the strongest proof of Christianity.' John was dreadfully earnest. 'I profess, sweetheart', said his father to his mother, 'I think our Jack would not attend to the most pressing necessities of nature unless he could give a reason for it.' At Oxford, with his brother Charles, he formed 'the Holy Club', a society of undoubtedly good works, but not without some priggishness. What changed him was contact with the Moravians. It was their missionary zeal which sent him out to Georgia. Three days after his arrival in America Pastor Spangenburg asked him, 'Do you know yourself?' Wesley was taken aback. The pastor went on, 'Do you know Jesus Christ?' 'I know He is the Saviour of the world.' 'True, but do you know He has saved you?' 'I hope He has died to save me.' Spangenburg was not satisfied with the answers, and went on, 'Do you know yourself?' Wesley answered, 'I do', but he did not, and he knew it.

He plunged into an incessant round of well-disciplined activity, but instead of being, as he hoped, preacher of the gospel to the Indians, he found himself parish priest to the settlers, and his period there, though not a failure, was not a success. After his return he wrote in his *Journal* (29.1.1738) 'I went to America to convert the Indians; but O! who shall convert me? Who, what is he that will deliver me from the evil heart of unbelief? I have a fair summer religion.' He had begun to know himself. A Moravian named Peter Böhler helped him on the road to faith, saying, 'Preach faith till you have it; and then because you have it, you will preach faith.' Then on 24 May, 1738 listening to Luther's Preface to *Romans*, 'I felt my heart strangely warmed. I felt I did trust in Christ, Christ alone, for salvation.' From there he did not look back. Over the next 52 years he journeyed 225,000 miles on horseback (reading as he went) or by chaise, wrote thousands of letters, and preached more than 40,000 sermons, sometimes to very large congregations, those in the London area being estimated at up to 20,000.

Wesley preached Jesus. He preached his teaching: witness the thirteen discourses on the Sermon on the Mount. He preached him as Lord. He preached his birth, life and death, his rising and his expected return.

> The person by whom God will judge the world, is His only-begotten Son, whose 'goings forth are from everlasting'; 'who is God over all, blessed for ever.' Unto Him, being 'the outbeaming of His Father's glory, the express image of His person' (*Heb.* i.3), the Father 'hath committed all judgement, because He is the Son of Man' (*John* v.22, 27); because, though He was 'in the form of God, and thought it not robbery to be equal with God, yet He emptied Himself, taking upon Him the form of a servant, being made in the likeness of men' (*Phil.* ii.6, 7); yea, because 'being formed in fashion as a man, He humbled Himself' yet farther, 'becoming obedient unto death, even the death of the cross Wherefore God hath highly exalted Him,' even in His human nature, and 'ordained Him,' as Man, to try the children of men, 'to be the Judge both of the quick and the dead'; both of those who shall be found alive at His coming, and of those who were before gathered to their fathers.   (*Standard Sermons* XLVIII)

Jesus is first God, then Man, and, as Man, Judge. Much of Wesley's belief about the person of Jesus is in that passage.

John's younger brother Charles was with him almost to the last, an attractive personality, more volatile than John, one who had been through his own conversion experience, struck by some words in Luther's *Commentary on Galatians* from which he learned to apply the words 'the Son of God who loved *me* and gave himself for *me*' (*Gal.* 2.20) to himself. Charles Wesley became one of the two greatest of all English hymn-writers, the other being Isaac Watts. His hymns, varied and ingenious in rhythm, strong in structure and rhyme, are a theological education. Bernard Manning said of the Methodist book: 'There is the solid structure of historic dogma; there is the passionate thrill of present experience; and there is the glory of a mystic sunlight coming directly from another world.' Charles's hymns are rooted in Jesus. Of the fraction of his output still preserved in *The Methodist Hymnbook* – not more than 4 per cent of the whole — thirty actually begin with the word 'Jesus', and four more with 'Christ'. The birth is there; in one familiar hymn the words have been modified from Wesley's original:

> Hark how all the welkin rings,
> 'Glory to the King of Kings,
> 'Peace on Earth, and Mercy mild,
> 'God and Sinners reconcil'd!
>
> Joyful all ye Nations, rise,
> Join the Triumph of the Skies,
> Universal Nature say,
> 'Christ the Lord is born to-day!

It is characteristic of him that, having greeted 'Jesus, our *Immanuel* here', he moves both to high theology and to personal prayer:

> *Adam's* likeness, Lord, efface,
> Stamp Thy image in its place,
> Second *Adam* from above,
> Reinstate us in Thy love.

Others, less familiar, show Wesley's riches of language:

> Stupendous height of heavenly love,
>   Of pitying tenderness Divine;
> It brought the Saviour from above,
>   It caused the springing day to shine;
> The Sun of Righteousness to appear,
> And gild our gloomy hemisphere.

or the magic use of the strong Latin word in

> Let earth and heaven combine,
>   Angels and men agree,
> To praise in songs Divine
>   Th'incarnate Deity,
> Our God contracted to a span,
> Incomprehensibly made man.

In 'Glory be to God on high' the thought

> See th' eternal Son of God
> A mortal son of man

moves to

> Jesus is our brother now,
> And God is all our own!

Other hymns show Jesus at work.

> O Thou, whom once they flock'd to hear,
>   Thy words to hear, Thy power to feel;
> Suffer the sinners to draw near,
>   And graciously receive us still.
>
> They that be whole, Thyself hast said,
>   No need of a physician have:
> But I am sick, and want Thine aid,
>   And want Thine utmost power to save.

Or again, in 'Jesus, Thy far-extended fame':

> Sinners of old Thou didst receive,
>   With comfortable words, and kind,
> Their sorrows cheer, their wants relieve,
>   Heal the diseased, and cure the blind.

Wesley in fact characteristically wrote short hymns on many scriptural passages. Of these 2,349 arise from a systematic exploration of the gospels, and nearly 700 more cover *Acts*.

A large number of his hymns speak of Jesus' sufferings and death. Wesley did not here achieve anything to match Watts:

> When I survey the wondrous Cross
> Where the young Prince of Glory died.

But in Wesley's hymns of the Passion we see above all that he has learned the lesson pointed by Luther. Here is a strongly personal sentiment matched curiously to an almost skittish verse-form:

> O JESUS, my Hope,
> For me offer'd up,
> Who with clamour pursued Thee to *Calvary's* top,

> The blood I have shed,
> For me let it plead,
> And declare, Thou hast died in Thy murderer's stead.

But if his Passion hymns are less memorable than some he celebrates the Resurrection unforgettably.

> Love's redeeming work is done,
> Fought the fight, the battle won:
> Lo! our Sun's eclipse is o'er;
> Lo! He sets in blood no more.

He follows scripture in seeing Jesus as presently exalted.

> Jesus the Saviour reigns,
> The God of truth and love;
> When He had purged our stains,
> He took His seat above.

The same hymn looks to his future appearance as Judge. This is more familiarly celebrated in 'Lo! He comes with clouds descending' where the one who comes is the true Messiah, the crucified Christ still bearing the tokens of his Passion on his 'dazzling body', and is at the same time addressed as 'JAH, JEHOVAH'.

Charles Wesley wrote hymns for all manner of occasions. There is one for a child cutting his teeth. Another is for the conversion of a prostitute. Another is for criminals being led to execution:

> Because Thou hangedst on a tree,
> And didst Thyself expire for me,
> Me and my dying mates receive,
> And bid our souls for ever live!

He wrote for children and young men and colliers. An extended quotation — though still only a third of the whole — from one of his best hymns will show his methods.

> O for a thousand tongues to sing
>   My dear Redeemer's Praise!
> The Glories of my God and King,
>   The triumphs of His grace.

> My gracious Master, and my God,
>   Assist me to proclaim,
> To spread through all the earth abroad
>   The honours of Thy Name.
>
> Jesus, the name that charms our fears,
>   That bids our sorrows cease;
> 'Tis music in the sinner's ears,
>   'Tis life, and health, and peace!
>
> He breaks the power of cancell'd sin,
>   He sets the prisoner free;
> His blood can make the foulest clean,
>   His blood avail'd for me.
>
> He speaks; and listening to His voice,
>   New life the dead receive,
> The mournful, broken hearts rejoice,
>   The Humble Poor *believe*.
>
> Hear Him, ye deaf; His praise, ye dumb,
>   Your loosen'd tongues employ;
> Ye blind, behold your Savior come;
>   And leap, ye lame, for Joy.

Charles Wesley's hymns are centred on Jesus, and celebrate his 'New, Best Name of Love'. That name is for him the link, the essential link, between the divine and human. In 'Wrestling Jacob' he wrestles with the unknown Traveller, demanding to know his name, and finds that it is Love, and then, and only then, knows him for Jesus. He sees Jesus always as he was on earth: those six verses are packed with allusions. He sees him firmly and clearly as God, and makes no bones about it, using no ambiguous terms or half-claims. And he always sees Jesus, God and man, existentially, in direct relation to himself, and so to any other man who will look with the eye of faith.

As a third example we may look at one who became a moderate Calvinist, John Newton (1725-1807). The Wesleys were brought up by devout parents. Newton had a pious mother, but she died while he was young. His father was a tough sea-captain. John's story reads like a schoolboy romance.

Summing-Up 225

He acquired a hostile stepmother, was taught by a brutal schoolmaster, went into business but was bored, went to sea, found a job managing a slave-plantation in Jamaica, came home, fell in love, was rebuffed, was pressganged, deserted, was flogged, became a godless blasphemer, deliberate and aggressive, became the servant of a slave-trader and his jealous African mistress on the Guinea Coast. He had nothing except his love for Polly Catlett; that sustained him. Eventually he was rescued, but had a year's further adventures, including being lost among mangrove swamps, narrowly escaping drowning, facing a hurricane, nearly starving, almost being thrown overboard as a Jonah. His life was immoral and unprincipled. His blasphemies grew ever more inventive. But on this voyage he idly picked up a copy of *The Imitation of Christ* and read the words: 'every work, and word, and thought, ought to be so ordered, as if it were to be our Last; and we instantly to die, and render an Account of it.' The hurricane burst on them, the boat sprang multiple leaks, Newton worked at the pumps for nine hours, had one hour's rest, then took the helm for eleven hours. He found himself saying 'If this will not do, the Lord have mercy upon us.' The words he had read and said remained with him. He stopped blaspheming. He began to read the New Testament. Words of Jesus struck home to him: 'If ye then, being evil, know how to give good gifts unto your children; how much more shall your heavenly Father give the Holy Spirit to them that ask him?' (*Luke* 11.13). They were rescued. He turned further to the story of Jesus. 'I stood in need of an almighty Saviour, and such an one I found described in the New Testament.' Back at sea he was done with blasphemy, but suffered still from 'black declensions' into loose living. But Polly now gave him grounds for hope, and on 12 February 1750 they were married.

Newton was now himself a captain, engaged in the slave-trade. He had some compassion on the slaves, but did not at this stage question the trade itself. Business came first. But Jesus Christ was meaning more to him, and he was becoming open to the arguments of the abolitionists. Then he had a fit, and never sailed again. He worked for a year or two as a Tide

Surveyor at Liverpool, but felt an increasing pull to the Christian ministry. Whitefield's preaching moved him. An old sailor named Alexander Clunie told him bluntly that he must declare openly what God had done for his soul. He wrote in his diary, 'If notwithstanding all my vileness I am made free from sin by the spirit of Life in Jesus Christ, what a wonderful instance am I, both of the riches and the freedom of Grace.' His lack of formal education was against him, but eventually, with the patronage of Lord Dartmouth, he became curate of Olney in Buckinghamshire. In his *Address to the Inhabitants of Olney* he spoke of his calling from God: 'He has placed me amongst you, that if I only pass you in the street, you may have a proof before your eyes of His gracious declaration that *all manner of sin and blasphemy shall be forgiven to men for the Son of man's sake.*' His preaching, nervous at first, was always Christ-centred. He wrote to John Wesley, 'I can think of but two things worth asking for, either to publish his grace and salvation here upon earth, or to quit the earth for good, and escape to heaven.' (He was commonsensical about preaching: 'I spoke near an hour and perhaps should have been shorter if I had had more to say'; 'Over-long sermons break in upon family concerns, and often call off the thoughts from the sermon to the pudding at home, which is in danger of being over-boiled.') Like all the evangelicals, he was charged with 'enthusiasm' and 'preaching people mad'.

His marriage was one of unalloyed happiness for forty years until Polly's last illness. She was herself deeply committed to Christ. Their only fear was that they might love one another too much. 'I am Husband-sick. . . . I worship My Golden Image', Polly wrote, and Newton responded, 'No time in your absence passes so pleasantly as when I am thinking of you, writing to you or hearing from you. I mean with the proper limitation. Dear as you are to my heart, you were not, you could not be, crucified for me. Nor do I live & move and have my Being in you but in Jesus. . . . May he be our supreme Lord, our Chief Beloved — and may his grace teach us to love each other in him, and then we shall not exceed.'

At Olney Newton was joined by the morbid, introspective

Summing-Up

poet William Cowper. Newton caught him up in a whirl of evangelical activity. Sometimes he called on Cowper to lead prayer or witness to his faith. It was agony for Cowper; he would be trembling for literally hours beforehand. Yet when the words came, they came with a mighty sincerity. Those listening felt that Cowper was wholly absorbed by the redemptive love of the Jesus of whom he spoke, and indeed that that Jesus was present with them. Newton and Cowper between them enriched their prayer-meetings with the little volume of *Olney Hymns*. Here Newton offered his testimony to Jesus in language which draws on the New Testament images, uses the orders or offices of the work of Christ, but is at the same time deeply personal.

> JESUS! my Shepherd, Husband, Friend,
> My Prophet, Priest and King;
> My LORD, my Life, my Way, my End,
> Accept the praise I bring.

Jesus was for Newton an immediate, warm, human presence and the ultimate divine power.

In 1780 Newton moved to St Mary Woolnoth in London. There William Wilberforce came to see him, a young man of large fortune, immense political promise, pietistic upbringing, followed by social conformity. Wilberforce was oppressed by the sense that something was lacking in his life. He had been led to read Philip Doddridge's *The Rise and Progress of Religion in the Soul*, and as a result had turned to reread the New Testament. His spiritual journey at this point, from a totally different background, curiously paralleled Newton's own. He told Newton that one sentence had leaped from the page at him. It was the very same which had struck Newton, 'If ye then, being evil, know how to give good gifts unto your children; how much more shall your heavenly Father give the Holy Spirit to them that ask him?' Two things ensued. First, Newton used his own experience to help Wilberforce and turned him from a depressed obsession with his own imperfections to a deep and more personal religion based on positive thanksgiving for grace. Second, Newton gave him advice which for his day was astonishing. He told Wilberforce that he was to serve Christ where he was, in politics; at the same time in politics he was to serve Christ. So was laid the foundation for the social and political work of the Evangelicals through the Clapham Sect. This had repercussions back on Newton, for he became strong in his opposition to the slave-trade, and his first-hand evidence was of prime importance to the movement.

A little before his death Newton said to a visitor: 'My memory is nearly gone; but I remember two things: that I am a great sinner, and that Christ is a great saviour.'

Many of the Evangelicals went through periods of unhealthy introspection. Their faith saved them from that, as it saved them from wildness and worldliness (of the wrong sort). Their theological understanding of the work of Jesus was not shared by everyone in their own day, and would not be today. Five things they brought. First, for Christians their centrality was right; Jesus Christ was plumb at the centre of their faith. Second, the Jesus Christ they knew was human; they saw him as a friend. He was divine; they revered him as God. Words tell us somewhat of those who use them. They called him Jesus more often than Christ, as did those who believed in him as Son of Man; they called him Lord more often than Master, as did those who believed in him as a Son of God. More than any other group in Christian history they held the balance and did justice to the unity. Third, in their sense of what Jesus had done for them they were radiant with joy, with gaiety ('Well, Henry,' said Wilberforce to Thornton after the Abolition of the Slave-Trade, 'what shall we abolish next?') In this they were in the company of Jesus. Fourth their gratitude was not and could not be self-satisfied and self-centred. They had been saved -- the word has been debased by casual religious usage — but for a man like Newton it was exactly true -- and their response was to seek to save others. They had accepted the love of Jesus, and they found that love reaching out through them. Fifth — and this has not always been true of their successors — they saw Jesus as transforming society as well as individual lives. It was not just the anti-slavery movement. Robert Raikes of Gloucester (1736-1811) was a newspaper proprietor, aware of the power of the media, and, as a Christian, using it to reform abuses. He campaigned for prison reform, as did John Howard and Elizabeth Fry, attacking insanitary and promiscuous conditions, separating debtors from other prisoners, helping the destitute to a bearable life. But this was treating symptoms and not causes. Raikes thought the causes of crime were unemployment (the drift to the towns without retraining) and ignorance. The Sunday School Movement began as a counter to this last. Wesley intervened against electoral corruption, organized the systematic (not casually generous) distribution of food, clothing and money to the destitute, instituted interest-free loans to the needy, arranged relief-work for the unemployed, including clothes-making for unemployed women, established medical dispensaries. The Jesus Christ who was the Lord of all was the Lord of their corporate life.

CONCLUSION

It is difficult to conclude a story which is not yet concluded. The day may come when the Christian religion is dead and the name of Jesus forgotten, but it has not come yet. Indeed there are signs that Christians are rejecting a too easy equation of Christianity with western culture and its acquisitiveness which is so deeply at variance with the words and way of Christ, and beginning to listen to voices from the Third World (a convenient, though unhappy phrase, since it suggests that we are at the last not one world). Not that the Third World is more objective in its approach to Jesus; it redresses the balance by being differently subjective. This may in turn lead to a revivification of the Church, partly in that the interaction of cultures is itself creative, partly in that the result of such confrontation is to send people back beyond the accretions of time and culture to Jesus himself.

The Christian churches have had to face their mission in a new spirit. In the first place, whereas in the nineteenth century there was a great driving vision of a world become Christian within a life-span, the immediacy of the vision has faded. The ultimate hope remains the same, but the churches are, consciously or unconsciously, realizing that there are many faiths, and are likely to continue to be many faiths in the world. Second, the countries of the west in general, and the USA and Britain in particular, have themselves become multi-faith communities; there are more Muslims than Methodists in Britain today. Hence the revolution in Religious Education in Britain; the traditional syllabus made no sense with a class two-thirds Muslim and one-third Sikh. Now Christianity is being seen in the context of other religions. Third, as there is closer encounter, so there is greater respect. Christians can no longer sing glibly

> The heathen in his blindness
> Bows down to wood and stone

when confronted with the majestic iconoclastic monotheism of Islam next door. Not many Christians would regard these world-faiths as works of the devil, or deny the genuine religious experience of those who profess them. 'I am the way, and the truth and the life; no one comes to the Father, but by me' (*John* 14.6) may be taken, by believing Christians, to mean, not that only professing Christians have any experience of God, but that all who find God find him through himself, through his eternal Word, through his expression of himself in creation and in inspiration as well as in Jesus. But, saying all this, Christians have to ask what is distinctive about the Christian faith. What has Christianity to offer beyond the insights of Judaism, Islam, Hinduism or Buddhism, or the worship of Olodumare or Chukwu, or any of the other names by which the withdrawn high-gods of Africa are called. The answer is, and can only be, Jesus. Therefore for Christians it is vital to concentrate on Jesus. And any who are searching, historically or existentially, to understand the essence of the Christian faith, should look first at Jesus. And any who are open to the various ways of life open to them, from Marxism and Scientific Humanism through the several religions, should look not at the churches but at Jesus.

His impact remains. Witness Napoleon on St Helena.

> You speak of Caesar, Alexander, of their conquests; of the

enthusiasm they enkindled in the hearts of their soldiers; but can you conceive of a dead man making conquests with an army faithful and entirely devoted to his memory? My army has forgotten me while living; Alexander, Caesar, Charlemagne and myself have founded Empires. But on what did we rest the creations of our genius? Upon force! Jesus Christ alone founded his Empire upon love; and at this hour millions of men would die for him. I have so inspired multitudes that they would die for me — but after all, my presence was necessary — the lightning of my eye, my voice, a word from me, then the sacred fire was kindled in their hearts. Now that I am at St Helena alone, chained upon this rock, who fights and wins empires for me? What an abyss between my deep misery, and the eternal reign of Christ, who is proclaimed, loved, adored, and whose reign is extending over all the earth!

C. Franklin Angus, Vice-Master of Trinity Hall, and perhaps the most brilliant classical lecturer of his day in the University of Cambridge as well as a great catalyst in conversation in his rooms far into the night, used to say in lecturing on Socrates that there had been three seminal figures in the history of mankind, Gautama the Buddha, Socrates, and Jesus — and Socrates was the only one of the three who had never been worshipped. Karl Jaspers in *Die grossen Philosophen* picked out four paradigmatic individuals, Socrates, the Buddha, Confucius and Jesus; no other has had a historical influence of equal breadth and duration, except perhaps Muhammad, who in Jaspers' view does not compare with the others in depth. Jaspers picks out similarities and differences between the four:

(i) The Buddha came from the aristocracy, the others from the commons (it might be truer to place Confucius in the middle class). All grew up in a society without roots.
(ii) All except Jesus were married, but all four were without family sentiment. All were strongly and naturally masculine.
(iii) None was an ecstatic visionary.
(iv) All were prophets, pointing to a deeper dimension of life, which all except the Buddha call God.

(v) All demanded of their hearers some form of transformation, rebirth or illumination.
(vi) All have a characteristic attitude to death. Socrates and Jesus were executed, and in them the western world has found two answers to death, one in a serenity which treats death as irrelevant, one in an attitude which finds obedience to God in suffering.
(vii) For all, human love is universal and unlimited, though only Jesus says explicitly 'Love your enemies'; Confucius rejects this.
(viii) Socrates, in the world, follows reason.
The Buddha tries to annul the world.
Confucius tries to shape the world.
Jesus is the world's crisis.
(ix) All communicate with others.
(x) All know the limitations of knowledge.

Jaspers picked out three aspects of Jesus' message: the coming of the Kingdom of Heaven; the way of life he proclaims; the need for trust in God. He saw the strength and strangeness of Jesus' character in the combination of gentleness and uncompromising militancy. But Jaspers goes on to say that Jesus is more than an interesting and unusual person with an interesting and unusual message. Jesus is what he is because of the certainty of his faith in God, a faith which is not a verbal assertion or intellectual tenet but is expressed in his whole life.

A seminal, paradigmatic figure. To study in academic detachment? To reject? To follow? To worship? The questions remain.

BIBLIOGRAPHY

Rationalism
G. W. Foote and J. M. Wheeler *Crimes of Christianity* vol. 1 (London 1887). No other was published: the authors are especially entertaining on the proliferation of relics. C. Bradlaugh *Doubts in Dialogue* (London 1909). The article 'Christian Priest and Sceptic on Christmastide' appeared in *National Reformer* 28 December 1884. Bradlaugh's temper in debate was admirable, and his constructed dialogues clear and fair.

Summing-Up

The Thinker's Library, and the Rationalist Press Association generally, put out a deal of valuable controversial literature.

Evangelicals and Wesleyans
I have treated this in *The Religious Revival in England* (Open University A202 Units 31-2, 1972). For a general picture see N. Sykes *Church and State in England in the XVIIIth Century* (Cambridge 1934); S. C. Carpenter *Eighteenth Century Church and People* (London 1959); L. E. Elliott-Binns *The Early Evangelicals* (London 1953). For John Wesley see G. E. Harrison *Son to Susanna* (London 1937). The primary sources are N. Curnock (ed.) *The Journal of John Wesley* 8 vols (London 1931); J. Telford (ed.) *The Letters of John Wesley* 8 vols (London 1931); E. H. Sugden *The Sermons of John Wesley* (London 1921). Also R. Davies and E. G. Rupp *A History of the Methodist Church in Great Britain* vol. 1 (London 1951). For Charles Wesley's hymns see B. L. Manning *The Hymns of Wesley and Watts* (London 1942); J. E. Rattenbury *The Evangelical Doctrines of Charles Wesley's Hymns* (London 1941). I have taken the text from *The Poetical Works of John and Charles Wesley* 13 vols (London 1868). For Simeon, H. C. G. Moule *Charles Simeon* (London 1892). Since I wrote there has appeared H. E. Hopkins *Charles Simeon of Cambridge* (London 1977). For Newton, B. Martin *An Ancient Mariner* (London[2] 1960), a thrilling adventure at bargain price.

Conclusion
I have drawn on material I used for the Open University in *What is a Gospel?* (A100 Units 19-20).

Index of Biblical References

Acts
1.7 : 162
2.9-11 : 12
2.22-4 : 25
2.36 : 88
2.38 : 89
3.14 : 57
4.11 : 104
7.48 : 104
9.1-19 : 82
9.31 : 82
12.12 : 29
13.13 : 61
13.22-3 : 100
17.24 : 104
21.10 : 45
21.40 : 15

Amos
9.7 : 3

Colossians
2.9 : 64

1 Corinthians
1.24, 30 : 93
2.8 : 88
3.2 : 116
10.3 : 104
15.6 : 82
15.22 : 97
15.45 : 96

Deuteronomy
1.31 : 61
8.3 : 38
8.5 : 61
18.15 : 72

Ecclesiastes
1.9-10, 17 : 15
2.3 : 15
3.16-17 : 15
9.11-2 : 15
23.1 : 61

Ecclesiasticus
24.3-4 : 92

Ephesians
4.5 : 88
6.19-24 : 157

Exodus
3.6 : 2
4.22 : 60
6.2 : 2
20.2 : 2
20.4 : 84
33.1-3 : 103

Ezekiel
19.10 : 95

Galatians
2.20 : 220

Genesis
5.18-24 : 97
14.18 : 98
45.3 : 99

Hebrews
1.3 : 220
1.5 : 61
4.15 : 55,77
5.5 : 61
5.7 : 71
5.12-13 : 116
11.8-10 : 98

11.17-19 : 98
12.2 : 71, 98
12.24 : 97
13.20 : 116

Hosea
7.11 : 4
10.1 : 95
11.1 : 35, 60
11.3 : 61

Isaiah
5.1-7 : 95
7.14 : 35
11.3 : 90
32.2 : 104
40. 13-28 : 7-8
53. 2-3 : 86
53.7 : 96
60.6 : 35
63.16 : 61
64.8 : 61

Jeremiah
2.21 : 95
3.4 : 61
16.14-15 : 2
31.9 : 61
31.33 : 6

Job
28.28 : 92

John
1.1 : 132, 199
1.4 : 95
1.4-5 : 94
1.14 : 55, 77
1.26 : 37
1. 29 : 96

Index of Biblical References

1.49 : 61
2. 18-20 : 104
3.6 : 141
3.17 : 141
3.19 : 91
4.6 : 55
4.7 : 55
4.7-13 : 99
4.42 : 89
5.17 : 62
5.22, 27 : 220
6.35 : 93, 95
6.41 : 93
6.48 : 93
6.51 : 93
8.12 : 94
8.15 : 91
8.41 : 34
8.42 : 62
10. 7-9, 11, 14 : 94
10.30 : 62
11.25 : 95
11.27 : 61
11.35 : 55
11.47-53 : 48
11.50 : 22
12.24 : 97
12.47 : 91
13.13 : 88
14.6 : 95, 162, 230
14.9 : 62, 116
15.1, 5 : 95
19.28 : 55
20.11 : 30
20.16 : 87
20. 17 : 171

1 John
4.1-3 : 65
5.7 : 187

2 John
7 : 65

Joshua
24. 12 : 2

Luke
1.28-35 : 162
1.47 : 88
2.11 : 88-9
2.40 : 157

2.49 : 62
4.22 : 34
4.41 : 61
5.8 : 60
6.20-1 : 43
6.36 : 62
7.50 : 89
8.36 : 89
9.55 : 57
10.25-37 : 44
11.13 : 225, 227
11.20 : 60
11.29-32 : 101
12.14 : 91
12.30-2 : 62
12.39-40 : 162
14.26 : 133
19.10 : 89
19.41 : 55
20.17 : 104
22.28 : 62
22.44 : 55
22.70-1 : 60
24.21 : 45

1 Maccabees
1.14-15 : 14
12. : 16

2 Maccabees
4.9-14 : 14
5.9 : 16

Mark
1.15 : 39
1.21-8 : 87
1.22, 27 : 59
1.41 : 55
2.17 : 42
2.28 : 88
3.5 : 55
3.11 : 61
3.30 : 36
4.38 : 55
5.7 : 61
6.3 : 36, 169
6.50 : 99
7.31 : 46
8.28 : 5
11.12 : 55
11.25-6 : 62
12.10 : 104

13.32 : 49
14.51-2 : 29
14.58 : 104
15.31 : 89
15.39 : 60

Matthew
1.21 : 88
3.17 : 61
5.7-10 : 43
5.17-20 : 133
5.41 : 44
6.33 : 38
7.3-5 : 36
7.21 : 62
7.21-3 : 59
8.25 : 89
9.5-13 : 59
9.21 : 89
10.32-3 : 62
11.27 : 62
11.30 : 36
11.39-42 : 101
14.30 : 89
14.33 : 61
16.16 : 61
16.41 : 101
20.1-14 : 198
21.42 : 104
22.15-22 : 134
23.8-10 : 87-8
23.35 : 97
25.31-4 : 162
26.6 : 104
26.63 : 61
27.40 : 61
28.18-20 : 162
28.19 : 102

Micah
5.2 : 35

Numbers
23.19 : 55

1 Peter
2.2 : 116
2.21 : 116
4.5 : 91

Philippians
2.6, 7 : 220

2.7 : 77
2.8 : 55
2.8-9 : 72
2.10-11 : 63

Proverbs
3.13-20 : 92
9.10 : 92
15.33 : 92

Psalms
2.7 : 61
8.4 : 55
16.11 : 95
22.6 : 117
27.1 : 94
30.3 : 2
45.2 : 85
45.8 : 35
72.15 : 35
80.8 : 2, 95
86.11 : 95
100.4 : 98
103.13 : 61
107.14 : 2
111.10 : 92
118.22 : 104
137. 1-2, 4 : 6-7

Revelation
1.8, 11 : 117
5.11-12 : 63
21.5 : 93
21.6 : 117
22.13 : 117

Romans
5.14 : 96
13.1-10 : 134
15.19-20 : 82
15.33 : 116

1 Samuel
10.18 : 2

2 Samuel
7.14 : 60

Song of Songs
3.6 : 35

1 Timothy
3.16 : 77

2 Timothy
4.1 : 91

Tobit
13.4 : 61

Wisdom
2.16 : 61
3.1-4 : 15
7.22-8.1 : 92-3
8.7 : 15
14.3 : 61

Zechariah
9.9-10 : 47
14.21 : 48

General Index

Abel, 97
Abélard, Peter, 130
Abercius, 94, 111
Abraham, 1, 30, 97-9; children of, 37
Acts of the Apostles, The, 12, 26, 82, 222
Acts of John, The, 66
Acts of Peter, The, 67, 86
Adam, 30, 108, 163; second, 96-7, 163, 221
Ademola, Dr George, 203-4
Adonai (title), 117
Adoptionism, 71-3, 78
Advocate (title), 117
'Aeon, infinite' (title), 115
aeons, 69-70
Africa, 9, 131-2, 162-3, 200, 209, 214, 230; church in, 73, 76; East, 164-5, 205-6; North, 108; South, 163, 197, 205; West, 162, 163-4, 202-4, 205-6, 225
African art, 199, 205-6
Age of Faith, 214
Age of Unfaith, 214
Ages, Dark, 213
Ages, Middle, 213-4
agnosticism, 193
Alexandria, 9-10, 12, 14, 66, 114, 128, 134; church at, 74, 79-80, 90
allegorical: interpretation, 73, 96-102, 110, 189; method, 16
All-Ruler (title), 117
Alpha (Beginning), 97, 116-17, 163
Ambrose, 86
America, Latin, 206-9
Amos, 5, 121
Anabaptists, 187
anchor, 110-11
Andrews, C.F., 198
And Was Made Man, 205

Angel (title), 117
Angus, C.F., 231
ankh (cross symbol), 113
Annunciation, 105
Anon. : By an Unknown Disciple, 196
Anselm, 149
Antioch-on-the-Orontes, 9, 14, 27, 29, 66
Antioch, church at, 66, 68, 72, 90
apocalypse, 27, 48-50, 56
Apollinaris, 76-7, 78-9
Apollo: as good shepherd, 86, 94; as Jesus type, 108
Apollos, 82, 90
Aquinas, Thomas, 135-7, 141, 144
Arabs, 168-9
Aramaic, 12, 15, 16-17
archaeological evidence, 3, 15-17, 22, 26
Arianism, 74-6, 213
Aristaeus as good shepherd, 108
Aristides, 64
Aristotle, 15, 121, 136, 200-1
Arius, 74-6, 187
Ark, as symbol, 103
Arm (title), 116
Armenian Church, 79
Arminianism, 217
art: African, 199, 205-6; Ascension in, 151, 152, 178; Byzantine, 91, 108, 109, 146-8, 150, 176-7; Chinese, 199; Christian, 86, 91, 95, 99-100, 102, 105-6, 107, 113, 147, 149, 199; crucifixion in, 148, 149-50, 152, 185; Graeco-Roman, 86, 94, 95, 105-6, 108-9, 183; Indian, 199; Judgment in, 91, 147-8, 149-52, 177, 183; Last Supper in, 107, 178, 184, 206; Lazarus in, 106, 178, 184; Madonna and Child, in, 109,

177, 205; mediaeval, 100, 148-52, 176, 183; Nativity in, 105, 177; pagan influences on, 86, 94, 95, 107-10, 112-13; Passion in, 107, 178, 185, 199, 205; Renaissance, 177, 183-6; Resurrection in, 107, 113; suffering in, 184-5; Transfiguration in, 147-8, 184, 205; *see also* gems; glass; jewelry; manuscripts; mosaic; painting; sculpture
arts and culture, 119, 125
Ascension in art, 151, 152, 178
Asclepius as healer, 105, 110
Asia, 165, 199-202, 214; *see also* India
assimilation, 120
Assisi, 174-7
Assyria, 4
Assyrian Christians, 78
ataraxia, *see* freedom from disturbance
Athanasius, 75-6
Atonement, 130
Augustine, 100, 101, 141-2, 143, 144, 200; *City of God*, 141, 142; *De Trinitate*, 87; *Epistula ad Deogratias*, 101; *Sermones*, 100
autarkeia, *see* self-sufficiency
authority of Jesus, 48, 59-60, 87
autocracy, 1, 17, 139
Aztecs, 158, 161

Babylon, 4, 6-7, 8, 101
Babylonian Exile, 6
bambino, cult of, 175-6
baptism, 97, 105; in art, 105, 177, 199; of fire, 102; of Jesus, 37, 62, 65, 72, 105, 110, 128, 192
Barnabas, 29, 82, 84
Barnabas, Letter of, 103-4
Barth, Karl, 127, 130-1
Basil, 147
Basilides, 128
Baynes, Norman: *The Byzantine Empire*, 145-6
bearded Jesus, 84-7, 109-10
beardless Jesus, 86-7, 106, 109, 151
Beckwith, John, 150
Beginning, *see* Alpha
Bellerophon and Chimaera, 110
Belsham, Thomas, 190
Benedict of Nursia, 126
Bernard of Clairvaux, 181

Bernini, 181
Bethune-Baker: *History of Christian Doctrine*, 73
Bevan, E. : *Jerusalem Under the High Priests* 13-14
Bible, authority of, 216
Bible of illiterate, 148
birth of Jesus, 33-5, 67, 105, 199
'bit for untamed colts' (title), 114
blasphemy, 46, 51, 61-2, 89
Bode, J.E., 195
Boehme, J., 154-5
Bornkamm, Günther, 25
Bradlaugh, C. : *Doubts in Dialogue*, 215
Bread (title) 117
bread: breaking of, 45, 50, 206; of life 93-4, 165
Bridegroom (title), 117
Britain, church in, 83
Brotherhood of Man, 131
Buddha, *see* Gautama
Buddhism, 200-1, 230
Bultmann, Rudolf, 41
Burckhardt, J., 121
Burkitt, F.C. : *Church and Gnosis*, 128
Byzantine art, 91, 108, 109, 146-8, 150, 176-7
Byzantinism, 145-8

Caesarea, 13, 19-20, 27
Caird, George, 39
Calf (title), 117
Calvin, J., 142, 156-7, 187; *Institutes of the Christian Religion*, 156-7
Calvinism, 217-18, 224
Camara, Helder, 126, 209
capitalism, 131
catacombs, 86, 96, 98, 99, 101, 102, 105, 106, 107, 109, 110, 111, 113
Catherine of Genoa, 180
Cellarius, Martin, 187
Celsus, 36; *The True Word*, 120
census of Quirinius, 19, 34, 202
Chalcedon, Council of, 78, 214
Channing, W.E., 190
Chapel-religion, 194-5, 216
Chavez, Cesar, 126
childhood of Christ, 32, 35-6, 106, 169-70
children, place of, 120, 197
China, 9, 90

General Index

Chinese art, 199
chi-rho symbol, 112-13
Christ (title), 83
Christian: architecture, 94, 151; art, 86, 91, 95, 99-100, 102, 105-6; 107, 113, 147, 149, 199; fathers, 33, 100, 123 writers, 4, 61
Christians, early, 55, 64-5, 87-96, 97
Christmas, 33-4
Chrysostom, John, 85
Chukwu, 230
Church: at Alexandria, 74, 79-80, 90; at Antioch, 66, 68, 72, 90; Armenian, 79; in Britain, 83; at Colossae, 64; at Constantinople, 77-8, 79-80; Coptic, 79; at Damascus, 82; at Ephesus, 78, 90; in India, 82, 198; at Jerusalem, 36, 82; at Rome, 27, 79-80
Church, Christian, 53, 62-3, 88, 95, 117-18, 119, 121, 215; authority of, 216; indifferent, 218; indigenous, 202; and politics, 207-10
church, symbols of, 100, 102
circus, 124, 129, 146
citizenship: obligations of, 133-4
Clapham Sect, 228
Clement of Alexandria, 86, 88, 94, 98, 108, 110, 112, 113-16, 117, 134-5, 144; *Hymn*, 114-15; *Protrepticus*, 108; *Salvation for the Rich?*, 134; *The Turor*, 114, 135
Clement of Rome: Letter of, 123; Second Letter of, 71
Clovis, 127
Collins, A., 189
Colossae, church at, 64
community, 40, 43, 61-2, 121, 142-3, 210; dedicated, 22-3; sharing, 45; symbol of, 45
Cone, James, 209
confrontation, 48
Confucius, 121, 231-2
conquistadores, 160
Constantine, 74, 112-13, 129-30
Constantinople, 129; Church at, 77-8, 79-80; Councils of, 75, 80, 96
controversy, 27, 40, 74-80
conversion, mass-, 160-1
Conybeare, F.C., 190
Coptic Church, 79
Corner-stone (title), 117

corruption, 140, 142, 218
cosmopolis, 9-10
Cosmos, 11
Covenant, 3, 6, 83, 99: New, 29, 50-1, 99
covenanted people, 5
Cowper, William, 227
Creation, 62, 65, 70, 74, 92, 140, 164, 208
creed, 26, 194, 203
cross, 46, 67, 98, 102, 120-1, 155; prefigured, 100; as symbol, 111, 112
Crowther, Samuel Ajayi, 162
crucifix, 149, 153, 161, 179
crucifixion: in art, 148, 149-50, 152, 185; of Jesus, 31, 52, 65, 66, 89, 129, 202; as punishment, 46
culture, Christ and, ch. 5 *passim*, 198, 199-206, 229
Culture-Protestantism, 127, 130-1, 195
Cyril of Alexandria, 78, 79-80, 100

Dale, R.W., 59
Damascus, church at, 82
Daniel, 101-2
Daniel, book of, 56-7
Daniel-Rops: *Jesus in His Time*, 168
Daphni, *see* Pantocrator
David, king, 3-4, 100-1, 107, 109
dead, living, 163
death: as annihilation, 11; gates of, 100; victory over, 102
Decapolis, 13, 39
Deism, 188-90, 218
Deissmann, Adolf: *Light from the Ancient East*, 89
deliverance: from Egypt, 2, 99; by Messiah, 5; from power of death, 102; spiritual, 89-90, 154
desarrollismo (developmentalism), 207
desire, 11
Desta, Gebre Kristos, 206
Deuteronomy, book of, 6, 61, 101
Diaspora, 8, 12-13
Diodorus Siculus, 13
Diognetus, Letter to, 134
Dionysus as Jesus type, 95, 109
disciples of Jesus, 41, 43, 46, 48, 50-1, 53, 63, 112
Dispersion of Jews, *see* Diaspora
divinity of emperor, 145

General Index

divinity of Jesus, 58-64, 65, 71, 76, 78-78-9, 80, 124, 144, ch. 6 *passim*, 168, 201, 213-16, 220, 227, 228
Docetism, 65-9, 78, 173, 216
Dodd, C.H., 42, 45, 49
Doddridge, Philip: *The Rise and Progress of Religion in the Soul*, 227
dogma, 193-4, 213-16
Dolci, Danilo, 126
Door (title), 117, 165
door of death, 94
door of the sheep, 94
Douala hymn, 163-4
dove, 112
Drews, Arthur, 159
dualism of culture, 137-40
Dura-Europos, 96, 105-6, 107

Eagle (title), 117
Ebionites, 64-5
Ecclesiastes, book of, 15
Eckhart, Meister, 154
economic greed, 137
ecstasy of mystic, 181
education, 21
Edwards, Jonathan, 142
Egypt, 1-2, 4, 6, 7, 8, 9, 12, 88, 89, 101, 208; Jesus in, 34-5, 99, 177
Egyptians, The Gospel of the, 66
Eisler, Robert 32
El Greco, 148
Elijah, 46
emanation, 66, 69-71
Emmanuel (title), 116-17
Empire: Christian, 129; Roman, 1, 9, 20, 74-6, 78, 82, 120
enamel work, 151
End, *see* Omega
Enoch, 97
Enoch, The Similitudes of, 56-8
Ephesians, letter to, 157
Ephesus, 27; Church at, 78, 90; Council of, 78
Epictetus, 173
Epicureanism, 10-11, 15, 86-7, 109-10
epitaphs, 110, 111
Equal (title) 117
Erasmus, 187
Erivwo, S.U., 204
Erosas Jesus type, 109
eschatology, 49, 90, 97, 131, 142, 164-5, 192

Essenes, 16, 22-3
ethical teaching, 31, 49
Eucharist, 98, 164
Eusebius: *Laudatio Constantini*, 108
Evangelicals, 217-29
evangelists, symbols of, 150, 151
evil, conquest of, 100, 110
Exile, 6, 46
excitement: irrational, 124
Exodus, 208
Exodus, book of the, 2
Ezekiel, 56
Ezra, 8

faith, 51, 98, 121, 232; age of, 214; justification by, 155, 218; multi-, society, 230
Fakeye, Lamidi, 205-6
Farrer, Austin: *A Study in St Mark*, 99
Father (title) 116
Fatherhood of God, 42, 52, 61, 62, 131, 187
feeding of the five thousand, 44-5, 170, 199, 203
festivals, 124
Figure (title), 116
Fire (title) 116
fire, baptism of, 102
First and Last (title), 117
First-born (title), 116-17
fish as symbol, 111-12
fishermen as symbol, 112
'fisher of men' (title), 114-16
Fletcher, Frank, 195
flood, 97
Florence Cathedral, 94
Flower (title), 117
folk-memory, 1, 6
food of life, 112
Foote and Wheeler: *Crimes of Christianity*, 215
forgiveness, 44, 199; of sins 40, 52, 89, 120
form-criticism, 27, 62
Fortune, goddess, 11-12
Fosdick, H.E., 196-7
Fount and Origin of God (title), 117
'fount of mercy' (title), 115
Fox, George, 219
France, Anatole, 31
Francis of Assisi, 174-6, 191, 216
Franciscans, 160, 175

Franck, Sebastian, 155
Franks, 76
freedom from disturbance, 11
free-thinkers, 215-16
free will, 217
Fry, Elizabeth, 229

Galilee, 15, 19-20, 39-42, 82
Gandhi, 126, 197-9, 209
Gate of Hell, 201
Gautama (Buddha), 121, 130, 158, 161, 162, 231-2
Gbonigi, E.B., 209
gems, 101, 112
Genesis, book of, 90
Gentile converts, 30, 82
Gentiles, attitude to, 32, 46
George and dragon, 110
Gibbon, Edward, 79, 120, 218
Giotto, 176-8
Gita, The, 197
glass, 86, 99
Glory (title), 117
Glover, T.R., 195-6
Gnosticism, 65-9, 70, 128-9, 159
God: as Father, 42, 51, 61; Fatherhood of, 42, 52, 61, 62, 131, 187; in Gnosticism, 66; impassibility of, 74; instrument of, 19; is all 11; of the Israelites, 2; Kingdom of, 22, 42-3, 49, 131; love towards, 43; names of, 116; presence of, 40; prophets of, 4-5; Son of, 58-64, 144, ch. 6 *passim*, 168, 228
God of Peace (title), 115
gods of city-state, 10
Good Samaritan, parable of, 30, 43
Goppelt, Leonhard, 97
gospel-cover, 105, 106
gospels, 25-31, 35, 55, 63, 155, 159; 189, 222; synoptic, 26, 30, 159
Goths, 76
Grabar, A., 110
grace of God, 120, 137, 226-7
Graeco-Roman art, 86, 94, 95, 105-6, 108-9, 183; *See also* mosaics
Graeco-Roman culture, *see under* Greek; *philosophies*
Grant, R.M.: *Gnosticism and Early Christianity*, 128
Greek: art, 86, 94, 95, 109; culture, 9, 12, 13-14, 16-17, 20, 123; influence, 1, 8-17, 187; language, 10, 12, 14-15, 30, 39; political structure, 9; science, 12; thought, 10-12, 15-16, 22, 135; *See also* philosophies
Gregory of Nyssa, 85
Grünewald, Mathias, 150
'guardian of righteousness' (title), 115
Guerdan, René: *Byzantium*, 146
Gutierrez, Gustavo, 206-9
gymnasium, 13-14

halo, 108, 184, 192, 199
Hand of God (title), 116-17
Harbour (title), 117
harmony, 112, 127, 199
Harnack, A.: *Mission and Expansion of Christianity*, 123
Hartmann, von, 159
Head (title), 117
healing, 40, 169, 203; image of Jesus, 105-6
Hebert, A.G.: *The Throne of David*, 98
Hebrew: tradition, 1-3, 5, 13, 15-17, 35, 61, 82-3, 116, 119-20, 123, 135; tribes, 3, 4
Hebrews, Gospel According to the, 33, 37, 98
Hebrews, Letter to the, 71
Hecataeus of Abdera, 13
Helios as Jesus type, 108
Hellenistic: Age, 9, 15, 61, 90, 126, 200; art, 86, 94, 95, 108-9; ruler-cult, 89
Hellenization, 16, 83
'helm for ships' (title), 114
Heracles, 121; as Jesus type, 108-9
Heraclitus, 90, 135
Herbert of Cherbury, Lord, 188
heretics, 128, 138, 187
Hermas: *The Shepherd*, 72, 94; *Similitudines*, 72
Hermes: as good shepherd, 86, 94; as type of Logos, 108
Herod: the Great, 14, 16-17, 18-19; sons of, 19-20, 34
Herondas, 129
hieratic art, 147, 151, 216
Hilton, Walter: *The Ladder of Perfection*, 178-9
Hinderer, Anna, 127
Hinderer, David, 162

Hinduism, 162, 197, 230
hippodrome, 14, 16
Hippolytus, 102; *Refutation of All Heresies*, 110
history: God lord of, 140; Jesus of, 118, 121, 155, 159, 183, 190, 192, 195-7, 200-1, 203-4, 208
Homoiousios, 75, 116
Homoousios, 75, 116
hope, 121, 229; Messianic, 5; of resurrection, 8
Horus and Isis, 109
Hosea, 5, 61
Hoskyns, Sir Edwyn: *The Fourth Gospel*, 141
Howard, John, 229
humanity of Jesus, 55-6, 58, 65, 68-9, 70, 76, 78-9, 80, 120, 124, 128, 144, 154-5, 156-7, ch. 7 *passim*, 213-16, 220, 227, 228
Hume, David, 190-2
humility, 121
Huxley, T.H., 192-3
Hymnal, EACC, 165, 201-2
Hymnbook, The Methodist, 220-1
hymns, 114-15, 163-4, 221-4
Hymns, Olney, 227

I AM (God), 2
I am (images of Jesus), 93-6
iconography, 147-8
identity: moral, 3; religious, 3
idolatrous emblems, 20
idolatry, 16, 101, 124
idols, 7, 161, 216
Idowu, F.B., 131-2, 202
Ignatius: *Epistula ad Ephesios*, 71; *Epistula ad Smyrnaeos*, 68-9; *Epistula ad Trallianos*, 68
Image (title), 116
images of Jesus, ch. 4 *passim*
image-worship, 146-7
Imitation of Christ, The, 178-9, 180-1, 225
immanence of God, 159
immortality, 15, 113, 120, 164
imperialism and Christianity, 198, 202-3, 214
Incarnate, Christ, 202
Incarnation, 208-9; Jacob's ladder type of, 99
India, 9, 196, 197; church in, 82, 198

Indian: art, 199; thought, 67
Intercessor (title), 117
intolerance, 120
Irenaeus, 85; *Adversus Omnes Haereses*, 67
Isaac, 98
Isaiah, 5, 121
Isaiah, book of 7, 46, 107
Isidore, 116
Isis and Horus, 109
Islam, 5, 78, 79-80, 162, 168-4, 215, 230
Islamic art, 151
Israel: image of (vine), 95; Kingdom of, 4, 5, 58; new 51, 56, 62, 99; sonship of, 60-1; religion of, *see under* Hebrew; tribes of, 3, 4
ivory, 106, 108, 146, 150

Jacob, 99
James, brother of Jesus, 36, 148
James, letter of, 155
James, William, 129
Japan, 201-2
Jaspers, Karl: *Die grossen Philosophen*, 231-2
Jefferson, Thomas, 131
Jeremiah, 6, 51, 61, 101
Jerome, 29, 30, 36, 37, 75, 86; *Adversus Luciferum*, 65
Jerusalem, 4, 6, 8, 12, 14, 18, 20, 27, 29, 47, 101; as image, 104; church at, 36, 82; Jesus in, 46-8, 50; Temple in, 4, 5, 6, 8, 12, 16, 18, 20, 32, 35, 47-8
Jesus: in art, 146-52, 176-8, 183-6, 199, 205; baptism of, 37, 62, 65, 67, 72, 105, 110, 128, 192; birth of, 33-5, 55, 155; childhood of, 32, 35-6, 106, 169-70; and culture, ch. 5 *passim*, 198, 199-206, 229; death of, 15, 21-2, 25-6, 27, 34, 47-52, 55, 65, 128, 155, 173-4, 201; divinity of, 58-64, 65, 71, 76, 78-9, 80, 124, 144, ch. 6 *passim*, 168, 201, 213-16, 220, 227, 228; ethic of, 130; humanity of, 55-6, 58, 65, 68-9, 70, 76, 78-9, 80, 120, 124, 128, 144, 154-5, 156-7, ch. 7 *passim*, 213-16, 220, 227, 228; impact of, 119-21, 144, 174-5, 178, 197-9, 207; to Islam, 169-74; the

liberator, 34, 45-7, 89; life of, 21, ch. 2 *passim*, 105-7; likeness of, 84-84-7, 186; mind of closeness to, 4, 6; ministry of, 15, 39-47; nature of, ch. 3 *passim*, power of, 27, 32, 40; priesthood of, 98; in prophetic tradition, 5, 30, 72, 83; resurrection of, 25, 52-3, 89; as Saviour, 66, 88-9, 112, 125, 132, 148-9, 163, 165, 200; symbols of, ch. 4 *passim*; teaching of, 27, 29, 32, 38, 40, 42-4, 105
jewelry, 149
Job, book of, 14, 15
John, the apostle, 28, 148, 149
John the Baptist, 20, 37, 39, 46, 96, 172
John: *First Letter of*, 122-3, 126; *Gospel According to*, 25-31, 35, 42, 45, 49, 50, 63, 73, 87, 90, 93-6, 116, 141, 187, 192
Jonah, 101, 110, 225
Jones, E. Stanley, 198
Joris, David, 187
Joseph, son of Jacob, 99
Josephus, 12, 16, 19-20, 21-2, 32, 36, 39, 46; *Antiquitates Judaicae*, 12, 14, 15, 16, 31-2; Bellum Judaicae, 12, 16, 39
Joshua, 99-100, 103
Joy (title), 165
joy, 71, 98, 179, 196, 228
Judaea, Roman province, 18, 20
Judah, kingdom of, 4, 5, 6
Judaism, 1-8, 17, 61, 64, 82-3, 158, 170, 230
Judas Iscariot, 41, 50-1, 173
Judge: title of Jesus, 90-2, 116, 165; Jesus as, 162, 220
Judgment, Day of, 193; in art, 91, 147-8, 149-52, 177, 183
Judgment, Last 97, 125, 151
judgment, 42-3, 50, 140; of God, 37; sound, 5
Julian of Norwich, Lady, 153-4, 179
justice, social, 5, 30, 119-20
Justin Martyr, 86; *Apology*, 108

Kallen, H.: *The Book of Job as a Greek Tragedy*, 14
Kalthoff, Albert, 158-9
Kautsky, Karl, 159

Keim, K.T., 192-3
Kekama, Job, 205
Kid (title) 117
King, Martin Luther, 126, 209
'King of the saints' (title), 114-5
Kingdom, 22, 42-3; of God, 131
kingdom: spiritual, 138-9; temporal, 138-9
Kiplayat, Bethuel, 206
Kitamon: *Theology of the Pain of God*, 201
Klausner, Rabbi, 119-20
Koyama, Kosuke: *Waterbuffalo Theology*, 132, 161, 200-1
Krishna, 158
Kukoji, David, 162
Kyrios (title of Jesus), 88

Lamb, 63, 117
Lamb of God, 96; as title, 117
Land, Promised, 103-4
Langland: *Piers Plowman*, 150
Lao-tzu, 130
Last Supper, 31, 50, 53, 88, 170; as symbol, 93-4, 98-9 in art, 107, 178, 184, 206;
Latourette, K.S., 160
Law, William, 155
law: and grace, 122-3, 132; and love, 51, 99; representation of, 105; and society, 136-7
Lazarus, 99, 106; in art, 106, 178, 184
legends of Jesus, 35-6, 84
Lenin, 120
Lentulus, The Letter of, 85
Leonardo da Vinci, 184
Leon-Dufour, Prof., 31
liberation, 2; of the soul, 67; theology, 206-10; violent, 38
liberator: Jesus the, 34, 45-7, 88-90, 163, 207; Moses the, 1-2, 99
Liberty (title), 165
Life (title), 116-17
Life of Christ. The: in art, 199-200
life: eternal, 113; glorious, 115
Light, 42, 50, 90, 203; Inner, 216; as title 116-17, 165; of the world, 94
Likeness (title), 117
Like-substanced, *see Homoiousios*
Lion (title), 117
lion symbolism, 101-2
Locke, John, 188-9; *The Reasonable-*

ness of Christianity 130-1
Logos, 62, 72, 74, 76-7, 88, 90, 108, 116, 187; *see also* Reason; Word
Lord (title), 116
love, 5, 43-4, 51, 121, 122-3, 135, 136, 165, 193, 198-9, 200-1, 215, 224, 227, 228, 232; contemplating of, 179; of enemies 125, 232; and law, 51, 99
Luis de Leon, 154
Luke, 29, 84-5
Luke, Gospel According to, 25-31, 35-6, 49, 50, 94, 157
lust, 124, 125
Luther, Martin, 138-40, 141, 155-6, 160, 200, 201, 219, 220; *Works*, 139
lyre as symbol, 112

Maccabees 16, 17, 21
Maccabees, books of, 15-16
Macedon, 8-9, 15
Macoba, Ernest, 205
Madonna and Child: in art, 109, 177, 205
Magi, 105
majesty, 156
Majesty, Christ in, 147, 150-2
Mâle, Emile, 151
Malinowski, B., 122
Mammon, 203
Man (title), 117
Mandela, Nelson, 216
mandorla, 150-1, 183-4
Manning, Bernard, 220
Manson, W. : *The Teaching of Jesus*, 57-8
manuscript, illuminated, 106-7, 146, 147, 151
Marcion, 66, 80, 138
Mark, John, 28-9
Mark, Gospel According to, 25-31, 35, 44, 50, 192
Martyrdom of Perpetua and Felicitas, The, 94-5
martyrs, 55, 97, 102
Marx, Karl, 120
Marxists, 130
Mary Magdalen, 87, 178, 183, 193, 196
Mary, mother of Jesus, 33-5, 36, 37, 109, 149, 153, 169, 173, 205

massacre of innocents, 34, 105
Master (title), 117
Mateos, Juan, 210
materialism, 131
Matthew, the apostle, 28
Matthew, Gospel According to, 25-31, 33-4, 44, 50, 62, 87, 192
Maurice, F.D., 142-3, 144; *The Lord's Prayer*, 142
Mbiti, John, 164-5
McGilvary, Dr Daniel, 161, 200
mediaeval art, 100, 148-52, 176, 183
Mediator (title), 117
mediator, Jesus as, 157
Melchizedek, 98-9
Melito of Sardis, 97, 99
memra (Word of God), 90, 135
mercy, 155
Mesopotamia, 1, 4, 12, 158
Messenger (title), 169, 174
Messiah, 5, 29-30, 34-5, 38, 45-7, 51-2, 58, 60-1, 65, 88, 89-90, 98, 127, 169, 173, 188-90, 223
Messianic: banquet, 45, 111; tradition, 44, 56, 58, 61, 107
Michelangelo, 91, 183-4
Midrashim, 61
militarism, 113, 127, 139-40
'milk from heaven' (title), 115-16
Mind (title), 116
miracles, 45, 65, 87, 106, 120, 141, 189, 190 191-2, 193-4; healing, 25, 32, 105-6, 191
Mishna, The, 17
mission, Christian, 127, 159-63, 198, 214
missionary activity, 29, 76, 82, 214
Mithras, 109, 158
Modalism, 73-4
Mohammed, *see* Muhammad
monasticism, 130, 139
money, 48
monogamy, 161
Monophysitism, 78-9
monotheism, 6, 10, 64, 71, 73, 168, 174, 230
Montalembert, De, 126
Montanists, 112
Montefiore, Hugh, 45
Montesquieu, 218
Moravians, 219
mosaic, 86, 91, 94, 95, 96, 99, 106,

108, 110, 113, 145, 148, 149
Moses, 1-2, 14, 76, 104, 109, 169; as type of Christ, 32, 64, 72, 99
Moses, Life of, 16
Moses, The Assumption of, 18
Mountain (title), 117
Mouth of God (title), 116
Muhammad (Mohammed), 121, 168-71, 199, 231
Murry, J. Middleton, 196
musician image, 4, 100
Muslims, 33, 162, 168-74, 215
mystery religions, 109, 120, 189
mystical: encounters, 2; experience, 46, 53, 60, 62, 152-5, 174-5, 178-83, 196
Myth of God Incarnate, The, 213-14
mythical message, 27, 66
myths, religion, 158, 163
Mzobe, Michael, 163

nabi, *see* Prophet
Napoleon, 230-1
nationalism, 10, 131
Nativity in art, 105, 177
Nazarene (title), 117
Nazarite (title), 117
neighbourliness, 43-4, 208
Nestorius, 77-8
Newman, J.H., 97
Newton, John, 224-8
Nicaea, Council of, 74-5, 79, 214
Niebuhr, H. Richard, ch.5 *passim*, 195
Niles, D.T., 165, 202
Njau, Elimo, 206
Noah, 97, 103, 112
non-attachment, 10
non-resistance, 119
non-violence, 199, 209
Notker, 117
Novatian: *De Trinitate*, 71
Nsama, Emmanuel, 206
Ntwasa, Sabelo, 209

oaths, 125
obedience, 8, 71-2, 121, 123-4, 232
Odysseus as Jesus type, 110
Olney, 226-7
Olodumare, 162, 230
Omega (End), 97, 116-17, 163
On the Sublime, 90
One who is sent (title), 117

Only-Begotten Son (title), 116-17
Orans, 110
Orient (title), 117
Origen, 30, 77, 86, 103, 120
orisa (subsidiary deities), 162
Orpheus, 121; as shepherd, 86, 94, 107; as type of Jesus, 105, 107-8
other-worldliness, 127
Otto, Rudolf, 216

pacifism, 113, 124, 126, 127
Padua, Scrovegni chapel, 177-8
pagan influences on art, 86, 94, 95, 107-10, 112-13
painting, 84-5, 91, 94, 95, 96, 105, 107, 109, 147-8, 149-50, 176-8, 183-6, 199-200, 205
Palestine, ch. 1 *passim*, 28, 82
palm, athlete's, 113
Pantocrator, Christ, 91, 147, 183-4
parables, 30, 40, 48, 173, 198; acted, 45
Paraclete (title), 117, 171
Passion: contemplation of, 179; in hymns, 222-3; scenes in art, 107, 178, 185, 199, 205
Patripassianism, 73-4
Pattison, Mark, 216
Paul of Samosata, bishop, 72-3, 75
Paul of Tarsus, 14, 26, 29, 31, 34, 64, 82-3, 84, 88, 93, 100, 110, 134, 143
peace, 5, 47, 51, 125, 142, 193
peacock symbol, 113, 149
Pearl, Hymn of the, 129
pelican, 113
Pergamum, 9, 17
persecution, 31, 48-9, 51
Perseus and Andromeda, 110
Persia, 8, 15, 78, 79-80, 146
Perugino, 184
Peter, apostle, 25, 29, 35, 38, 51, 58, 88, 106, 148
Peter of Ghent, 160
Peter, The Gospel of, 66
Pharisees, 16, 19, 21-3, 120, 196
Philip, apostle, 41, 82
Phillips, Rev. Dr W.L., 218
Philo, 12, 16, 90; *In Flaccum*, 12; *Legatio ad Gaium*, 12
Philosopher, type of Christ, 86, 88, 105, 110

philosophies: Gnostic, 69-71, 128; Graeco-Roman, 10-11, 15-16, 62, 83, 90, 93, 95, 120, 135, 138, 158; *see also* Epicureanism; Platonists; Pythagoreans; Stoicism
phoenix, 113
Photius, 168
Pilate, 19-20, 26, 31-2, 52, 185, 205
Pisano, Nicola, 176
Plato, 15, 109, 121, 130, 135
Platonists, 65, 90, 187, 190; Christian, 96
Pleroma, 69-70, 128
Pliny, 31, 63
ploughman symbol, 114
pneuma, 67, 70
polis, 9-10
political: action, 206-9; authority, 134, 138; quietism, 21-3; withdrawal, 22-3, 125
Polycarp, 85
portents, 25
Potency (title); 116
poverty, vow of, 174-5
Power of God (title of Jesus), 93, 124
power politics, 137
Practice of the Presence of Christ, 180-1
prayer, 42, 61, 109, 154; figure in, *see* Orans
predestinarianism, 217
Predestination, 157
Priest (title), 117, 165
Priestley, Joseph, 189-90
Primal Man, 56
Prince (title), 117
prison reform, 229
probability, 191
procurators, Roman, 19-20
Prophet (title), 117, 169
Prophets, books of the, 15; *see also* Daniel; Isaiah; Zechariah
prophets, tradition of, 4-5, 15, 37, 46, 169, 174; *see also* Amos; Daniel; Elijah; Ezekiel; Ezra; Hosea; Isaiah; Jeremiah; Jonah
Proverbs, book of, 92
Providence (title), 116
Psalms, book of, 4
Psalms of Solomon, 47
psyche, 67, 70, 74
Ptolemies, 9, 12, 88, 110

purification, 5
Pythagoreans, 16, 95, 121

Quakers, 213
Qur'an, 168-74, 199

Rabbi (title of Jesus), 39, 87-8, 105
Raikes, Robert, 228-9
Ram: as title, 117; in thicket, 98
Ramakrishna, 162
Raphael, 184
Rationalists, 157-9, 190-4, 213, 215
Rauschenbusch, Walter, 131
Ravenna, 86, 91, 106, 108, 112, 113
Reason (Logos), 11, 188; *see also* Logos
redemption of world, 123
Reformation, 155-7
Refuge (title), 165
relevance of Jesus, 132
religious: community, 22-3; narrowness, 21; observance, 22; outlook, 23; pietism, 22; purism, 21, 22
reliquary, 107
Rembrandt, 184-6, 216
Renaissance, 155, 176, 187-8; art, 177, 183-6; post-, 213
Renan, Ernest, 192
Renesse, Count Camille de, 193
Reni, Guido, 184
repentance, 37, 39, 155, 188
resurrection, 8, 52-3, 89, 120-1, 165, 188, 201, 223; in art, 107, 113; and life, 95; type, 101-2
Resurrection and Life (title), 165
Revelation, book of, 96, 104
riches, attitude to, 134, 172-3
righteousness, 5, 135
Ritschl, Albrecht: *Justification and Reconciliation*, 131
'road to heaven' (title), 115
Robertson, J.M., 158, 190; *Christianity and Mythology*, 158; *Pagan Christs*, 158
Rock (title), 117, 165
rock as image, 104
Rolle, Richard, 150
Roman Empire, 1, 9, 20, 74-6, 78, 82, 120, 158, 200; Christian, 145
Romanization, 1, 9, 17-21
Romans, letter to, 155-6, 219
Rome, 10, 18, 29, 31, 32, 129;

church at, 27, 79-80; New, 129; power of, 41, 45, 52 S. Clemente, 149; S. Costanza, 95, 113; S. Maria Antiqua, 110; S. Maria Maggiore, 99-100; St Peter's, 94, 95, 108
Rosy Sequence, The, 181-3
Ruskin, J. : *Unto This Last*, 198

Sabaoth (title), 117
Sabbath observance, 32, 40-1, 88, 133
sacraments, 194
sacrifice, 5, 51, 96, 97, 98, 132; human, 161
Sadducees, 21-3, 120
sadism, 124
salvation, 30, 47, 48, 97, 112, 135, 141, 155-6, 207, 228
Samson, 100, 109
Santa Sophia, 93, 147
Sarapis, 88, 110
sarcophagi, 86, 95, 96, 97, 101, 102, 105, 106, 110, 113
Satan, victory over, 100
Saviour: Jesus as, 66, 88-9, 112, 125, 132, 148-9, 163, 165, 200; title of Jesus, 88-9, 116-17
Sawyerr, Harry: *Creative Evangelism*, 164
Schweitzer, Albert, 49
Schwenckfeld, Caspar, 155
sculpture, 86-7, 91, 94, 96, 100, 101, 105, 108, 109-10, 149, 151-2, 176, 199, 205
Second Coming, 162, 165
Sedulius, 117
Seleucids, 9, 111
self-discipline, 11, 136
self-righteousness, 61
self-sufficiency, 10-11
Septuagint, 12, 88, 96
Sermon on the Mount, 197-9, 220
Servant (title), 169
Servetus, Michael, 187
service, 50
sexual symbolism, 181
Sheep (title), 117
sheep and goats, 91, 94
Sheol, descent into, 163
Shepherd (title), 117, 165
shepherd and sheep, 44, 94
Shepherd, (Good), 86, 94-5, 102, 107-8, 110

shepherd image, 97, 100, 110, 114-15
ship as symbol, 112
signs, 25, 45, 170
silverwork, 109, 149
Simeon, Charles, 217-18
Simon of Cyrene, 67
simplicity of life, 199
sin: in man, 137; original, 124; victory over, 188
slavetrade, 225, 228
socialism, 143
society, Evangelicals and, 228-9
Socinus, Faustus, 187-8
Socrates, 33, 121, 130, 231-2
Solomon, 3-4, 60
Son of God, 58-64, 124, 144, ch. 6 *passim*, 168, 228; *see also* Jesus, divinity of
Son of Man, 38, 43, 46, 48, 55-8, 64, 144, ch. 7 *passim*, 228; *see also* Jesus, humanity of
Son of Man: in art, 199-200, 205
Song of Songs, The, 15, 181
Sophia, *see* Wisdom
soul, Christian, 110, 153-5
Sovereignty (title), 116
Spangenburg, Pastor, 219
Spirit: title, 116; of God (title), 124; Holy, 11, 37, 51, 53, 65, 72, 110, 171
spiritual guidance, 127
spiritual Kingdom, 138-9
Splendour (title), 116-17
Spring (title), 117
Stephen, martyr, 55, 99
stigmata, 176, 191
Stillingfleet, Bishop, 189
Stoicism, 10-11, 15-16, 22, 62-3, 90, 134-5, 138
Stone (title), 117
Strabo, 12
Strauss, D.F., 192
Strength (title), 116
Student Christian Movement, 196
Suetonius, 31
Suffering, 29, 65, 66-7, 73, 101, 149-50, 153, 199; in art, 184-5; Servant, 46, 58, 86, 96
Sun, 10, 117; and moon emblems, 129, 149, 151; of righteousness, 94, 108, 129; Unconquered, 129
Sunday, 129; School Movement, 229

Sun-chariot, 146
Sun-wheel, 112, 113
Sundkler, Bengt, 163
supernaturalism, 157-8, 161, 189, 196
supernatural powers, 169
superstition, 159-60
'support of our labours' (title), 114
Susanna, 102
Suso, Henry, 179
symbols, 45, ch. 4 *passim*
synagogue worship, 21
syncretism, 74, 113
synthesis of thought, 16, 116, 133-7
Syria, 1, 9, 17-18, 129

Tacitus, 31
Talbot Rice, David, 147
Tao, 90, 132, 199
taxation, 19-20
teacher: Jesus as, 105, 170, 174, 193, 198 Muhammad as, 170
teaching of Jesus, 27, 29, 38, 40, 42-4, 59
Temple: in art, 177-8; at Elephantine, 8; as image, 104; Jerusalem, 4, 5, 6, 8
temporal Kingdom, 138-9
temptation of Jesus 38, 55
Teresa de Jesus, 153, 179, 181; *Life*, 179, 181
Tertullian, 123-4, 126; *Apology* 123-4
Testament, Old, 62, 66, 70, 72, 80, 83, 89, 90, 96-102, 103-4, 117, 147, 197
Testament, New, 10, 13, 33, 61, 72, 80, 83, 87-93, 93-6, 122, 124, 131, 133, 136, 143, 159, 162, 187, 197, 209, 210, 225, 227
Thailand, 200-1
theatre, 14, 124
Theodorus Anagnostes, 109
Theodotus, 72
Theologica Germanica, 179
theology: black, 209-10; liberation, 206-9
Theophilus of Antioch, 116; *Ad Autolycum*, 116
Thérèse of Lisieux, 181
Thomas, apostle, 63, 82
Thomas of Celano; *Dies irae*, 91, 152
Thurman, Howard, 209

Tindal, Mathew, 189
Toland, John, 189
tolerance, 12, 188
Tolstoy, Leo, 124-5, 126; *The Kingdom of God is Within You*, 197; *What I Believe*, 125
Torah, 2, 15, 16, 17, 21-2, 32, 38, 40-1, 64, 83, 105, 122, 133, 135, 138, 169-70
trade routes, 9, 15, 39
Traherne, Thomas, 179-80
transfiguration, 46, 60, 62, 147-8
Transfiguration in art, 147-8, 184, 205
Trappists, 197-8
travel, 9; mystic, 153
Trinity, 74, 102, 152-3, 168, 187
Truth (title), 116
Truth, The Gospel of, 128
tsuraso (redemptive suffering), 201
tsutsumu (Involvement), 201
Turgeniev, 186
Turin shroud, 84
Twiceborn (title), 116
Twining, Louisa, 98
tympanum, 151-2

Underhill, Evelyn: *Mysticism*, 179
Uniformity of Nature, 191
Unitarianism, 186-90, 213
United Nations, 126
unity of mankind, 10, 229
universalism, 3, 7, 32, 46, 48, 58, 61, 109, 132, 168, 188, 193, 198, 200, 202

Valentinus, 69-71, 128
Vallejo, Cesar, 208
values, cultural, 122
Vandals, 76
Velasquez, 184
Veronica, 84
vice, 11, 123
vine (image), 95
Vine (title), 117
violence, 5, 46, 49, 125
violent: protest, 22-3; uprising, 16, 20-1, 32, 36, 38, 47, 51
virgin-birth, 33-5, 55, 157
virtue 11, 37, 65, 188
virtue (title), 116-17
virtue, way of, 123
Virtues, cardinal, 15, 136

Vorster, John, 216

Water: Jesus giving the Living, 99; of Life, 149
Watts, Isaac, 220, 222
Way (title), 117, 199
way of Jesus, 123
way of world, 123
way, truth and life, 95, 162
Weber, Hans-Ruedi, 206
Weigel, Valentine, 155
Wells, H.G., 194
Wesley, Charles, 219-24
Wesley, John, 142, 217-20
Wesleyans, 217-24
Whale, J.S., 121, 156
Wilberforce, William, 227-8
'wing for sure-coursed birds' (title), 114
Wisdom (title), 115, 116-7, 124, 165
wisdom, Divine, 15, 70, 72, 74, 92-3, 128
Wisdom of Solomon, The, 15
women, place of, 30, 41-2, 120, 160, 197, 200
Wood, H.G.: *Did Christ Really Live?*, 157-8
Woolston, 189
Word (Logos), 55, 62, 69-70, 72, 74, 90, 114-15, 116, 124, 135, 165, 230; *see also* Logos
Word, Incarnate, 78
Worm (title), 117
worship, 164
wounds of Christ, 176

Xavier, Francis, 160

Yahweh, 2, 3, 4, 5, 6-7, 16, 22, 50, 60-1, 62, 70, 83, 88, 92, 97; Servant of, 8
yang (male principle), 199
yin (female principle) 199
youth, type of divine, 84-7, 108

Zacchaeus, 84
Zalmoxis, 121
Zealots, 22-3, 36, 38, 41, 48, 208
Zechariah, 47, 48
Zeus as Jesus type, 109-10
Zion, 4, 6
Zoroastrianism, 6, 170

For Product Safety Concerns and Information please contact our EU
representative GPSR@taylorandfrancis.com
Taylor & Francis Verlag GmbH, Kaufingerstraße 24, 80331 München, Germany

www.ingramcontent.com/pod-product-compliance
Lightning Source LLC
Chambersburg PA
CBHW070558300426
44113CB00010B/1306